RETURN OF THE
SOUL DOCTOR

The 2nd Ashington Casebook,
from the diaries of Dr. Jack Rivers

Other Books by Caitlín Matthews:

The Barefoot Book of Princesses
The Blessing Seed: A Creation Story for a New Millennium
The Celtic Book of Days,
The Celtic Book of the Dead
The Celtic Devotional
Celtic Love: Ten Enchanted Tales
Celtic Memories
The Celtic Tradition
The Celtic Spirit: Daily Meditations For the Turning Year
Celtic Visions
Celtic Wisdom
Celtic Wisdom Sticks: An Ogam Oracle
The Celtic Wisdom Tarot
The Complete Lenormand Handbook
Da Vinci Enigma Tarot
The Elements of the Goddess
Fireside Stories,
How To Be A Princess
In Search of Women's Passionate Soul: Revealing the Daimon Lover Within
King Arthur and the Goddess of the Land
King Arthur's Raid on the Underworld
The Little Book of Celtic Lore
Mabon and the Guardians of Celtic Britain
Psychic Protection Handbook
Singing the Soul Back Home: Shamanic Wisdom for Every Day
Sophia, Goddess of Wisdom: Bride of God
Tales of the Celtic Lands
This Ancient Heart
Voices of the Goddess: A Chorus of Sibyls
While the Bear Sleeps: Midwinter Tales
Diary of a Soul Doctor
Untold Tarot: The Lost Art of Reading Historical Tarot

Written With John Matthews:

Animal Tales
The Arthurian Book of Days
The Complete Arthurian Tarot
Celtic Myths
Christmas Tales
The Complete King Arthur: Many Faces, One Hero
Elemental Encyclopaedia of Magical Animals
Encyclopedia of Celtic Myth and Legend
Encyclopedia of Celtic Wisdom: A Celtic Shaman's Sourcebook
Faery Magic
The Faery-Tale Reader
The Fourth Gwenevere (with John James)
Ladies of the Lake
The Little Book of Celtic Blessings
The Little Book of Celtic Wisdom
Mad Professor's Laboratory
Magic Toy Box Sea Stories
Storyworld
Tales from the Haunted House
The Trick in the Tale
Walkers Between the Worlds:The Western Mysteries from Shaman to Magus
The Lost Book of the Grail: The Sevenfold Path of the Grail and the Restoration of the Faery Accord

RETURN OF THE
SOUL DOCTOR

The 2nd Ashington Casebook,
from the diaries of Dr. Jack Rivers

by

Caitlín Matthews

Return Of The Soul Doctor:
The 2nd Ashington Casebook, from the diaries of Dr. Jack Rivers

Copyright © 2020 by Caitlín Matthews

Caitlín Matthews has asserted her right to be identified as the Author of this Work. All rights are reserved, including the right to reproduce this book, or portions thereof, in any form. Reviewers may quote brief passages. This is a work of fiction. Names, characters, businesses, places, events and incidents are either the products of the author's imagination or used in a fictitious manner. Any resemblance to actual persons, living or dead, or to actual events is purely coincidental.

Book Design by Jeremy Berg
Cover Photo by Dave Smith

Starseed Books
An Imprint of Lorian Press LLC

ISBN: 978-1-939790-41-5

Matthews, Caitlín
Return of the Soul Doctor/Caitlín Matthews

First Print Edition: August 2020

Printed in the United States of America,
the United Kingdom and other countries

www.lorian.org

Acknowledgements

The poem on p.4 is by Caitlín Matthews and first appeared in *Fireside Stories: Tales for a Winter's Night,* Barefoot Books, 2007.

The works of the playwright in the *Masque of Antimony* in case 7 have been expanded and partially mined from the work of the real Jacobean poet, John Marston, who is not responsible for what I have created here.

The ritual outlined in *Out of the Ashes* originated with my teacher, Dolores Ashcroft Nowicki in the 1980s: this version of the Reconsecration Ritual comes from the adaptation that I developed with Felicity Wombwell. It has spread all over the world to help heal those who still feel unclean, traumatized, or violated.

I am grateful to Damh the Bard for permission to use his wonderful picture of the Long Man of Wilmington. You can find more about his work here: https://www.controverscial.com/Damh%20The%20Bard.htm (accessed Jan 2020)

The first Soul Doctor book in this series is called *Diary of a Soul Doctor* (2017) and is available from Lorian Press LLC. The work of my own shamanic practice continues, while my books and courses can be found at www.hallowquest.org.uk

    Caitlín Matthews
    Oxford, January 2020

Dedication

This book is dedicated to the memory of my dear shamanic colleague, Jane Dagger (9th December 1959- 15th September 2009), who acted as my 'Jack' for so many years in our healing work and teaching; ever reliable and insightful, she was one of the great bringers of delight who restore the light when all is dark. In the words of Jane's song, may Lady Willow lift all pain from your suffering:

> The willow song is here for you,
> She bends and bows the whole day through,
> La-laa, la-laa, la-laa, la-laa,
> She bends and bows, her heart is true.

Contents

Introduction: Return Of The Soul Doctor	1
Case 1: The Return Of The Native	5
Case 2: In The Shadow Of The Long Man	29
Case 3: Out Of The Ashes	59
Case 4: An Old Master	89
Case 5: The Ghost Of Shotley Moor	115
Case 6: The Companion	139
Case 7: The Mask Of Antimony	167
Case 8: The Stalker Behind Bars	195
Case 9: Closing The Circle	215
Case 10: The Path To The Sanctuary	249

Pictures

Outline of the Long Man of Wilmington	30
The Restored Reliquary	58
Emblem of Antimony	174
Lupus Metallorum	175

Introduction:
Return of the Soul Doctor
From the Desk of Dr. Jack Rivers.

Full to the brim of the wondrous past, I felt the wondrous present.
   Richard Jeffries– *The Story of My Heart*

Over the course of the last few years, I have received many letters demanding to know what became of Ash and to hear more of our case histories. Urged on by these requests, and by my wife Jane's insistence, I have collected a few more of these together, I hope for everyone's satisfaction. I have been much moved by the reports of people reading and re-reading these old cases, and very amused by others who have wanted to move into the Beacon right away so that they could live there forever.

Things were not always so rosy in those days, and the many frustrations we experienced were often the result of a health system that didn't quite connect or cover the kinds of problems our guests brought to us, which is why we existed in the first place. Writing today, I can see that this problem has not abated: the lost, the lonely, the depressed, the confused and the midisagnosed still fall between the cracks, and the need for our work has not grown any less necessary. To make things less easy, the half-trained, the untrained, the crank, and the phone-psychic have rendered many of our guests' problems yet more confused.

Going back over our case-books has brought to mind our life at the Beacon in the early days very vividly: the wonderful and imperturbable McLains and their ability to create a hospitable welcome; the beauty of the Beacon's setting on the South Downs in as rural and peaceful a place as you can still find in these days of overpopulation and frenzied activity; the idyll of living and working with the one I loved, and with the one whom I honoured above all other colleagues.

Ash's extraordinary life was lived below the horizon of notice, in most instances. Only those touched by his work know how very extraordinary a person he was. For those who have not read my previous collection, I append a very short and unconventional biography – quite unlike anything that might appear in a professional journal.

Dr. Richard Ashington, who was always known as 'Ash' to everyone from colleague to patient, was born in the Vale of Pewsey in 1946. After reading Psychology, Philosophy, and Linguistics at Oxford, he went on to do a general medical training in Aberdeen, and to specialize in psychotherapy with the

Guild of Ecumenical Psychology in London. Running beneath this training, you have to imagine his fortuitous meeting and collaboration with Melanie Rydale, who had been one of 'Jung's women;' she was the author of many remarkable books, including the influential *Thresholds of the Mind* (1956), and its companion, *Portals of the Soul* (1958), which shocked everyone by departing entirely from the psychological premise of the first book, and introducing many more esoteric ideas than the medical profession of the time was quite ready for. She co-founded the Guild of Ecumenical Psychology with Rabbi Ariel Klein, but her main influence upon Ash was her magical and alchemical work, about which I can give no further report. Ash certainly attended a lodge at Aldhampton once a month, which Melanie had founded. She took up with him and guided him to be the practitioner he became. At her death, her house, the Beacon, which had become a place of healing for those suffering from undiagnosed forms of mental affliction or psychic disturbance, came into the keeping of Ash.

The last collection of cases, *Diary of a Soul Doctor*, describes how I came into that household and found my life's work. Ash continued to live and work at the Beacon, with brief intervals away, after which it was signed over to myself. I continued to run it with Ash's help. In the interval between this book and the last set of case histories, you may wish to know that, while I lacked Ash's deep esoteric training and knowledge, his mentorship and guidance sharpened up my instinct and insight, so that I could continue his work.

As I was writing just then, I had a distinct sense of him, almost as if he had walked through me. My impression of the Beacon, its sure and certain welcome, its tasteful furnishings and pictures, fused together, leaving me with a sense of extreme blessing. My wife has just come in with a cup of tea, remarking how nice it was that I was using Ash's old cologne, but I really had not done so. I don't even possess that distinct, old-fashioned brand of Aqua di Palma. I suppose I must have been about to doze off, but if that was meant as a blessing from you, Ash, I accept it gladly.

When I compiled the case notes for the first collection in *Diary of a Soul Doctor*, it had been a matter of choosing among many cases to make a final selection. I had little idea of writing up more of them, but such has been the response to my first collection, that I have been forced to reconsider, and so this volume provides another set of cases that Ash and I worked upon. As before, theses cases range widely over the time that I worked at the Beacon. Some seem to come from a different world, prior to the invention of the internet, when things were at a quieter pace. At the Beacon, we strove to maintain that, in order to make an enclave of peace.

Among my own retired acquaintances, these stories seem to have found a kind of notorious acceptance: now that most of them no longer have medical reputations to ruin, it is apparently alright to accord Ash the recognition they chose to withhold from him during his career. But I have also had several letters of appreciation from those who knew Ash first-hand, and loved him for what he was, and even more from fans and readers who imagine that he is still practising, and could he perhaps just pronounce on their interesting cases himself? These seekers I have had to disabuse of their pipe-dream, for those days are past.

As always, there are usually one or two who think the cases I have written up are all fantastic rot. Only the other day at the theatre, I bumped into Miles Kingston, my old bête noir, who congratulated me on a rip-roaring good read although, of course, he couldn't help implying that nothing like these cases in this, and the second of the Ashington Casebooks which you hold in your hands, could possibly have taken place.

Veracity about case histories is a difficult thing for professionals: in the interests of discretion, it has become the way to fuse together cases of similar kinds and make a kind of composite case, for the purposes of professional study in books and for student seminars. While I have changed person names, locations, and some details, I have left these stories mostly unvarnished: they happened as I have told them. My own part in them is subjectively documented exactly as written. Truth, as they say, is often stranger than fiction, just be aware!

For those who just want to read these casebooks as stories, and not worry about whether they are true or not, then I would say to you, 'Go ahead and enjoy them!' I certainly will not be offended, and if it helps Ash live on in your imagination, then, so be it!

Caitlín Matthews

Case 1: THE RETURN OF THE NATIVE

> Come you in and rest your head,
> Smooth the sheets upon the bed.
> All the cares that strewed your way
> Find their rest at ebb of day.
> No more wandering, no more war,
> Come you in and close the door.
> **Caitlín Matthews** – The Wanderer's Welcome Home song

The New Year began very still and drear. That winter, there had been none of those happy, bright blue days with a touch of frost, just a miserable overcast sky and much rain throughout November and December. The boiler had been intermittently troublesome over Christmas, and now the upstairs toilet bowl had sprung a leak on New Year's morning, so I was down on my knees with soaking towels and grouting, since Gillespie was still in a state of post-Hogmany delicacy, unable to help, due to the two bottles of whiskey with which he had been gifted. Fortunately, we had no guests currently staying at the Beacon.

I thought I had stayed the worst of the water when I heard the rattle of the bell-pull being lifted. The deep resonant ringing from the hallway lifted my flagging spirits, for I was urgently expecting the plumber whom I had persuaded to come out with the bribe of a bottle of good malt whiskey, and payment of time and a half, it being a bank holiday.

Taking the stairs two at a time, I leapt to the door and flung it open in welcome relief. On the threshold, staring lovingly through the door glass into the porch at the image of Melanie, the founder of the Beacon, stood a tall, thin man with utterly white hair. But no plumber's bag did he have in his hand, only a battered old backpack. With a characteristic turn of the head, his grey eyes looked straight into mine, he said, 'Hello, Jack!'

'Ash?... Oh my God! *Ash!*'

My old employer stood modestly on the threshold of the nursing home that had once been his and which had been signed over to me on his departure. He was back from his three-year retreat in Nepal without any warning. At his going away, I somehow felt I would never see him again, it had seemed so final.

'I thought I'd come back for my birthday,' he said simply, by way of explanation.

All thought of plumbing gone from my mind, I wrapped him in my arms and shouted with joy, bringing the McLains, our housekeeper and caretaker, running.

Wendy called anxiously ahead down the corridor, 'Has the leak got worse?'

'Man, will ye hold yer wheest....' Gillespie followed, stumbling along the hall, still clutching his head. But when they reached the threshold, beholding Ash, they drew him into the hall with cries of rejoicing and many tears.

So it was that the bewildered plumber found us, in the middle of a kind of Te Deum-cum-hysterical-Indian war-whoop. I detached myself most unwillingly from Ash and showed the man upstairs.

After paying off the plumber a much dryer hour later, sending him home to his own hearth with a very expensive bottle of Islay Malt from sheer relief of heart, I found the others in the living room before a roaring fire. Wendy sat as near to Ash as she might, her right hand in his, while her left hand wonderingly strayed to touch his whitened hair, 'But it was so black before!'

'The snow was quite intense,' was all he was say, enigmatically.

I sat opposite him, drinking him in, 'What *have* you been doing with yourself, my friend?'

'I have been meditating on Mahakala, the God of Time, among other things.'

There was no good answer to this.

'Man, ye've become a shadow of yerself!' Gillespie observed, 'but I'll give it to them Nepalese chappies - they must have been supplying ye with the waters of life! You've lost years...'

Thinner he was, certainly, but younger? Three years' absence from the Beacon had somehow rendered him remarkably youthful, almost boyish, despite his white hair: he'd always possessed the skin of a 30 year old, so it had never been easy to guess his age. He had gone away tired, exhausted from years of maintaining a remarkable service, sorting out what his confrères regarded as the impossible cases, and solving the conditions of mysterious causation by his own set of esoteric skills. His current thinness was not unhealthy, but rather whippy and wiry, like a young greyhound ready for the racetrack. Whatever he had been doing, he had been renewed in body.

'You remind me of T. H. White's Merlin. Have you been youthening like him?' I accused him, feeling how unfair it was that the rest of us had grown older while he had had some kind of spiritual make-over.

'Possibly. But for now, I just need to lie down. I've been on the road a long time. It's been 36 hours since I slept. We'll catch up later....' He set down his cup.

Wendy and I exchanged awkward glances. I began to explain, 'Ash, I took over your room when Jane and I....'

'I fully expected that, Jack. I can sleep in your old room, if it's free.'

I shouldered his backpack and led the way upstairs, 'Is this really all the luggage you have?'

'It is.'

'And you don't mind this…?' I indicated the rather sparsely furnished room I used to inhabit.

'It looks like a wonderful place to sleep….' He cast himself down and was instantly gone. I covered him up with the quilt, putting his backpack on the chair: it felt pretty light, considering how long he had been gone.

I crept downstairs where Wendy and I hugged, 'It's like having the very best Christmas present,' she said, squeezing me tight with joy.

Clapping my hand to my head, I cried, 'Oh my goodness, when *is* Ash's birthday?'

'It's on Epiphany,' she said. 'You know - the 6th of January - surely you must remember? Plenty of time to sort something out.' Of course, this didn't stop her from making a start on a cake that very night, by soaking the dried fruit in brandy.

There was so much to catch up with, but there was one sorrow that we could not spare him: Cinnamon, his beloved marmalade cat, had been killed by a motorbike who had turned into our lane by mistake, not seeing the dead-end road sign. The biker had failed to slow down as the lane turned towards the Beacon, and Cinnamon had died instantly as she ran out of the gate. I broached the news carefully, but Ash merely answered, 'I felt her go – a couple of Junes ago?'

Astoundedly, I nodded, 'Yes, we buried her in the Wilderness under her favourite plum tree. Gillespie could hardly speak for days. He planted a circle of cyclamens on her grave that bloom every autumn.'

However, we had kept one of her kittens, Harlequin, a pugnacious white and black tom who had inherited only a couple of patches of his mother's colouring, on the left side of his head and his right flank. It wasn't long before an importunate white and black paw came scratching at his leg to come up. Ash made space on his lap and the cat leapt up, pushing his head against the long fingers. As Ash riffled the ruff around his neck, Harlequin collapsed into an abandoned heap on his lap, giving up great purrs of contentment.

'A cat, a fire, and friends… It's very good to be back. …Is there more tea? I am much too be-catted to reach the pot.'

His white hair was going to take some getting used to, I thought; it made his dark rimmed grey eyes seem enormous, but while I poured another cup, he had been observing me, 'You're looking very prosperous…'

'You mean, overweight?' For I had put on a pound or two since Jane and I married.

'No, I mean you look as if you are flourishing.'

I took this to mean the Beacon's work, and began to render an account of myself, giving him a potted review of the last three years. It had been hard at first, especially when referrals realised that Ash was no longer there to help them, only my plodding and un-esoteric self, but slowly the guests had started to come back, only now they were gratifyingly coming because I was there.

He listened to my account, nodding, saying only at the end, 'It sounds as if you have done splendidly… But Jack, I don't see Jane? How has that worked out?'

Jane and I had soon learned that the Beacon was bigger than both of us. While Ash had been optimistic in the way things might play out, I had taken on more than I knew when I took over the Beacon at the same time as a new wife. Jane's sense of responsibility would not let her instantly resign from her post as bush nurse in the Australian Northern Territory until a replacement could be found for her. She'd said, 'You know I'll miss you terribly, but I have to finish off and hand over to someone for the sake of the community I've served. Maisy is going to have to train up a replacement she can rely on.'

Reluctantly, I agreed. Removing Jane from the bush would be like removing me from the Beacon. It was my anxiety that we would never be together. We'd clung together at the airport like babes in the wood, before she was consumed in the tunnel leading to customs and baggage scanning, and her blonde ponytail could no longer be seen. But she *had* come back a few months later, when the replacement had been trained up. We'd had a little time together, then almost immediately she had begun a mental health degree, in order to be more helpful at the Beacon; the only drawback was that the course was in Manchester, so we had been parted once again. She came home for the holidays, usually, but that Christmas and New Year, she had had to fly home to see her parents in Melbourne because her father had had a health scare. She had just two more terms of her training to go before we might be together. We seemed destined to be half a world away from each other.

'It was a lonely time, the first few months. I got in a succession of assistants that didn't quite work before I found Will Walton.' This young doctor was both eager and spontaneous enough to run with the hare and race with the hounds, and wasn't too fazed by the Beacon style, as I liked to term it, though I had many quizzical looks from him in the first few months. 'You'll get to see Will in a few days: he's with his family for the New Year.' Will now held the fort at the Beacon while I saw the Harley St cases on my set London days, just as I used to do for Ash. I consulted just two days a week in London now, and our accountant was wondering whether it was really worth all the expense of keeping up a city clinic, something I wanted to discuss with Ash, yet he showed no desire whatever to return to the traces.

I burbled on about the accounting, 'Alan Burcott has given us a clean bill of health, financially, but he questioned whether we are getting all that we might out of the London clinic…'

Ash didn't stir, but sipped his tea calmly, 'I'm sure that you will make the best decision, Jack. Can we talk about that another time? I just need an interval to step back into things, if it's alright?'

'Oh course!' My relief that he was contemplating coming back into things was great, but at the same time all my carefully woven plans were going to have to be unravelled, and I had already busily started shuffling rotas in my head. Ash was back, and soon Jane would return too, but would we be able to keep on Will Walton as well, I worried? I tried to head off the weight of decision, by asking Ash about his retreat, 'I can't imagine what it's like being alone for that long. It must be overwhelming to be with people again.'

He smiled slowly, 'No, though the airports at both ends were hells of cacophony. It was the silence that nourished me. Stillness, silence, spaciousness. Becoming a mandala of the cosmos, being full with all that is. – That's all I can say about my time there.'

'Well, you take your time to settle back in. – We will need to make some decisions, but I won't worry you about them now.'

I had truly missed our talks. While I have had my own mystical experiences, I had become less capable of speaking about them with others. Now, in Ash's presence, I felt the iron reserve I had kept about such things fly out of the window because, although the language of the soul is not the discourse of everyday, Ash made any such discussion feel normal again.

Wendy's concern for Ash's slender frame played out over the next week in the provision of piles of toasted crumpets, mountains of scones, and offerings of milk drinks. It began on his birthday. Facing a veritable mound of food, Ash noted, 'I shall become as stout as Toad of Toad Hall if I'm not careful, Wendy!'

'Ach, ye wilna fade awa, that's for sure!' Gillespie observed, shovelling half a crumpet into his mouth sideways as if inserting a pair of false teeth.

At Ash's request, we invited no-one to the birthday tea, but bided together around the fire of apple logs, speaking of old times, as the frost began to pattern the windows. Looking fondly over our old team, I felt that the spirit of the Beacon had not dimmed. The deep indwelling that you sometimes feel at Christmas had extended itself right up to this Twelfth Night; it was a blessing to hear Ash's laughter as we read out the daft mottos from the Christmas crackers we had kept back for this evening. The MaClains sang carols, and we joined in the choruses with gusto: *We Three Kings*, for Epiphany, and *In Dulci Jubilo* because we all liked it, and we could sing all the parts between us, if I attempted an alto falsetto. Gillespie sang the wistful '*Oh Men from the Fields,*' in his glorious bass-baritone and we all felt something had indeed 'come softly within' to join us. Wendy recited one of her favourite poems from the winter anthology on the shelves:

> Bring in more logs, the day grows chill!
> It's time to gather round the fire.
> Across the fields, the snow lies still,
> The beasts lie safely in warm byre.
>
> When wind blows down the chimney steep,
> And red-gold sparks leap in the dark,
> It's time to open the book of story,
> And learn of winter's hidden glory.
>
> Peer in the blaze: where elf-caves glow,
> Where dragons breathe and beanstalks grow;
> Where lost companions find their way,
> Where jewels and secret treasures lay,
>
> To hear what has been told before
> By those who sat in times long past,
> Round fires where children begged for more:
> 'Don't let this story be the last!'
>
> And still in winters yet to come,
> When starlight sings the snowflakes' song,
> When moon is bright and dull is sun,
> And all these tales to you belong,
>
> Remember then this winter night,
> When snow lay thick and wind blew cold.

Tell the glad tales round hearth-fire's light,
For your own child to have and hold.

As they peered into the depths of the fire, I looked around our little circle. Wendy and Gillespie's children had long ago grown up and made lives of their own: they had done their part. If children were to come to myself and Jane, then their coming was still unknown to us. As far as I knew, Ash had no children. He had signed over the Beacon to me on the understanding that I would continue his work. Considering your own unborn children puts you in a strange and unsettled mood, I found, or maybe it was just the fruit punch that Wendy had made? Before I got too weepy, missing Jane, I stretched and went to make another pot of tea for us all.

Later, on the way to bed, I found Ash attending to the shrine light before Melanie's photograph.

I said, 'I've kept the flame going, just like I promised.' In the quiet of the porch, the words sounded like self-justification, and I kicked myself for striking a sour note on this most perfect day.

Ash contemplated Melanie's image, 'I felt how well you were keeping it. Every time the wind blew up a snowstorm, I could feel the Beacon, standing solid and dependable, like you, Jack. – I do hope that Jane will return to help you soon: you need your helpmeet beside you.'

I laughed, 'I bet no-one's ever called her that!' But he was right. I needed her beside me. I was ready to open a new chapter and stretch myself.

The next morning began with proper Plough Monday plunge into the mundane preparations for work, which always mark the passing of the Christmas season. At 6am. we all heard a terrific bang when Ash went to run water for a shower. The old boiler had finally given up the ghost, it appeared, and we had to begin negotiations with our plumber for a new one. Over that week we were to be reduced to boiling kettles and saucepans in order to have any hot water, which severely cramped our activities. Fortunately, the Aga still functioned and so the kitchen remained the warmest room; but since we all gravitated towards it, Wendy had to keep swishing us away to get on with her work.

'We will wash in the sink, just like during the war' Wendy pronounced, when Ash bemoaned the lack of a shower. 'No reason not to keep clean,' but I was still glad that I had had a bath the night before. The laundry would be taken to the laundrette in Chistledon, it was decided, as that week wore on and the date for a replacement boiler went on receding into the middle of January.

At 11am, Will Walton returned from his holidays with a streaming cold that was soon diagnosed as flu. Wendy sent him promptly to bed with a dose, fearing a flu outbreak if he was not confined. Will's blue eyes started out of his head at seeing Ash, who had become a fabulous being in his mind, one worthy of admiration and awe, 'I really had thought he was mythical, you know,' he remarked as I drew the curtains and gave him some cough linctus.

Ash still took no part in my deliberations. As first, I felt an awkwardness at trying to involve him, but something had shifted, and nothing was quite right: there was a reluctance in him to discuss the business of the Beacon, which I tried to put down to his period of re-integration in our rhythms.

Outdoors, to make it more difficult, the wind had turned to the North East, sending down crystal needles of sleet, making the plumber so busy with burst pipes and the like, that our boiler situation threatened to turn into a fortnight of freeze. Laying one fire and cleaning it every day was all very well, but now we had to lay one in Will's room also, and when Wendy herself began to come down with the flu, there were just us menfolk to manage everything.

So it was that the dismantling of the Christmas decorations was being handled by Gillespie and myself, while everyone seemed out of sorts, except Ash, who was still pottering about, finding his feet at the Beacon again. The midwinter enchantment was over for another year with a great crash and bang.

At 1.30pm the phone went. Expecting it to be the plumber who had left one or two off-hand messages about the difficulty of locating the correct kind of boiler, I picked it up, speaking abruptly into the speaker, 'The Beacon, Jack Rivers speaking.'

From the other end issued a series of stop-start noises not unlike that of our boiler, while it was still on life. Finally, a patrician voice of great age uttered peremptorily into the speaker, with the kind of crisp diction required when wearing dentures, 'Tryphena Hands here. I wish to speak to Dr Ashington.'

'He is just back from a long trip, madam, and may not be available to consult,' I informed her.

Another series of noises ensued, suggesting that the elderly lady at the other end might be dealing with the aftermath of a stroke, but she was quite firm about things when she replied, 'Well, he will speak with me!'

Not wanting to gainsay so august a lady, I went reluctantly in search of Ash, finding him in the sanctuary. He was sitting quite still and all I could do was breathe stertorously while he meditated. Without opening his eyes, he said, 'What is it, Jack?'

'Sorry, but an old woman rejoicing in the name of Tryphena Hands is on the phone demanding that you come. She sounds like Dame Edith Sitwell, and must be all of a hundred and three. I told her…'

His eyes snapped open instantly and he rose, making a swift salutation to the shrine, and moving speedily to the office phone, 'Phena? Is that you?' He sounded strangely glad and relieved.

Her response could be heard from where I stood, 'Ash? They told me some ridiculous story that you were in Tibet or somewhere outlandish. I need you, dear heart. Can you come over and get me? It is time, I think.'

While he made arrangements for her to come to the Beacon, I kept up a hopeless pantomime, trying to convey to him how unsuitable it would be for an elderly person to stay with us right at the moment, with neither central heating nor hot water. But he completely ignored me until he had rung off.

I nearly shouted, 'What are you thinking of? We have flu in the house and no heating or hot water.'

Unperturbed, he said, 'Phena is an old friend, and she will have every comfort we can provide, if you will allow it?

Speechless with frustration, I finally nodded, 'Alright, but we need to make sure she is comfortable.'

'Don't worry, I will start pulling my weight, but can you drive me into Nutbourne? I need a little longer before I drive again, I think.'

I flung up my hands, 'You know that Wendy has come down with the flu as well as Will? It will be just me and Gillespie running things, you know? Let me just check with her.' I knocked on the door of the flat and let myself in, calling out to Wendy, 'Sorry to disturb, I have to go to Nutbourne with Ash. Are there things to buy I can gather on the way?'

Wendy croaked, 'Come in and take a list. We'll be out of so much by now, I imagine.' Sitting up in bed with difficulty, she dictated a full list of supplies, and firkled in her handbag to give me the Beacon credit card. 'Bring me some more honey and lemons as well,' she begged before sliding wanly back down into the pillows.

As we set off through the icy lanes towards the junction where we could pick up the Eastern coast road, I asked Ash to fill me in, 'Who is Tryphena Hands?'

'An old associate of Melanie's. We were in the same lodge, but she has not attended for a while now.' He was talking about his monthly lodge meetings at Aldhampton, where his magical group still convened. I never asked about it, as it was not my business.

'Has she had a stroke? She sounded a little uncertain in her speech…'

'No, she just doesn't see many people these days. – It always takes her a little interval to get started. She is over a hundred now, I believe.'

I enquired, 'Is this another case for us, or just a friend in trouble?'

'Both,' he said, infuriatingly terse on the detail.

'You know I will need to pick up supplies for the house; Wendy's worried that we will get snowed in again and not be able to get out for a while: things are very low.'

'Low supplies in Wendy's book would probably keep us alive through a siege, I imagine,' he grinned, like his old self again. 'Concentrate on the fresh produce, I would.'

We somehow managed the drive into Nutbourne across the Downs, which is only normally a three quarters of an hour drive, skidding and sliding in places as the cold winds overcame the wintry sun's effect and refroze the black ice of the previous night. Coming over the brow of the last hill, we rejoiced at sight of the sea, as we usually did, and slipped finally onto the wider A roads which were cleared and gritted. I made a stop at the big supermarket outside Nutbourne, running around the aisles like a lunatic, and probably forgetting all kinds of things; then, suitably laden down, we continued into the town. It had taken us about an hour and half, and I was anxious about the journey home in the dark.

Tryphena's abode was a fine red-brick town house of the Arts and Crafts era with a beautiful wrought-iron gate piercing its street wall. A blue plaque on this wall announced the house behind it as the dwelling of the Arts and Crafts artist and ceramicist, Sebastian Ellis Hands, her uncle, who died young. Within the gate, little shrouded rose-bushes hid their pruned heads under sacking, like mourners along the southern side of the house, which was up a steep street, a mile from the harbour below. Now that we were nearer to the coast, we could discern that the waves seemed to be semi-frozen. The sea hadn't frozen properly for 10 years - always an uncanny sight to see the tides halted by the surface ice. Over the porch was a stone sea-goat and the house sign, 'Capricorn House.'

Tryphena answered our knock slowly, pulling Ash like a long-lost son into her frail arms. She was once, I would guess, a tall woman, but age had shrunken her stature. He kissed her tenderly on the cheek. Piles of hair were coiled about her head under a silk scarf, and she must have been a great beauty in her time.

I was introduced and given a very courteous handshake. I took care not to squeeze the crooked, much-beringed arthritic hand, but I did feel like the driver who should be banished to the back premises to have a cup of tea while his betters conversed. Ash conveyed that I was his employer and partner in our work. Tryphena's deeply hooded eyes stretched wide, attempting to encompass me within this description and, from her dubious expression, evidently failing.

We were ushered into an elegant sitting room with a viridian green tiled fireplace and many small pictures on the walls. I fell into an embroidered chair, flabbergasted, to consider the prospect of myself as Ash's employer. The scales fell from my eyes. Now it all made sense: the hiatus since Ash had arrived, and my strange sense of missing a step: he had been patiently waiting for me to re-employ him! I cursed myself for a fool.

While Ash went to fetch tea, Tryphena regarded me, craning out from the depths of her armchair. I realized that she was scanning the area over the top of my head in the way that Ash used to do, 'You do not bear the signature of one who follows the Work?' I could hear the capital letter in her enunciation.

'No, but I am very warmly at home with it in our *work* together,' I responded, injecting the same lower-case emphasis in my words. She was, of course, referring to the Great Work – what she and Ash were doing in their lodge together: the meeting of heaven and earth through the practice of ceremonial magic.

She sat back, satisfied, 'Umm. But, young man, the day is coming when you will incorporate it further, I would say! Put on more logs, if you would be so good!'

I obliged, wondering what she could be thinking of. I had never expressed any curiosity about their lodge, nor any desire to be part of it, leaving that kind of thing to Ash. I remained sceptical about magical associations in general. Back in the days of my first appointment as a mental health doctor, when I was seeking a better post, I had been warmly invited to join a Masonic lodge: it had been intimated to me, on the side, that 'they would take care of me,' but such rampant nepotism so disgusted my socialist soul that I never pursued the invitation further. I daresay, had I followed that path, I would now be in some comfortable sinecure of a job, part of a well-respected community of specialists who trotted out their standard responses for a goodly fee. Instead of which, here I was running the Beacon, understaffed, confused, and put out that Ash had no sense of what was fitting.

Over the very good China tea that Ash brought back on a huge red lacquer tray, Tryphena brought out some documents for Ash to sign. I was required as a witness, and duly appended my signature. They looked like testamentary documents: wills, and transfers of property or holdings. Only when we were done, and the documents consigned to a briefcase, did Tryphena offer a plate of *petit fours* so delicately exquisite that I fear I made a bit of a pig of myself.

'You will give the documents into the keeping of Hesselton's?' she enquired of him.

'We can do it on the way,' he assured her. 'Is there anything else to pack?'

Tryphena looked around the room very slowly, as if taking it in for the last time. Something about her manner brought me to realization of what our visit was really about. We were taking Tryphena Hands home to the Beacon to die. I don't know how I knew it, but Ash nodded at me, seeing that I had realized the cause.

'The only things I need you to sort out have been put together already,' she replied. 'I trust that we can bring them with us?'

Tryphena selected the coat and wrap that she wanted for the journey, pulling on a pair of long purple gloves over the rings, and I helped Ash load her suitcase and a long black bag into the boot. After locking the house, she gave one set of keys into Ash's keeping while the other set were posted through the letterbox of the house next door in an envelope, for her neighbour, Martina, who had promised to look in on things.

Sniffing the winter sea air appreciatively, Tryphena was folded into the front seat of the car with an auxiliary blanket over her lap. Although cars are heated today, her memory of past journeys still demanded that little comfort.

The briefcase was duly dropped off at the solicitor's office and we started home in the twilight.

A hard-pressed Gillespie had been holding the fort alone and was clearly glad to see us, telling us the good news, 'The plumber chappy has promised tomorrow will see a new boiler, so we wilna freeze!' While he brought in the shopping, Ash and I conducted Tryphena into the house. Just like Ash, she stopped in the porch to regard Melanie's picture on its shrine, then, with a touch of her purple gloved finger to the frame, she nodded at us, 'You can show me my room now.'

The journey had been as smooth as I could make it, but it had been too much for her. 'Shall I bring you something on a tray?' I asked.

'Just a little Bengers for me,' she replied, already closing her eyes with weariness. I looked quizzically over her head at Ash: Bengers – a powdered foodstuff that was mixed with milk and advertised for people with delicate digestions, hadn't been made for several decades, to my best knowledge.

'I think we have some Slippery Elm food, if you like. It's like Bengers,' Ash responded, to which she assented.

We had just one downstairs bedroom, usually kept free for any disabled guests. It was freshly made up and a fire laid in it, as Ash had called ahead to Gillespie. I went to make the Slippery Elm with some milk on the Aga, while

Ash settled her in.

When I brought Tryphena her supper in a beautiful china bowl on a tray, with more tea, she was looking more diminished: I realized that her teeth had been removed, as well as her coil of hair, leaving her scalp hidden under a concealing turban. 'Thank you, young man! I shall sleep after this I think. Good night.'

We retired to the living room.

Ash looked contrite, 'I'm sorry to manage you into this, but ...'

'You had a prior agreement with her, didn't you?'

He looked relieved, 'Yes.'

I was curious: 'How did she know you were back in the country?'

'I sent her no message, but she sent one to me – I picked her up and knew I had to come home, that the time was near. Initiates of our lodge meet in the same location in the Otherworld, so I was aware of her.' He contemplated me carefully, 'You don't mind? ... I mean, it is not my place any more to decide things here. The Beacon is under your care now, not mine.'

In a voice of pretend importance, I said, 'As it's a special case, I'll let it go this time ...' Then carried on, 'Oh, goodness, Ash, you must know that any case you consider urgent has my full attention! Surely, you can't expect me to take the decisions after all these years together?'

He grinned, 'I didn't want to overstep the line, but you will need to draw up a contract for me, so I can work here again.'

I cast up my eyes and shook my head, 'All right! But please don't give me any more cause to get above myself. We both know who the expert is here!'

I tutted, 'Contracts indeed! Now tell me about Tryphena...'

It was very clear that both love and loyalty bound them together. I gathered also that Tryphena was the last link to Melanie. Born when Queen Victoria was still on the throne, she grew up as an Edwardian, which explained her beautiful manners and her patrician voice. Ash told me that her uncle, Sebastian Ellis Hands, was friends with Melanie's father and that he had been responsible for the remodelling of the main building of the Beacon which was itself wrapped around an older, medieval manor house: the only part of that original structure remaining was the medieval sanctuary at the heart of the Beacon. The porch and front range of the house had been added on, with a new wing to extend it. The staircases had moved to accommodate these changes – which explained why the internal hallway was so large – it had been originally part of the older house.

Medically, Tryphena had the usual problems of extreme old age: everything was worn out, and our job was to keep her comfortable and let her take her own time dying.

'We do not know how long that will be,' I cautioned. Death, like birth, may be inevitable but it takes its own time.

'Nevertheless, I will be paying for her stay. Her care will not be a drag on the Beacon, I promise. In any event, I don't think she will be with us long.'

He spoke pensively, but not sadly.

That night, I rang Jane to tell her the good news of Ash's return. Her father was making a decent recovery after a heart scare, having been diagnosed with angina, and she was reassuring him that it was manageable. We talked about arranging her flight home. The last year of her degree course in Manchester didn't begin until the third week of January, and I earnestly hoped that we have at least the best part of a week to be together, quite apart from really needing her back at the Beacon, as I told her.

'You must be in two minds about having Ash back?' she said, immediately putting her finger on the awkwardness I had been feeling.

'Well, I can't tell how things will work out yet, but it is good to have him back.'

'When your boss comes back asking for a job, it's a bit weird, surely?'

I had to agree.

'I'm really curious, Jack,' she said, 'How can a woman in England summon home a man from Nepal without a phone? Do ask him for me! I know that it's kind of normal here in the Northern Territory, among the tribes – we have people walking into the clinic who've come hundreds of miles on a pick-up truck, but they still know all our local news - but I've never heard of a Western example.'

I reported what he had told me, urging her to come home as soon as she could.

With Will and Wendy both out of action still, the daily running of the Beacon was complex, with all the fires to lay and grates to clean. Fortunately, the boiler was finally fitted with the minimum of fuss and the temperature of the house became stabilised – ironically, precisely when the icy snap seemed to ebb, leaving us with one of those bright blue January days that are clear and cold.

Tidying up the living room, I asked Ash, 'How exactly did Tryphena alert you that you needed to come home? And would you have returned without her calling you?'

Ash put down the pile of magazines he was sorting through, 'She did so by thought, plain and simple.'

I protested, 'I really don't believe that you can influence people that easily – it isn't possible!'

Ash turned to look out of the window where Gillespie was tying up some stray branches of the espaliered apple trees he was training against the southern wall of the house. With a smile, he said, 'Look and listen. I shall make Gillespie sing "My Love is like a red, red rose."'

Disbelievingly, I stationed myself at the window, cracking it open a space. Sure enough, Gillespie's rich bass started humming the same tune a few seconds later, breaking out into,

'O my Luve's like a red, red rose
That's newly sprung in June;
O my Luve's like the melodie
That's sweetly play'd in tune.'

Ash wasn't even looking at Gillespie, but sorting the pile of magazines still with his back to the window.

'How did you do it?'

'Just by thinking.'

I asked suspiciously, 'Do you ever plant such thoughts in my head?'

'No, you are free to think and feel as you will, and so is Gillespie. This was just a harmless example by way of demonstration.'

'Reading or influencing other people's thoughts is a scary prospect, though!'

'Believe me, no respectable esotericist would ever presume to eavesdrop or influence anyone. That would be presumptuous. – Of course, a well-placed thought based on a reiterated suggestion will influence a normal person easily. But then, every advertisement in the world is already doing that. – Think how many times have you been unable to speak to Wendy after she's gone out shopping: your thought and need got through and she brought you what you wanted anyway, even when it wasn't on her shopping list?'

I conceded that one, 'But you were thousands of miles away!'

'Distance is not usually a problem. Tryphena's urgency was unmistakable. It penetrated to my meditation, and I was as aware of her as you of me now. And yes, I had aimed to come home soon, though not quite as early as I did.'

But I still shook my head in puzzlement as Gillespie's fine voice rose in affirmation,

'Till a' the seas gang dry, my dear,
And the rocks melt wi' the sun;
And I will luve thee still, my dear,
While the sands 'o life shall run.'

Despite her fragility, Tryphena seemed to practice her meditation like Ash, every day without fail. At first, she would ask to be got up and sit in a well-padded armchair bolt upright, hands along the chair arms and feet together like an Egyptian divinity. She informed me: 'I meditate every day for half an hour, except on bad days when I meditate for 2 hours.' This seemed to be the by-word of their lodge. This ability to draw oneself into a deep stillness certainly helped maintain their equanimity. For Ash, just returned from his retreat, I imagined that one hour's meditation must have seemed a very short time. I contemplated a bizarre supposition that the longer you meditated, the younger you got, for time had laid its fingers very lightly upon him, though Tryphena's own span of years seemed to have finally run out.

I was up in the night to get some water when I heard movement downstairs and ran down to knock on Tryphena's door, 'Are you alright?'

An inarticulate sound came from within, so I went in to find her slewed sideways in her bed, in the act of trying to fetch a miniature from her table, in some distress. A moment later, and she would have slipped to the floor. We really didn't have the right beds for geriatric nursing: it was something I would have to consider getting in. I lifted her gently back into place and gave the tiny frame into her hands: the image was of a young man with longish dark hair, with a violin resting against his chest. The miniature had evidently been designed to hang from a chain. Tryphena clutched the image, held it before her eyes, then cast her hand back onto the coverlet, 'It's no good, I can't see it anymore.'

I offered her the magnifying glasses that she wore sometimes, but she shook her head, wearily, 'It doesn't matter, now.' The effort had exhausted her but she continued to clutch the miniature.

Her pulse felt febrile and erratic. I took the decision to bring in an oxygen cylinder, fitting the mask as gently as I could. Her breathing and pulse settled down shortly.

I monitored her for about half an hour and went for a cup of tea. On looking back again, her eyes had the calm, brown velvet softness of pansies, and she had recovered entirely from her panic. They fixed on me now, 'I wondered about Ash's assistant. I see now why he chose you – you have a kindness and deftness that all doctors ought to have, but something more – a humility that lends you grace.'

I blushed with pleasurable embarrassment. 'We're just here to serve.' We both knew she would not be getting better, that for her, the healing was into and beyond death.

She reached for my hand, 'I have lived a long time, but I will not be a long time dying, I assure you.'

I realised afterwards that I had been witness that night to the last denial that sometimes falls away before death, to be replaced by an utter calm. There are only a few deathbeds where you witness that clarity.

'Is there anything more I can do for you?' I asked, wondering whether I should go and awaken Ash.

'You may take off my rings,' she said, with solemn finality. 'No! Not the amethyst or the signet ring.' I helped her remove the other rings, placing them in a saucer nearby. Some did not want to come off, and I had to use some liquid soap to persuade them. This left just the amethyst on her left hand, the stone as big as a bishop's ring, while on her right was the little jasper intaglio of a sea-goat. Her hands looked strangely undressed without their adornments, but she must have felt considerably less burdened without them.

'You may adjust my pillows and then I will sleep.'

'Is there anything else?' I asked, as I settled her down.

'Is there a candle you can bring to my room? I should like one lit and this bothersome light turned off please.' She indicated the bedside lamp.

I fetched one of the sanctum lights from the porch cupboard. When I returned, she shook out from the back of the book she had been reading, a laminated picture of the Praying Hands by Durer, shooing it towards me with a finger, 'I should like that to be put near the candle.'

With the picture and the candle arranged on the shelf where the light would be safe, she seemed satisfied, so I switched off the bedside light.

From that evening onwards, Tryphena ceased to eat, taking only a few sips of liquid daily. Ash was beside her all of the way, meditating as she moved in and out of consciousness, praying and being present to her last journey. During that week, several individuals came and went - members of their lodge, I assumed, come to make their farewells. None of them stopped to socialise with us over a cup of tea, but went straight in and out, anonymously.

As the door-bell rang for the third time that day, I went to open it to the next visitor, only to find my own wife on the doorstep with her suitcase.

'What a wonderful surprise!' I kissed Jane, lifting her case inside, feeling strangely shy, excited, and just a little annoyed that I had not had the chance to pick her up myself, which I would have been glad to do.

'Happy New Year, my dear!' She patted my cheek, 'Don't frown! I took the earlier flight and hired a car from Gatwick to be here quicker.'

All was forgiven in her embrace.

As soon as Jane was clear of her jet-lag, she took over the main nursing of Tryphena. 'I've never known a patient so calm and accepting. I suppose it must come from her great age?' she said.

For her part, Tryphena said little, but something truly wonderful was beginning to happen in that little downstairs bedroom. We were all keenly aware of being in the presence of a great wisdom as we went in to change the bedding or examine her. Like Ash, she was youthening – an effect that you sometimes see in a corpse where the appearance seems to grow younger; the years fall away - something to do with the laying down of burdens, in my view.

Jane said, wonderingly, 'I know it must have hurt her when I replaced the tape on the cannula this morning' – we'd had rigged up some intravenous fluid for Tryphena, so that she was sufficiently hydrated - 'But she didn't even flinch. I know she still has sensation, because she responds when I smooth arnica on the bruising.' Like many elderly people, Tryphena tended to bruise around the IV points.

She was dying of extreme old age, slowly withdrawing from us, but her own deep awareness of something much greater was flooding into the room at the same time. Gillespie came in regularly to massage her feet with oil, singing very softly in a rumbling burr, and Tryphena would make joyous sounds in descant at the pleasure his hands were bringing. He was always very quiet afterwards. His take was, 'That leddy is bringing us closer to heaven.'

Will and Wendy were both much better and were back on light duties, but they kept away in case of bringing infection into the room. But on the Friday of that momentous week, Ash told them both that it could do no harm now, as Tryphena was nearer and nearer to the brink, if they wanted to look in. Carefully not touching her, Wendy surveyed the form of our elderly guest with infinite compassion, 'How beautiful she is!'

She was right. As life withdrew, Tryphena grew in grace and beauty, reminding me strangely of someone, but I couldn't bring to mind who.

Will, who had been utterly contrite in bringing flu into the Beacon, now held back, but when Wendy moved out of the way, his mouth fell open. 'Is it me or is there something golden – I don't know what it is? Look!' he pointed.

All of us saw it at the same moment, the sheath of her soul rising in a golden net. Jane clutched my hand, the tears pouring soundlessly down her cheeks, 'Oh my goodness!'

Gillespie sank to his knees at the foot of the bed and we all drew back to let Ash come forward, 'Don't be afraid!' he said. 'She is returning to her own familiar place.' His calmness steadied us.

We watched with wonder as the golden net slowly withdrew, rising towards the ceiling until it vanished and dispersed.

On the bed, Tryphena's face was utterly transfigured and we knew without a doubt what a great soul she had been. It was a privilege to have attended her passing, but now we had all swung too high, as Ash realised, 'I will keep vigil with her,' he said, dismissing us gently, 'If you will bring me another sanctum light, Jack...?'

The others made their way to the kitchen to digest what they had witnessed while I brought a new candle. On my return, Ash was sitting beside the bed, one hand upon her solar plexus and the other on her forehead; he seemed to be praying, so I left him.

Tryphena lay in state for 24 hours while we made the necessary arrangements. There was no need for a post-mortem examination: she had been under our care and had died of natural causes, so Ash and I signed her death certificate, and sorted out the funeral.

'Help me get her ready, please,' he asked us.

'I think Tryphena would prefer to be seen naked by women, gentlemen!' Jane said, shooing us out, so it was she and Wendy who washed her body, and dressed her in a linen nightdress. Then together we all helped dress her for her coffin, laying her out in her plum-coloured robes, with the golden mitre-like headdress that Ash said was from her time in the Order of the Ancient Mystery back in the 1920s. With his own hands, he placed the silver lamen of their lodge around her neck - an arch of stars over a pair of offering hands - and crossed her arms over the wand that he took from the long black bag that evidently held her magical equipment. Of her many rings, only the one amethyst remained, glowing in the light of the many candles that had been brought to surround her. So attired, Tryphena resembled an ancient queen prepared for her pyramid.

Anointing her with fragrant oil for her last journey, Ash solemnly kissed her on the forehead. Outside waited Ben and Eric Railton, the undertakers from Sumpton in the Vale, with a wickerwork coffin. We helped them place Tryphena in the coffin, fastened the straps, and bore it out to the waiting cart. Farmer Jelley stood on the stoop of his cart with hat raised as she was safely stowed, then turned to click on his two shire horses, Betsy and Barton. So began Tryphena's last journey, in a hay-cart heaped with early daffodils and narcissi flown in from the Scilly Isles by one of her confrères.

We followed on behind in a slow procession on foot, up the lane and along the road westward, turning off onto the path leading to the Downland Forest Burial Ground, where we met with the other mourners. Ash told me that Tryphena had been delighted to learn of its existence and had bought a plot for herself where a tree could be planted over her. Many people seemed to have already availed themselves of this service; both saplings and more established trees were already planted. In a few decades more, this place would be a forest in truth: but at present, it was a windy and unsheltered spot on a January day. Jane had worn her cherry anorak and a faux-fur hat to keep out the cold. With her mittened hand clutched in mine, she clung to my side as we made a circle with the others about the grave as the cart tail was lowered.

Members of the lodge stepped forward with Ash, to bear the coffin from the cart and lower it into the hole that waited. Men and women drew close as it descended and Ash proclaimed,

> 'O, Keeper of the Arching Stars,
> In service to the earth below,
> We bring to you a fallen star
> To raise to glory in your bow.
> Grant her a way that shall endure,
> An endless joy forever sure!'

The members of the lodge chanted together and bowed to the grave in farewell. Such utter simplicity felt right for Tryphena who had lived so long. Like a story read before bed when a child falls asleep at the end, there was a rightness to it.

The Downland Forest Burial Ground people had assured us that they could backfill the grave for us with a JCB, but by common consent we chose to fill it spadeful by spadeful ourselves, with all but the most elderly mourners taking their turn in that bitter wind. By the time it was done, the twilight was gathering along the line of the Downs.

Finally, the grave was filled and Gillespie, in full Highland rig, brought forward the hornbeam sapling that had been selected. Ash held the slender trunk as Gillespie planted it, patting the earth down with a spade with the blessing of his own green fingers. He stood straight as a soldier to salute it, then Wendy brought him his pipes. He played the *Flowers of the Forest* as a lament, eliding it into a wandering tune I didn't know - one of his own, I suspect, which expressed what we had all felt while attending to this great lady. The dreich echo of the pipes was answered by blasts of Arctic wind from the North East, and I took a professional decision, escorting Wendy and Will back to the carpark where the mourners were streaming back, getting them a lift onwards lest they relapse after their flu.

The rest of us walked back to Ted Jelley's farm, where he had kindly opened his barn for the funeral reception. After the chilly Downland Burial Ground it was very welcome to have a hot cup of tea. Ted's daughter, Elaine, had laid a wonderful spread to which Wendy had contributed. We were also glad of the braziers that had been brought in to warm us after our labours.

Ash spoke to each of the mourners. I was keeping a keen eye upon him, wondering how he was coping, but only the professional Ash was present that day.

Over the funeral bake-meats, Gillespie drew me to one side, passing me a quick nip of his whiskey flask under the tablecloth. 'Have a dram, laddie. Keep the wind oot of your bones!'

I took an unashamed long drag on the flask, 'Is Ash alright, do you think?'

Gillespie cast a considering eye, 'Aye. He'll be fine the noo, but later, mind...' He shook his head. 'I shall remember that dear lady's going to the end of my days. That we should ever dee so well!'

I agreed with him. Will Walton stood rather apart, looking lonely and left-out. I brought him a plate of jam tarts to try. At his hesitation, I added, 'It's alright, they don't count when you've been shovelling earth in such a wind!'

He took one, with a sideways look, 'You said when I started here that I would experience some out-of-this-world things. I thought you were joking, you know? I still don't know whether what I saw was real...'

'Well, rational knowledge is one thing, but the witness of your own senses is another.... Reality has many sides to it, and we see more ways round it at the Beacon than anywhere else I've ever worked,' I advised him, wedging a lemon curd tart into my mouth, which put paid to further discussion.

Feeling like a latter-day Ash myself, I found myself saying to him afterwards, 'Those who deal with the soul and its care have to stay alert and not dismiss what shows itself. With Ash back, not only will our caseload double, but you'll be seeing more of that sort of thing.'

Will looked into his cider, 'I'm not sure I'm up for it. It's kind of out of my remit.' He suddenly looked young and vulnerable, not like the keen young doctor I'd taken on to support the work.

'Well, it was once out of mine, too,' I assured him. 'When I first came to the Beacon, I could scarcely credit the kinds of cases we saw. Ash used to tell me that we were men under orders, not under our own steam, and that's still a good guide. Keep your nerve and drink up your cider, I would! I am very happy with your work here.'

When we returned, stiff and cold, there was only Tryphena's room to put to rights.

'I'll strip the bed and tidy up,' said Jane to Wendy who was looking a little wan again. 'You go and sit down: you look all in!'

I went to help Jane, but as we opened the door, we were met with the smell of the fragrant oil with which Tryphena had been anointed earlier; it seemed to have become enhanced, blooming to fill the space with an intensity of perfume. You would have sworn that someone had been incensing the room since we left.

Jane said in an awed voice, 'I've heard of the odour of sanctity, but I've never smelled it till now! I thought it was just a metaphor...' She had been raised as a Catholic, and seemed surprised to find things to be just as spiritual tradition asserted.

When we had tidied up, she picked up the miniature of the young man with the violin, which still lay on the bedside, addressing it with, 'And who are you? Well, you're a dish and no mistake!'

'It is of Vivian Rich, the violinist,' said Ash from the doorway. 'He was her lover.'

'Well, I can see there's quite a story to tell ...' Jane made an opening, but Ash did not rush to fill in any more detail.

'So, where should we send her things?' she asked, tidying Tryphena's effects into a linen basket.

'They will stay with me,' said Ash, holding out his hands for the basket, also placing the miniature into it, 'She was a member of my family, after all.' Ash never spoke about his family, so I assumed he was using the word to cover his extended esoteric acquaintance with her.

I thought again of the documents we had witnesses in Nutbourne. 'And what happens to Tryphena's house?'

'It will be held in trust, but everything waits on probate,' was all he would say.

The inevitable day dawned when Jane had to travel up to Manchester: I would not see her again until Hilary term ended with the Easter Holidays. No more snuggling in bed under the warm quilt, hiding from winter's cold with my beloved in my arms. No more walks on the Downs hand in hand.

Jane was adamant that she would drive the hire car back to the airport herself, 'However would you get back? Anyway, you know you will just make yourself miserable.'

As the car splashed through the puddles in the lane, I waved her off, knowing that Ash was right. She was indeed my helpmeet and I was incomplete without her but, at that moment. the winter seemed suddenly stretched into infinite emptiness.

'Will you come for a walk, Jack?' Ash appeared at my shoulder after the car was lost from view.

It was too wet and muddy to go up Hartsworth Beacon, so we took a tour of the garden, hunting for any sign of snowdrops. We found some up in the Wilderness, at the back of house - strangely in the most wintery part of the grounds that rarely got the sun. Ash carefully dug up the plant, roots and all, putting it into a porcelain planter, 'I always take the first snowdrops in to show Melanie,' he said.

I smiled, indulgent of his fancies, then something struck me, 'Where is Melanie buried?' For I had never known him visit a cemetery. The Downland Forest Burial Ground was very recently started, and she had died many years ago.

'She isn't,' he said, matter of factly. 'She was cremated and her ashes scattered over Hartsworth Beacon. It was what she wanted.'

'How are you now?' I asked, after a while, knowing how greatly Tryphena's going must have affected him.

Shading his eyes, he looked out over our glorious view and considered, 'I am glad I was back in time to say farewell... I will miss her guiding hand and her wisdom... She trained me, you know. Melanie was my sponsor, but Tryphena was the head of the lodge, and she initiated me. It is a link that remains unbroken.'

We walked round to the Spinney where the sugar maples and birches grew, running our hands across the lavender and rosemary bushes as we went. The sun suddenly shone on the back of his hand, and I saw Tryphena's red jasper Capricorn ring was on his ring-finger.

'She gave you her signet ring?'

'Yes. It is a family heirloom.'

I was puzzled, 'Does she have no descendants to pass it onto, then?'

'Oh yes.' He looked at me with a secret smile. Then I suddenly remembered who Tryphena reminded me of - the same depth of the eye socket, the straight nose – how could I have not noticed?

'But.... When you said that she was family, I thought you meant she was one of your spiritual family, not a blood relation?'

'She is both. Tryphena was also my grandmother. Of course, I didn't know that for many years, but I worked it out. My mother was her daughter, the love child of Tryphena and Vivian Rich....'

'...who was your grandfather! – But why did you not say something to us all?'

'She knew that I knew, but it was her secret to keep while she was alive. We never acknowledged our bond, and that was fine by me. My grandparents did not have a conventional relationship, you understand, and my mother was brought up as part of another family. It took a deal of detection to follow the leads. She and my father are dead now...'

'So, you are the last of your line?'

'As far as I know.'

I flung an arm around him, 'My dear friend, I am so sorry.'

But while I held him, the words from St Matthews' gospel echoed unspoken between us, "Who is my mother, and who are my brothers?" And the answer resounded within me, "Here are my mother and my brothers."'

And I knew that meant myself and all who worked at the Beacon.

It was the last day of January, and new cases were beginning to arrive. The snowdrops adorned Melanie's shrine in the porch, ready to welcome them. Deep winter was coming to an end, and we were ready for the onset of our year. There was just one more component to put into place.

I called Ash into the office and asked him formally if he deemed himself fit to be re-employed, and he duly signed the papers that our solicitor, Jimmy Stenson, had drawn up. It felt very strange to be on the other side of the desk and I would never get used to it, I told him, 'I liked it best when we sat side by side.'

'As soon as the GMC gives its approval and restores my registration, I can join you. Until then, you are in charge, and I will stay this side of the desk' he asserted, grinning. Since he had had a significant break from practice, we had to go through the formalities.

He had gained a little weight due to Wendy's cooking endeavours that month, but Ash would never be anything other than slender, I thought, but he was looking alright – a restored, if white-haired, version of the old Ash who had once welcomed me here as his assistant.

This was my friend but, until things were regularised, I was still – bizarrely – his employer.

Standing, I formally shook his hand, 'Welcome to the Beacon,' I said, warmly. 'It's so good to have you back!'

Case 2: IN THE SHADOW OF THE LONG MAN

> We who have seen (the old divinities) pass in rattling harness, and in soft robes, and heard them speak with articulate voices while we lay in deathlike trance, know that they are always making and unmaking humanity, which is indeed but the trembling of their lips.
>
> **W.B.Yeats** – Rosa Mystica

Living as we do, in the shadow of the South Downs at the Beacon, we cannot fail to be moved by their splendour every day. Their bright magnificence upon the southern skyline somehow hints at the sea that lies beyond them, while their sturdy, springy backs provide the pathway of all our walking. The Downs listen kindly to all the sorry tales that we have trudged through, while their slopes support our sometimes staggering steps with the softness of their chalk, and the refreshing rigour of their flint.

For lovers of chalk down-land, there is the additional delight of the chalk hill figures that antiquity has left us. Some of these giant figures were made millennia ago, or rather more recently - archaeologists and historians argue just how long - for how can you estimate a process that involves the generational scraping back the turf to reveal the chalk - with any great certainty?

The Long Man of Wilmington is the nearest figure to the Beacon. He is one of the more uncertain hill figures, in terms of dating. Unlike, the White Horse of Uffington on the Berkshire Downs, which has been maintained by regular community gatherings to scrape back of the turf for over 4000 years, the Long Man himself fell into disrepair back in the 19th century, and could only be faintly discerned in low sunlight or in snow. His outline was finally preserved by the unfortunate expedient of laying some yellow bricks upon his outline, which were finally replaced in the 1960s by pre-cast concrete blocks – a less authentic method of preservation than the traditional scouring of the chalk, but at least we can always see him now.

The Long Man looks north from the steep side of Windover Hill – the bare outline of man with his outstretched arms each clasping a staff, or so most people describe them. He stands 226 feet high, with about 30 yards between each staff. Like a white gingerbread man with sticks, outlined by the green turf, he has stood there since at least there was a medieval Abbey at nearby Wilmington. Along the ridge of the Downs, he is surrounded by much older Neolithic tumuli, with both long and round barrows. But no-one is sure of his origins: he is Odin, say the Old English enthusiasts; while antiquarians swear he was carved by monks to represent and encourage pilgrims; or he was an agricultural figure with scythe and hay fork, say some early records, but recent investigations report that he may be post-Reformation after all.

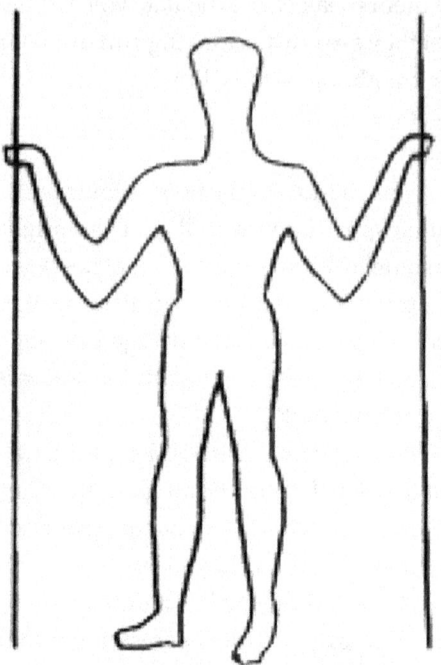

Outline of the Long Man

To me, I have to say, he has never seemed very modern. Whenever I have driven past this chalk hill figure, I have not seen the two uprights on which he rests his hands as staves, but rather as the edges of a doorway which he is holding open. And that was my opinion a long time before we had Ned Bryher under our care, when my perception of these doors became critical to his cure.

I had just dropped Ash off at Capricorn House down in Nutbourne, where he was going to sort through Tryphena's things, now that probate had been proved, and he was going to stay over the night there. In my soul, I was so glad that Ash was with us again, and that the weight of responsibility for the Beacon that I had carried in his absence could be shared with him once more. In sheer lightness of heart, I decided to take the longer road past the Long Man on my way home - since that chalk figure feels to me like the guardian of the Downs. Like telling the bees that someone has died, I somehow felt that giving the Long Man tidings of Ash's return seemed only right and proper.

It was just as well that I did. The day was drear, with flakes of snow beginning to descend, but I was keen to see the chalk hill figure before he put on his winter array and became totally invisible to view. I drew level with Windover Hill, slowing the car, meaning to briefly park in the pulling-in place opposite. But before I could even put on the hand-brake a wild-looking woman in a black poncho leapt across the road and threw herself onto the bonnet of the car. Her straw-coloured hair was in disarray and her expression desperate.

'Oh, thank the Lady!' she breathed, as I rolled down my window. 'Can you come? He's too heavy for me carry ... and with the snow coming down... There's nobody about.' She was Canadian, I knew, from the way she said 'aboot.'

I got out and appraised her: a woman in her early thirties, I judged, with a broad face and appealing green eyes. 'What's the trouble?'

She gestured up towards the Long Man, 'It's my partner, Ned... I can't get him to stand up.'

'Has he had an accident, or does he have a prior medical condition? I am a doctor.'

She sighed with relief and pulled me bodily across the road, indicating a figure in a red anorak lying at the feet of the Long Man: from the car, I had assumed the redness to be some piece of stray plastic sheeting blown away from some local farm.

'We were walking and he wanted to meditate, but now he won't move. He's got no condition that I know of.'

To calm her distress, I asked, 'We will deal with it, but you will have to tell me which is the best way to get to where he is.'

'Up here,' she pointed to the path leading up the South Downs Way, trying to pull me towards it. Neither my car, nor any emergency vehicle could make it to where he was lying – only a helicopter - so it would have to be shank's pony.

'Hang on, we're going to need a few things!' I got some supplies from the car, including the car-blanket, thrusting it into my pack-back.

By the time we reached the recumbent young man, the snow was coming down thicker, settling on his curly brown hair. His legs were still crossed and he had merely slumped forward. The woman wrapped the blanket around him while I examined him thoroughly. He seemed uninjured but there was something about him that reminded me more of Ash in trance than with a man who had lapsed into unconsciousness from some *a priori* condition.

He needed to be out of this weather, and the nearest medical unit would be Lewes, 'He seems to be alright, but just in a deep state of meditation,' I said to the woman, wonderingly.

She bit her bottom lip, 'Oh, not again!' She sounded prosaically annoyed.

My head went up, 'Has this happened before, then?'

She nodded, 'When we were on Orkney – that was mighty inconvenient, too.'

'Are you sure that he's not taken any substances to account for this?'

She sighed, brushing off the snow settling on his chest, 'They all ask that one! No, he's clean. I wouldn't be with him, truly, if he were that way inclined. Anyway, Ned's too fastidious for that.'

Whatever this was about, we would clearly have to carry him back to my car as the snow was thickening: the only other way to get him off the hill would by helicopter if it got worse.

'Are you able to help me?' I slid both of my arms under his to get a sense of the weight requirement: he was of slender build, fortunately. 'I think I can do it as a fireman's lift, if you lend a supporting hand.'

The woman stepped forward, 'I'm strong. We can manage him together if we cross hands.'

Her big-boned body could have carried a grown sheep or a calf, I reckoned, but a man? However, she was not joking: we chair-lifted Ned down the slope between us, and managed to get him down to the road-side, where I could back up the car, and slide him across the back seat.

As we waited for the heater to engage, and the windscreen wipers to take effect, I told her, 'I'm going to run you into Lewes, to the Victoria Hospital – they only do minor injuries, but they are the nearest. Now tell me your name and about when this last happened.'

'A hospital will just shake their heads and not know what to do, you know – that's what happened last time. On Orkney, I got him to the Balfour Hospital in Kirkwall and they had no idea. – Oh, and I'm Wilma Graceson.'

I pulled off my glove to shake her formally outstretched hand. 'Pleased to meet you, Wilma. I am Jack Rivers. - How did Ned come out of it, last time?'

'He just came to in his good time, a few days later. He's had all the tests, but he kind of zones out for long periods.'

Even as we sped along the road to Lewes, I was feeling that this was a case that might be more up our street than the hospital's, but the Beacon was still another 50 minute's drive or longer, if the weather worsened. Capricorn House was much nearer, I realized, but I did not want to drop an unconscious man into what was already a house of bereavement.

Wilma told me that she had followed Ned all over the country, looking at sacred sites: from Orkney to Scilly, from Bardsey Island in the West to Lindisfarne in the North East, traipsing over hill and under dale in search of antiquity and sacred tradition. These visits had been paid for out of Wilma's unlimited allowance, for she came from a moneyed family, while Ned's parents had long since split up, neither much caring about where, or with whom, their son travelled, so long as he never came home again. They had had enough of him and his sweeping enthusiasms.

There is a brand of explorer who cares not for the facts and figures so much, as for the myth and mystery, and it was clear to me that Ned was the king of those pilgrims, with an appetite for ancient stones and local folk traditions that was never sated.

'What do you think causes it?'

'I don't know, it's like his fascination for antiquity gets him high.' She rolled her eyes in self-mockery. 'Yeah, I know. Sounds stupid, but that's the bottom line.'

I spoke to her a little about our work, as we drove, to the extent that she said, 'I sure would like him to see your partner. He sounds perfect for this.'

In the face of her sudden hope, I said, 'Well, if the hospital finds nothing wrong with him, then contact us. Our card is just there under the dashboard. – Oh, I forgot to ask, how did you get to the Long Man?'

'We parked in a village about four miles away. – Don't worry about it. I can get a taxi back and pick up the hire truck.'

I saw them both safely into the hospital in Lewes and drove home in what turned out to be the worst blizzards of the year.

When I next drove back that way, the Long Man was entirely invisible, still caked with layers of snow which had frozen hard. I was going to pick up Ash and confer with him about Ned, since Wilma had phoned me the next day after I lifted them both into Lewes. The hospital had put Ned under observation overnight but was keen to have him removed to a larger hospital, since they said they didn't have the facilities to deal with him. 'But it's more likely they don't know what to do about him,' Wilma observed. 'I got a taxi over to pick up the truck, so I can bring him over to you, if you have the room. I can pay,' she'd said over the phone.

Back at Capricorn House, I found Ash surrounded by piles of papers which he had been sorting through. They were stacked all over the big dining table from end to end. As promised, I had brought him more file boxes to put them all into, but I still had to run down to the local supermarket and beg a few tomato boxes for the overspill. It was still a shock to see his prematurely-whitened hair.

'I was hoping that I would have this all straight before you came, but you know the problem, I have spent too long reading everything.' He looked drawn and thoroughly over-extended from his efforts. His old blue sweater, thrust upon him by Wendy before he set out, hung about him voluminously, a reminder of how much weight he had lost. The wrists protruding from the long sleeves were still way too thin.

'Look, it's awful going through family stuff without help. Do you want me to sort through Tryphena's clothes for you?'

'It's already done. Martina next door is going to take the usable stuff to the charity shop. Tryphena's magical equipment is all packed up, and I will take that to the lodge next month.'

I looked around the beautiful front room with its elevated, unobstructed sea-view, 'And what will happen to the house?' I knew he had inherited it from his unacknowledged grandmother when the will was read.

'I am going to keep it on,' he said, staggering a little under the weight of the papers. I promptly took the box from his arms and made him sit down again, automatically examining him, concluding that he had not been taking care of himself, 'And when did you last eat?'

Distractedly, he admitted, 'Probably yesterday.' Taking in my hard stare, he smiled, 'I know, but it's difficult to remember to eat regularly when you've only been eating once a day for so long.'

Marching into the kitchen, and muttering darkly about people who go off to Nepal, I looked into the depleted larder. I heated some tinned consommé well past its sell-by date, throwing in a capful of brandy for good measure, and spread some crackers with marmite, thrusting this scratch meal down on the table before him with, 'Now, eat that, and then we will go home.' Grief is never good on an empty stomach, and Ash was still not looking as hale and hearty as I would like.

While he ate, I told him about my encounter on the road.

He spooned soup, 'What did the hospital say?'

'They declined to comment, but they must have run a few tests to see what might be going on. They want Wilma to take him to a bigger hospital for a larger battery of tests. Ned is just unconscious, but it looks more like when you "go out" than anything else, to my view.'

He nodded, 'It sounds intriguing. Yes, let's have him come to the Beacon, if the doctors are happy to discharge him into our care.'

'I think they will gladly relinquish him to Wilma: she is a force of nature.'

After Wilma had delivered Ned to us, and Wendy had made him comfortable, Ash looked him over thoroughly, 'You are right. He is not unconscious, just in a deep state of meditation. Though I'm astonished he hasn't been brought up to the surface by all these moves. I wonder what training he has had?'

'Training?'

'Well, few people of my acquaintance can sustain this depth of meditation without prior spiritual training or some spectacular natural aptitude. Had he been a Tibetan monk, I could understand it...'

'He looks a bit young for much of that kind of malarky - er, thing.' My careless words hovered in the air, and I kicked myself for being so dismissive. I covered it with, 'So why is Ned so prone to these lapses, do you think?'

'I suspect because his deep fascination with the myths and legends of the places he visits has made his soul bodies unstable, though Melanie would have said, "the faeries have cast the glamour o'er him."' He mentioned his mentor so infrequently, I looked up, realizing that some of the papers he was going through must have brought her to mind. We passed her photo on the hall shrine every day, but I sometimes forgot from whence Ash's wisdom arose.

Ash had already told Wilma, 'Ned needs a lot of grounding before he does much more exploring.' She had merely turned down the corners of her mouth in a dubious way, 'Well, I have tried.' She was downstairs with Wendy, waiting for our prognosis.

I asked him, 'What can we do?'

'You will watch him while I go out and act as a Soul Shepherd, bringing him back. If you see any movements towards consciousness, you are to start calling him gently but insistently by his name - like an annoying alarm clock that won't switch off.'

Ash sat opposite me, on the other side of the bed. He made a few passes with his left hand over Ned's body, as if measuring the subtle but unseen soul-bodies. Then, uttering a sequence of overtones, he entered into a deep stillness.

I watched, occasionally gazing out of the window at the sky, as the snow-heavy clouds began to gather beyond the Beacon. The room darkened within, even as it grew nearer to sunset without, where a pure gold and magenta tinted the sky. A lone gull called a melancholy cry, and flew landwards away. The golden rim of Hartworth Beacon briefly illuminated the darkening room, its reflected light falling upon the deeply sleeping man on the bed, and upon Ash's face, now shuttered with searching. The shadows took on a deeper plum-coloured tint from that February sky, as I waited.

It is hard to concentrate when time is empty, so I tried, just for a few minutes, to sense what Ash was doing, closing my own eyes, seeing if I could perceive where Ned was. Then, mindful of my instructions, I found I had to shake myself into wakefulness since the snow-heavy sky threatened to claim me also. I began to count the pattern of Ned's breathing, as I have done many a time with a dying patient, but this time seeking to mark the return of life, rather than note its ebbing away. I took off my watch to time the slow rise and fall of Ned's chest. It seemed that, after 15-18 minutes, the breath was picking up pace; after 20 minutes, I was sure of it. Finally, Ned began to shift like a man in dreaming REM sleep; as he came out of the deeps depths where he had been submerged, his feet arched back and forward.

As I began to call, 'Ned' in a low urgent voice, he started to turn his head from side to side, as if trying to forbid me. I increased the volume, checking to see how Ash was doing as well – it felt to me as if he was driving Ned back towards me, as a sheepdog turns a flock of sheep into a pen, slowly but surely. His own eyes fluttered open, looking into mine. I nodded, indicating how Ned was coming into consciousness. Ash rose, leaving the room, as I called, 'Ned, Ned, Ned!' as insistently as I could. The door opened and Wilma was ushered in.

Her mouth was one arrested O of astonishment, as Ned opened his eyes upon her with a deep sigh, 'Oh, Wilma, what a wonderful dream I've had.'

'What was it, hon?' her voice vibrant with relief. She sank to her knees at the bedside, clutching his hand, and kissing it, 'You had me so worried, you bad boy.'

Now that Ned was awake, his character was more clearly apparent. In the curl of his lip and wings of his nose, there was a self-indulgent, even willful, expression, spoiling his thin face.

'I was with the Deep Ones in the valley. They were dancing....' His eyes began to close, seeking that dream world again, but Ash was having none of it. In a sharp, clipped voice, he announced, 'It is 12th February and 11.30am. Time for you to wake up.'

I was amazed to see the old Ash, just as he had been before he went away, but with a grimmer tone than I had ever heard before.

Ned's eyes snapped open at the unfamiliar but commanding voice, as he took in myself and Ash, and his unfamiliar surroundings, looking sheepish, 'Have I had one of my long sleeps again?'

'You sure have, hon! ...been gone the best part of three days. These kind gentlemen have a clinic here and they helped you come back.'

Ned looked straight at me, struggling to rise on one elbow. By his ruckled brow and truculent mouth, it was clear that he not at all thankful, so Wilma calmly thanked us on his behalf.

I shook my head, 'I did very little, save call your name. It was Ash who did the bringing back, not me.'

Ned turned his head reluctantly, his face whitening as Ash's eyes bored down into his. I had no idea what was happening between them, but I would swear that Ned recognized him. The instant passed, as Wendy knocked at the door. She had been primed to prepare one of her champion teas downstairs, and now she brought tea and toast to our errant sleeper, watching with satisfaction as he wolfed it down. 'Is there any more?' he asked plaintively.

Ash pre-empted Wendy's answer, 'There is indeed, but you will have to get up and come downstairs for it.' His voice had less steel in it, but enough to show that he was not prepared for any acting up.

Wendy blinked at Ash in surprise, tempering her employer's unwonted tone with an encouraging, 'There's a roaring fire downstairs. Gillespie just built it up for you.'

Wilma helped him into a dressing gown that had been left by a forgetful guest, and Ned was brought down to the cosy warmth of the sitting room, where Wendy had laden a table full of delights: sandwiches and little pies, a divided glass crystal plate of tomatoes and beetroot, twinkling with home-made pickles, and a plate of crumpets ready to toast on the fire. Wilma watched Ash wield the toasting fork and then, declaring herself smitten with the whole idea, asked to take it over and toasted some more to keep up with Ned's prodigious appetite. I was allowed to superintend the teapot while Wendy went and fetched in an array of Welsh cakes, and a freshly made Black Bun, followed by an anxious Gillespie, determined not to lose out on this, his country's native Hogmanay delicacy. Such was his desire for this pasty-wrapped dark fruit cake that Wendy had to make it regularly throughout the winter months.

I watched Ned carefully as he ate and drank. Wilma was hunched over the tea tray anxiously watching him as well. I shared some of her anxiety, flashing her a complicit look over the Welsh cakes as I passed her the plate. Over the last pot of tea, we hit the crunch. Ned drained his cup down, and began to look about him. To that moment, he seemed to have taken every service as his due. Now he stroked his chin, fastidiously realizing that he had not shaved for a while, 'I'm sorry to have put you out like this. I'd like to shave before we go, if that's alright.'

Wilma's face fell, but before she could protest, Ash said evenly, 'Mr Bryher, you have been out of consciousness for nearly 72 hours. Not only do we not know what caused this, we also don't know what kind of effect it has had upon your system. I would strongly advize that you stay here for at least another few days until we are clearer what has happened.' Even as Ash said this, I had the impression that he already knew very well.

'But I often fall asleep like that when I'm going around the sites,' Ned breezed a wide smile.

No-one smiled back, especially Wilma, who thrust both sets of fingers into her thick blonde hair in frustrated protest.

Ash maintained his professional veneer, 'Nonetheless, your unexplained lapses into unconsciousness are a considerable worry to your companion, who has to deal with your condition, in often very remote locations.'

Wilma burst into silent tears, at this rare and unaccustomed solidarity from another human being. Ned flashed his charm at Wilma's back, puzzled that she was being so uncooperative, 'Wilma's been great. She can deal with me, no trouble, eh?'

Slowly and with great dignity, Wilma turned herself to address him. 'No, Ned, she can't do it anymore. Either you get this problem sorted out once and for all, or I go back to Ontario.'

Ned's face dropped, like a boy who has been told he will not be having another ice-cream at the seaside ever again. He blustered, 'But we were going to go to Karnac to see the stones….'

'The stones will still be there when you get better, Ned. But if you want to go on and see them, then I think there's a ferry to Brittany from Frisdon, but you will need to organize that for yourself.' To underscore her words, Wilma rose, shouldered her backpack, and walked towards the door.

It had been made clear to us that Ned had taken little responsibility for either the funding or the organization of his pilgrimages, being wholly dependent upon Wilma's largesse and on her arrangements to reach his destination, so his dismay was considerable. He struggled to rise, but wasn't yet strong enough to get far. Gillespie stepped in and lent an arm, with a gruff challenge, 'Are you just going to let that braw lassie go, or are you going to stand by her?'

'Well, she's not going to stay by me!' he wailed in a childish pet.

'Mebbe she is waiting for the boy to wake up and become a man?' Gillespie suggested to the air at large, completely unmoved by Wendy's sharp turn of the head in his direction. But tough love was what Ned needed.

'Shall we go call her back?' Gillespie pulled at Ned's arm.

A battle royal was playing out in that narrow chest, clearly, but he nodded miserably, and shuffled towards the hall where Wilma was hefting her backpack onto her shoulder. She put one hand on the front door handle, and dealt him her ultimatum. 'I'm going away now, Ned. I'm going to find a hotel nearby, and I suggest you think hard. If you stay here and get this sorted out, I will pay for your treatment, and I will come back, and we can talk about how it's going to be. But if you leave this place before the week is out, I wash my hands of you. If you go off visiting some other site without getting sorted, then I am going home to Canada for good.'

He crumpled to his knees and clung to her ankles in an extremity of supplication, 'Wilma, my dear one, don't leave me, please!'

Wilma's heart was rent, but she did not stoop to detach him. She opened the door, letting in a blast of icy air, 'I'm going now. Just think, Ned. I can't deal with this mystery any more. It hurts too much, and you just don't care enough.'

She shuffled a few steps into the cold before she finally shook off his clasping hands, and strode to her van. I came to her side, holding open the back doors against the icy blast, as she loaded her backpack, assuring her, 'He'll be ok with us. We've had one or two reluctant guests before. Time and Ash usually tell on them.'

She nodded, 'Thank you. I knew I could depend on you the moment I set eyes on you. Look, send me the bill whether he stays or goes – I'll let you know tonight where I am staying. Just let me know whether there's any hope.'

Wilma waved to me as she turned the van into the lane and was gone. Lying across the drive, Ned stared after the retreating vehicle with all the *horror vacui* of a man lost in the Arctic wastes without a compass.

'No! most definitely not!' An emphatic Wendy was almost shouting. I looked out of the art room and saw Ned slinking away hurriedly with his tail between his legs. Coming into the kitchen, I found Wendy inarticulate with rage, with a raised wooden spoon in her hand. 'That man – that man – ' she swallowed, trying to get control of her emotions, '… needs a mother.' Which was a fair assessment, I thought. Wilma was clearly tired of being Ned's, which is why it was expedient for her to keep away from him for a while. I sat Wendy down and poured her a cup of tea, prepared to listen.

'He's been down here, pestering me every hour of the day, wheedling and whining like a little lap dog,' she explained.

'What does he want?' trying not to smile.

She shot me a peeved look, 'He wants a substitute Wilma, I imagine, and he's not finding one in me! If he comes into my kitchen one more time, I will hit him.'

'You mean he was coming onto you?'

She pressed her lips together, 'A flick of a wet tea-towel would fend off the likes of that, no! He's been trying to find out where Wilma is from me by devious means. I hope you have her details locked up, because he's out to get them. He just tried to touch me for funds too, as he's not got a penny on him. I'd not put him beyond stealing some money to hire a taxi to take him to her and make a grand gesture. He pretended it was her birthday, when I know perfectly well she's a Cancerian, because we had a talk about astrology. The wretch!'

'Leave him to me. We'll make the kitchen out of bounds,' I promised.

After Wilma had departed, we'd had a difficult time with Ned who revealed just how childish and manipulative he could be. Since neither pleading nor tantrums would move us, he reverted to a stubborn silence, looking more and more like the Elephant's Child developing his trunk, from Kipling's *Just So* story. Leaving Ned with Gillespie, I went to confer with Ash, finding him reading in the main office. The temperature within was almost glacial.

'It's freezing in here, how can you stand it?!'

Ash put aside his book and drew the silk scarf tighter around his neck, 'I hadn't noticed, sorry.'

I poked up the extinguished fire, quickly laying some kindling and pear-wood logs around a new firelighter, 'I suppose I should apologize for inflicting him on the Beacon?'

'Well, we've had more willing guests, but I think we will not proceed far until we have some cooperation. You were perfectly right in your diagnosis, by the way, Jack. He was just "out" but in a kind of way that is willfully self-destructive.'

I appraised him, 'What was all that about earlier, when he was coming round? You sounded almost cross with him.'

He nodded, 'Yes, I was! You have no idea what trouble he was to bring back. He has all the cunning of a wagonload of monkeys. I had to take some extreme measures to extract him from several hiding places that he has been holing up in.'

It was unlike him to be so grim, 'So I gather that this case is more serious than it appears?'

'Indeed so! There is something directing his movements that has a will of its own. Added to his own mischievous and selfish desires, it is an unpleasant combination, and will be no end of trouble to control. He's lucky that Wilma has been so compliant till now, but since her patience is exhausted, we must expect more upheaval.'

'When you say, "directing his movement", are you saying he's not responsible for his own actions?'

'That's the annoying part: if he exercised some normal restraint and self-care, he would be perfectly in charge of his life. Instead, he chooses to go from pillar to post, chasing the next sacred site.'

I scratched my head, 'Well, I've heard of "island-bagging," but sacred site bagging is a form of collection I can't get my head around.'

'I believe that what started as a perfectly understandable interest in ancient sites has turned into something more dangerous, at least for him. I spoke truly on the first evening: "the faeries have cast their glamour o'er him" indeed, or one particularly difficult faery has.'

My brows rose, 'Whenever I think I've heard everything, you still have the power to confound me! Fairies? What next?!' I held my hands nearer to fire.

'There's no need to sound so disgusted! We are not talking fairies – the winsome dragonfly-winged brigade from children's picture books - but *faeries* – the ancient inhabitants of the earth who live beside us and who have their own separate existence.'

I sat gob-smacked. My undisguised disbelief in everything he was saying was total.

Sighing, Ash took up his vain attempt to persuade me by another tack, 'Have you never been faery-led? You know, when you start out in one direction and find yourself in a totally other place, and utterly lost?'

Something began to stir in memory. There was the time when I was with my parents in the New Forest. 'I don't really know about faery-led – lost, certainly. When I was about 5 or 6, -...I don't recall now.... we'd gone for some kind of car-rally holiday organized by dad's workmates from the car-factory, a kind of work's outing weekend. The car blanket had been spread out and Mum was preparing the picnic, but I wouldn't leave the food alone, and so she sent me off to play. I remember stepping through a gap in the hedge and finding myself somewhere else. Gone was the large field with cars and picnickers, with dads, mums and children running about, and I was quite alone. I couldn't even hear anyone else.' I fell silent, remembering my distress and panic, and the humiliation of having lost everyone in my life by that one thoughtless action. 'I don't know how long I was gone, but it seemed like an age. I remember being hot and thirsty, and getting more and more panicked.'

'How did it end?'

'I cried out and when no-one came, I tried to find the gap in the hedge, but I couldn't find even a crack anywhere round the field I was in. A horse showed me in the end, though I swear there had been no horse in the field previously, but suddenly it was there and I followed it through – I was miles away and a farm-worker drove me on his tractor down a country lane into the field where the cars were parked. My sister says that I was gone for about 3 hours, and I'm inclined to believe her because my parents didn't usually make any kind of fuss, but they were so relieved to have me back. It felt to me like maybe a panicky quarter of an hour. We never spoke of it again, but I think they must have called the police, because I remember the policeman putting his big helmet on my head to make me laugh.'

'And what did you think had happened?'

'I don't know... I have no explanation, except I probably got panicked and turned around, with no sense of direction.'

Unmoved by my explanation, Ash nodded in confirmation of my tale, 'Like I said, "faery-led." A perfect example: child falls into fairyland and is finally retrieved. The Hidden People love children. Now, remember what it was like to be that lost in time and space, and consider Ned: he falls out of time and space every time he goes to a sacred site: he thinks to himself that he is doing this incredibly spiritual thing, when he is really just opening himself up to be stolen away. He's done it so many times, it has become addictive.'

'How can you know that?'

'Because I saw him and how he behaved when I was trying to bring him back. I also saw what was with him, leading him away. One day soon he is going to go to a lovely landmark, lapse into that state again, only no-one will be able to bring him back. He will not come back. He will become just another footnote in some future folklorist's account of faery-led people who fall out of time, only to return hundreds of years later.' His voice held a certainty that chilled me to the bone.

'What was it leading him? What did it look like?' Then I remembered, 'Ned seemed to almost recognize you when he came round. Have you met him before?'

'No. It is not *Ned* I've seen before... Do you remember when we treated Philip King*, when I helped you see what I see?'

'You mean, when you made me crouch down and you put one hand upon the top of my head and the other under my heels?' This transfer of the second sight was an old method that could be conferred by one seer upon a non-seer. 'It was a method that Tryphena got from Vivian, who got it from an old Scottish travelling woman, who also taught him some old airs for the violin.

Tryphena passed it to me, and I will have to pass the way of it onto a woman, someday – that's how the knowledge runs, woman to man, man to woman.'

I sighed with relief, not wanting to be the bearer of that kind of knowledge.

'So, would you be prepared to experience that again? I think you have a

*See 'Singapore Sling,' in *Diary of a Soul Doctor*

stronger rapport with Ned than I do, you being the one to rescue him from "the bare hill-side."'

I thought deeply; while it had been amazing to witness the trails of ritual movement, to see the ancestral presences that only Ash could see, I was not sure I wanted to do that again.

'What use would it be to Ned, if I did?'

'To have the support of a man who has a healthy dose of scepticism but can still see the dangers nevertheless? I think that would count for a great deal.'

Fate had thrown myself and Philip King together in a way that had resulted in my first acquaintance with Jane, and led to our whirlwind romance, so I felt very warmly towards him, but Ned was a wholly unattractive proposition, with his sneaky, wheedling ways.

'Well, I can see that Ned can't be allowed to just lapse into these states, drifting like a ship without anchor... but you said he knows what he is doing?'

'He does, and he hasn't taken care about how and when he does it.'

Alarmed, I asked, 'You wouldn't want me to go out after him, would you?'

'Not without guidance and companionship, certainly. After all, two sheepdogs work better than one....'

'Very well. When and how are we going to do it? Philip King was desperate for our help, but Ned is another story! He actively wants to court the danger. Would we not be acting without consent?'

'A fireman doesn't ask whether someone in a burning building wants to stay there.'

'Is it that serious?'

'I believe so. That's why we need to be vigilant.'

'And that's why you want to do the same thing again?'

'Yes.' He looked deeply into me, 'The only question is, are you strong enough to withstand the lure of the one who is leading him?'

'The faeries, you mean? – Some particular faery?'

Ash nodded curtly, 'Yes.' Then, more confidentially, 'You were right, I *was* recognized, but not by Ned himself – rather by the faery that wants to lead him from this world. It is unfortunate, since that being knows who and what I am rather too well. I can't go into details about it, as it is not my story to tell, but suffice it to say, that your presence in this case will be more helpful to Ned. I am going to have to take a back seat.'

I suspected that whatever Ash's past history with this being, that it pertained to a member of his lodge in some way, hence his circumspection. 'How do you want to proceed then?'

'I'm hoping that the bell jar of the Beacon will enable Ned's own resilience and good sense to reassert itself, to give you time to get to know him better. I can manage the other cases with help of Will, but I'd like you to make your best attempt to befriend him.'

'You mean I'll be the good cop?'

'Indeed! And I'll keep on being the bad cop, which should give you a better chance of his confidence.'

'I'm not sure we can trust him very far.'

Ash's face remained grim, 'No, but if we help him forge a strong enough connection, we might stand a chance of hauling him back before he gets in any deeper' He shook his head, 'If only he had a more mature will-power!'

'Well, he can be stubborn enough when it comes to visiting the sacred sites…'

'But not when it comes to considering his own good, unfortunately'

Putting my head on one side, I asked, 'When you said "faeries" – I always thought that they were supposed to be beneficent beings?'

'Faeries come in many different varieties, like human beings, they can be mainly harmless, but when provoked, it may be another story.'

'Why would a faery want to lead Ned astray?' I puzzled. 'What would be the advantage to the faeries of a human being as annoyingly weak-willed as him?

'The one who was luring him closer seemed to be keen to have Ned with them.'

'Well, I know he is the nearest candidate to being "away with the fairies" I've ever met, but what did you see?'

'A faery being who is beginning to ravel Ned up like a parcel, prior to removing him from this realm completely.' He didn't smile at this absurd metaphor. 'I think Ned is seen by them as more of their realm than of ours.'

'So, what am I to do?'

'As I said, make an effort to befriend him. Take him for walks, if he's up for it, but absolutely *not* out of these grounds. I don't trust him not to make a bolt for it.' Ash picked up the fine ball of shaped chalk that lived on his desk, and threw it to me, 'And spend some time getting to know the Long Man.'

'You are serious?'

'You know how to meditate. I think you are going to need a few allies in this case. The Sanctuary is always available to you, you know.'

In the following days, I did my best with Ash's instructions. I was the one who led the interviews, while around the house Ash remained as stark and frosty to Ned as the weather outside, making me feel like an amiable fool by comparison. This had the effect of making me slightly more trustworthy, I believe, but Ned was a hard nut to crack.

Ned's headlong story was based largely upon his reactive response to overly-strict parents who didn't have a historical bone in their bodies. History had been his first love, and when he discovered that these things had a spiritual background, it was their spiritual pre-history that began to occupy him. At university, he had indulged this preoccupation to the point where his tutors had given him over as a New Age mess, so that he left without a degree. For a few years, he had patched his life together with odd jobs, living on sufferance at home, until he was offered a job as the assistant to a small company who went out to the United States every year, selling products at Renaissance fairs. It was while attired as a medieval tinker that he had met Wilma one hot summer in Virginia, and they had been together ever since. Her money and support began to underwrite his ambition to visit as many sacred sites in Britain as he could, until he had begun to lapse into deep meditative states at some of these sites.

Getting this much information out of him took the patience of a saint, for Ned could spend whole sessions sulking or replying monosyllabically. I would have to remind him that Wilma was waiting to see some change or improvement from him, only for him to recommence his wheedling, trying to find out where she was staying. He really resented not being able to have his mobile phone – something we didn't allow at the Beacon until the last few days of anyone's stay.

I had to be cunning, pumping him about his love of sites and why this had gripped him so strongly. 'What's your favourite site?'

He gave me a slantwise look, 'Of all the ones I've visited, the Long Man has the strongest call.'

'Why-so? The concrete blocks shaping his outline aren't exactly traditional! And the site isn't thought to be so very ancient.'

Ned shook away that statement, 'It's …like this place. Like the downs themselves – it continues something begun much earlier.'

I readily agreed with him, eulogizing about chalk down-land in general with unforced sincerity.

'Wilma says these are not really hills, not by Canadian standards, that is.' And the wistfulness returned to his voice.

'Well, I believe they have some impressive mountains there… But you said the Long Man called you…? It didn't sound like a figure of speech.'

He leaned forward, cocky boastful and certain, 'Oh, I hear the call of lots of places, but they have different sound signatures – like musical instruments do.'

'You mean they produce music, or something else?'

'They make inscapes in my soul – that's what you want to know isn't it? They are landscapes my soul can visit.'

I nodded encouragingly, 'And does Wilma share this facility?'

Loathe to criticize his love, he launched into a series of excuses for her, none of which sounded very plausible, ending with, 'Wilma hasn't been doing this as long as me, and she isn't from here.'

I ventured a theory that I found attractive, even if it could not be conclusively proved, 'Some scientists say that our mitochondrial DNA has a kind of epigenetic memory and that wherever its carriers have moved, we remember the places our ancestors once walked.'

Ned fizzled with excitement, 'But that's exactly what I experience! The ancient places are the ones that have the wisdom.'

'And that's why you visit them?'

'Yes.'

Drawing him even further out, I launched into an account of the times when I've felt the spirit of a place as a tangible force, 'Standing looking out on the Beacon or lying in the grass behind the house, I often feel part of things… Do you feel that too?'

I had overstepped the mark, I realized, for he began to be more guarded from this point, trying to circle nearer to the spirits he was aware of at these places. Reporting to Ash afterwards, I said, 'It was almost as if a shutter came down in him.'

'He didn't want to bring his faery friend to our notice, I imagine. What else were you aware of when you were with him alone?'

'I can't put it into words very well, but there were moments when a kind of wariness descended, as if someone watched me out of his eyes.'

'What else?'

'A sort of – this will sound stupid – well, a sort of rippling or shifting round him. And his expression takes on a kind of sharpness… Although he looks nothing like him, Ned reminds me very much of a boy we had at school, Matthew Bruton: he caused no end of chaos wherever he was: dropped chalk, spilt milk, trodden on exercise books was the least of it, even good friendships foundered. He was an arch muddler in himself, but a tangler-up of everyone around him as well. I suppose we would say he had Attention Deficit Disorder today, but he had a way of mangling any plan.'

Ash looked thoughtful, 'That is a good description of what is around

Ned – he is wrapped up, tangled up indeed. And how are your Long Man meditations doing?'

I exclaimed, 'But how did you know that I should meditate on that? Ned singled out that site as the most important in his travels to date.'

'Well, let's hope that he gets to visit more sites, but that one might become his last visit, if he is not careful.'

'I wish you would tell me what you know... Do you want me to read the riot act over him?'

Ash shook his head, 'It would only entrench him further at this point... So what of your meditations?'

I had dutifully gone to the Sanctuary every morning after my walk, sometimes accompanied by Harlequin, our black and white tom who, though strictly forbidden to enter, would try almost anything to push inside. There was one particular spot he loved, just under the image of St Margaret and her dragon, where he would curl up, though it was not particularly sunny or even warm there.

Sitting in front of the Spiral sculpture, I had acknowledged the light burning in the hanging sanctum lamp, and gone in spirit to the Long Man, seeking to understand him more. Some days it was just me sitting there, at other times, it was me and the Long Man, who seemed a kind of cheerful guiding spirit. He was often accompanied by a group of men with digging equipment or other tools, while at other times, I was aware of the monks who had once made their foundation near Windhover Hill in the middle ages.

'The Long Man seems to have a lot of companions,' I explained. 'He has a long eye that helps people see far and deep. I think he's also some kind of guide – maybe along the downs? I don't know. What were you expecting me to get?'

Ash smiled, 'Whatever you experienced. Jack, I want you to keep holding strongly to your contact with him. It may prove the key to all this.'

It wasn't really Gillespie's fault, but he'd left the keys in the van with the engine turning over, ready for another run out for more supplies before any more snow came down. He'd just unloaded the last bag of feed for the wild birds, laying the sack in the lea of the wall, when Ned darted out from the shelter of the yew hedge and drove off in the van.

'I never spied the shadow of him,' he confessed, when Wendy berated him for carelessness. 'That yin has the luck of de'il, and the craft of the Kelpie!'

We gathered round the Aga with a cup of coffee for a quick consult, 'Well, we all have a shrewd idea where he might be, either with Wilma or at a local sacred site. Which?' asked Ash.

'With Wilma, I'd say,' Wendy said.

'Aye, I reckon with the lassie,' Gillespie nodded.

Ash looked at me, 'Jack?'

'I'm certain he's gone back to the Long Man. I didn't know why, but I could feel in my waters that something was pulling him back there.'

'Thank the Dear I put the chains on the tires!' Gillespie said.

Wendy looked between us, then decisively poured the rest of the pot of coffee into the thermos, thrusting it at me with a couple of packets of biscuits, 'Go! If Jack thinks he knows, then he really knows!'

Ash and I drew on our winter coats, and went to pack his car with supplies. Will came running out with a red coat, scarf and gloves, 'I just checked his room. His coat was still there. He must have taken his chance to escape, and won't have a thing on him to keep him warm!'

I opened the driver's door, but Ash directed me to sit in the passenger seat: 'I'll drive! You keep your strength for what we find at the other end!'

Reluctantly, I relinquished the keys. Ash had not yet driven himself anywhere, to my best knowledge, and I was still holding him as less than competent in my own mind, I realized. I sat in the passenger seat as an act of trust, letting Ash take back control.

As we sped eastwards, I asked, 'Should we phone Wilma?'

'Not until we get him back, if we can.'

We found Ned's body lying just where I'd discovered him the last time. He lay at the foot of what I saw as the Long Man's door, wrapped only in the van's ragged old grey car-blanket. Ash sped ahead of me up the slope like a deer and bent over him. When I saw the slump of his shoulders, I feared we had lost Ned from hyperthermia. On puffing up behind him, I saw that Ned was indeed still breathing, but Ash's countenance was grievous, 'He has gone from us,' he said in a voice of finality.

And I knew that he meant Ned's soul had gone out.

'Let me try and bring him back!'

'You go in peril of your life – there…'

'Let me at least try!'

The snow began swirling down again. Ash wrapped Ned up as well as he could, sheltering his body from the prevailing wind with his own form.

He turned to me, saying, 'Then if you go out, I will be your anchor man. I cannot be there for you both. If you are unable to fetch him back, I will pull you back alone.'

'Agreed!'

It was not how, when, or where we had planned it, but now was the time for me to crouch down. Ash placed one hand upon my head and one under my heels while reciting the formula that conferred the second sight on a non-seer.

I stood up and through the billowing snow faced the Long Man. My sight was doubled, as I saw both what was and what was not visible. Demanding entrance to his hill, I called upon the powers of the light that shines in every dark place, into shuttered minds, and desolate hearts. The Long Man opened his doors to me and I stepped through. My experience this time, was very different. Instead of the shimmering light, I was much more inside the physicality of knowing.

There was a wedge in my hand – the kind of object a mason might use. The words 'beetle and wedge' were running through my mind like tickertape. I wasn't even sure I knew what a beetle was, never having set eye or hand upon one of these tools.

My mind was not my own – something shaped over mine, bringing me to attention beyond myself. I suddenly had wider thoughts, and hands bearing knowledge. A long procession of men with tools were moving, hand over hand, with me, into me, and I knew with a communion of knowing beyond my own short remembrance. This was a great comfort to me, for I feared I might be taken over by the faery that was leading Ned.

The wedge twitched in my hands, and I knew with an urgency that I must use it and quickly too. I did what the larger knowing dictated, I placed the wedge in the frame of the door that was going to close with Ned and myself inside the hill. As I did so, I found I had an iron mallet in the other hand. As I hammered in the wedge, I knew with a countryman's witness, that the wedge also had a sliver of iron in it, that it would keep the door from closing. Words came to me with certainty and I uttered them aloud. They were not in any language of this world, but they might once have been.

As the wedge struck the door frame, time itself shuddered, and splintering echoes of reverberation mounted like a scolding of magpies. Someone or something was seriously displeased with me, I knew.

I thrust my mallet-bearing hand out to where the fading shimmer of Ned was held, commanding him back, with all the authority of his ancestral kindred. He had only to touch the iron to be brought safely home, but still something failed to stir in him. With greater and more distinct command, my voice – a voice overlaid by a disorderly scree of male voices – made the slope by which he might still bridge the worlds and not be lost.

Beside Ned was a troubled ripple that I had been careful not to notice or look directly at until now. Like a man about to catch a nervous horse, my mind had kept aloof from it, so as to be operative without disturbing it, but now the ripple shivered through severing shards of appearance, beginning to shape itself more clearly. I knew I had to look away from it.

Gripping the mallet resolutely for its iron rather than for its physical power – as a thing forged by men in the white fire of the furnace, laid in a mould, as woman lays child to her womb – I did not dare claim combat, but I did stand resolute to give Ned the last chance to break free from that rippling influence.

Slanted, uneven perspectives poured forth as water through a bulging dam, framing into a shape that I now recognised as something that had always been playing about Ned and giving him little peace. Its continual presence had faded his native courage and essential will, fracturing him along fault lines that had flaked him like flint.

And now the ancestral line of men within me were roused to anger, for that rippling shadow had trespassed on the edge of an inviolable and sacred place – one that belonged to men – not to the children of the hidden earth – and a warning was finally called out from the shout of a thousand voices.

The watery ripple that bulged into form was stayed for a fraction of an instant, a whisker's shaving of time with eternity, into which I leant down and pulled Ned out, his hand finally gripped upon the iron.

The rippled form bulged forward, hastening too late. The wedge began to slip. Snow swirled. And I was holding Ned against me in the turning of time. High above us, the Long Man drew his door shut with a firm hand. Earth closed, and the line of men who'd dragged their descendant out with me fell backwards like a tug of war team, and were gone. Just a sigh in the wind, snatched into the slope of Windhover Hill forever.

Fierce and sudden, time ran on once more, dropping the pair of us to earth. We were shunted back to weight, gravity, cold. Through weaving wraiths of blizzard, Ash still sat holding the space, his eyes wide open, dark against his pale face. Ned hung from my arms like wreckage from some cosmic accident. The strain of this return to gravity and time dragged me to my knees. I tried to speak but the mighty commands of that generational bellow I had uttered that night had departed into the night, leaving me hoarse.

Ash was upon me in that instant, staring into my eyes for sign of intelligent identity. 'It's me, don't worry,' I rasped. He hugged me to him swiftly, then turned to care for Ned. Together we poured neat brandy down his throat, before lifting him for the second time from this hill down to the road. We were in sight of the car when Will came running up towards us, to help us down, this time with a stretcher that he had brought with him.

Will was all for taking Ned to hospital, but Ash and I tacitly knew we had to bring him back to the safety of the Beacon, and not only to a bed, but to the Sanctuary itself. As we drove back through that blizzard, the sight that had been conferred briefly upon me was still in place, and I had to close my eyes against its power. I felt drained and hollow, realizing that this was how Ned must have been feeling. But the after image of that faery being was struggling at the edge of my vision, so I had to open my eyes again.

Will drove, while Ash sat in the back to care for Ned who lay over his lap. In the passenger seat, I gripped the car door, willing my feet back to sensation once again. I was once more aware of the trailing lights of everyone's body field: Will's tight and resolute, Ash's bright as crystal, Ned's a dull yellow but unmixed with any other influence. My own cape of light was visible to me, and I was aware that I was like a building blazing with spotlights. I consciously began to pull the cape tighter and dim it down a little.

Gillespie and Wendy were ready for us.

'Take him straight to the Sanctuary,' Ash commanded, as Gillespie and Will took the stretcher.

I stood on the threshold of the Beacon, transfixed by the blaze of beauty that was Melanie's shrine, until Ash pulled me in, 'For God's sake, Jack, come in from the cold!'

'It really is the House of the Perfect Eaves!' I exclaimed stupidly in the hallway, as I took in the rich welcome of the Beacon with the gift of my enhanced vision.

Wendy tucked another blanket over Ned as he was borne aloft to the Sanctuary. I stumbled after.

'Where do you want him? Across these chairs?' Will asked.

Before Ash could answer, I remembered Harlequin's place, 'No, lay him there under the painting of St Margaret!'

Ash nodded to them, saying, 'Leave myself and Jack to deal with him now,' gently pushing Wendy out of the room, 'You can prepare some soup for him, but don't bring it until I ask.' Gillespie gathered a protesting Wendy into his arms and out, while Will shot us unbelieving looks at what appeared to be our medical negligence.

'Why on that spot, Jack?' Ash asked me.

'Because it will help Ned feel himself again,' I said with a certainty I couldn't back up.

'So, before you lose the sight, how does he look? Is there anything we need to be worried about?' I looked with my magnificent vision, seeing that Ned's cape of light had changed to a yellowish green once again. There was no trace of the overlay that had so nearly claimed him, no sign of the interference that had him under its spell. 'He looks entirely clear.'

'I concur. Let's look him over, then.'

Ned appeared to be sleeping normally this time. I can only say that I wished then that I might have this gift of vision selectively when diagnosing, but not for everyday use, or I would have run mad. When we were satisfied that there was no lasting damage, I said, 'Whatever that being was, the spirit of the Long Man barred the door to him. But I couldn't have brought him back without Ned's ancestors to help me,' and I told Ash how it had been. 'Now, for goodness' sake, please will you take this confounded gift away from me?'

I crouched down once more, and Ash restored me to myself and my ordinary senses. On standing up, I found I was less steady than I would like, and he deposited me into a chair.

'You must go to bed with a hot drink after your exertions. I'll stay here with Ned until he wakes. Just call down and let Will know he can come in now, or he'll never forgive me, and tell Wendy to make up a thermos of her good soup for later, and let her make a fuss of you.'

The little trefoil window was entirely perfected framed with an deep edging of snow and the sanctum lamp burned steadily, shining down upon the sleeping Ned.

With one hand on the door, I turned, 'So, what would have happened to the physical Ned, had we not got him home?' I ventured to ask, more to exorcise the thought from my mind than anything else.

'He would have withdrawn into a coma-like condition and probably been put in a hospital until someone deemed it necessary to turn off his life-support.'

'You mean, he would have just died?'

'No, though his body would have been destroyed by then, Ned himself would probably have made it back to this side of the worlds eventually. Just not within the era of anyone now alive.'

I gulped, 'And then what?'

'He would have probably begun to do exactly what the faery had done to him, in order to gain another body.'

I wished I had never asked the question, not to have that answer circulating as I lay sleepless under the blankets that night. Why could I not have just left it alone?

It was a couple of days before Ned was up to being interviewed. He had awoken naturally and slept in a bed, none the worse for his time on the snowy hill. In the cold light of day, he was strangely more biddable. With an unaccustomed humility, he said, 'I'm so sorry I've been such a trouble. I had no idea what kind of danger I was in, but I understand it now.'

Ash scanned Ned's aura, nodding, 'It is good to see you are clear of the one who was calling you away. When did it begin?'

'It was a couple of years back, when we were touring the sites around Avebury. We travelled over to see the Alton Barnes White Horse, and I went to sleep on Adam's Grave – you know, the long barrow? Wilma couldn't wake me up. It happened a few more times. Every time, it was so beautiful, I didn't want to wake up. I just wanted to stay there. It was a land where all the sacred sites were somehow joined up, you see.'

Ned put into words something I had always felt.

'And the being who was calling you?'

Ned shivered, 'I wasn't aware of him until I came to the Long Man. When I meditated there, I had a really strong contact with the ancestors...' Frowning, he said, 'He kind of came through them - like he infiltrated them, does that make sense?'

Ash looked at me for confirmation, 'Oh, yes, I understand you completely,' I said, remembering the line of forefathers who had stood for him.

Ned said to Ash, 'I've been thinking about what you said... you know, about going to sites and not taking enough care? Maybe I could write a guidebook to the sites with notes about how to approach a site, and what to be careful about...? Could I ask your advice about that?'

Ash's pinched look faded at hearing that plan. In warm tones, he said, 'Indeed you can. That would be a wonderful service for you to give to others, now that you have this experience. The first thing is to travel safely yourself. Not every site is awake; some are dormant and need to be left sleeping, others have a kind of hyperactivity of their own in which we should not be involved. It is a fine art to judge which.'

Ned was silent for a long time. Then, rousing himself up, he took my hand and squeezed it, 'Thank you, Jack! I don't know how you did it, but I will never forget how you looked up there by the Long Man, nor what you did.'

I asked him, as we had asked many times since we brought him back from the hill, 'Do you want to speak to Wilma?'

He shook his head, 'I need to show her I can be trusted again first.' The puzzlement to him, was just how to achieve this.

Since Ned wasn't well enough to come down in the living room, one or other of us would sit with him in the evening for a while, to keep him company.

Wendy brought up her basket of felt to work upon. Ned's eye lingered a long time on the array of colours. Finally, he summoned up courage to ask her for some small offcuts from the toy she was making for her grand-daughter in Canada. Over the next few days, with Wendy's help, some scissors, and a hot iron, he fashioned a love gift for Wilma. It was a little book made of felt, with the offcuts felted onto its pages as words. We were none of us privy to its contents, save Wendy, and she kept her own counsel, until the day it was finished, when she said over supper, 'I think Ned is ready to see Wilma now.'

Ash lowered his fork, 'Why do you think that, Wendy?' Of all of us, Wendy had had the most trying time with Ned's intransigence.

'Because he has created a proper apology for her. He's made something all by himself. It's very sincere, in my opinion. I know he's not entirely back on the straight and narrow, but they have to make a bridge from both ends if they are to meet in the middle.'

Gillespie pointed with his knife, 'My guidwife, the great romantic!'

Wendy blushed, replying in his own accent, 'Only a felted Cupid, ye ken!'

We had, of course, kept Wilma abreast of Ned's progress, but she had sworn not to step foot in the Beacon until there was at least some sign of change and progress.

'Well then, let's ask her round to see him and she can make up her own mind,' Ash smiled.

Ned sent his gift via Wendy, and Wilma called that same afternoon. We left them the privacy of the sitting room to sort it out. After an hour or so, Wilma knocked on the kitchen door where we were all gathered.

'Come in, dearie!' Gillespie called, as she hovered on the threshold.

Wilma's cheek had begun to lose the little pucker that had become imprinted from her dancing attendance on Ned. She surveyed us all, 'I don't know how to thank you! I didn't really want to go back home alone, but I knew I had to put him on the line, or we'd be playing that same game for the rest of our lives until I lost all respect for him. - He actually looks and sounds like he used to.'

Wendy passed her some coffee, 'Do you have a plan, dear?'

'Yes, we do! You know I have a lot of money in trust for me? Well, I only use the interest to live on at present, but now Ned and I are thinking of founding a small institute for the study of sacred sites, somewhere we could teach people about them in a good way, with trips and visits as a part of it. But, before we even go there, we're going to Canada for a rest cure. I want Ned to spend some time at my folks' place, then meet and mix with some ordinary people and a real family... and then...' She waggled her blonde mane, 'Eat poutine, do some sport, watch some movies, and be a regular guy. – I know, it's a tall order! But as normal as he's ever going to be.'

'That sounds like a plan!' Will said, 'But is Ned ready to leave?' he looked sideways at Ash for confirmation.

'I know that Ned still has a long way to go,' Ash said, 'But he is on the mend, and there can be no better guide than the love of a good woman. If you are ready to take him home, then he is ready to go.'

After Wilma had paid for Ned's stay, along with a very generous donation to our funds, she took me aside, saying, 'Ned told me what you did for him! I am just in awe of what you do here.'

I felt uncomfortable, because the praise should be shared with Ash, 'I was only the unskilled labour, believe me. The real master here is Ash. Without his wisdom and care, I don't think Ned would be with us.'

'I know that,' she said, then kissed me on the cheek, 'But that's for bringing my bad boy home again!'

We waved them off in a very different spirit from their first arrival.

Not long after Ned and Wilma departed for a trip to, we began to have electrical problems upstairs which Gillespie could not fix himself. The electrician diagnosed elderly wiring; so began a very inconvenient few days in which we had to move a lot of things. The worst disruption to Ash was that part of the Sanctuary floor would need some floorboards taking up. I was present when the discovery was made, for I was deputed by Ash, who was up in London that day, to ensure that nothing was unduly disturbed within.

There was never much daylight in the Sanctuary at the best of times, so I had to help with the illuminations, becoming the electrician's mate that afternoon, holding up the work light which had to be plugged via a trailing socket from the adjoining room. The floorboards that needed to be raised had not been touched since the introduction of electricity, and the dust was dreadful.

The electrician, who had entered the Sanctuary with incurious eyes, being of that breed of workman who is stoically unspeaking about other people's weird furnishing choices, was lying on his side, with an arm outstretched into the void, trying to trace where the wiring went, when he exclaimed, 'Here! There's some kind of box!' He brought out of the void a filthy box of curious design, and unwisely blew upon it, raising a dust storm.

Flourishing it aloft and shaking it, he declared, 'It's probably some kind of time capsule thing!'

Immediately, I knew that this object should not be touched until Ash was present. I drew off the cotton handkerchief I had wrapped around my nose and mouth, which was the cleanest thing about me, and took the object from him.

'I don't think so,' I said, setting it swiftly down on a chair, for I had caught sight of plaques of red and blue enamel under the encrusting dirt.

'Aren't you going to open it?' The electrician peered over at it and back to me.

'Not till the owner returns, no! This is his house.'

'No finder's fee for me then!' he said, in a resigned fashion.

After Ash came home that night, we were all in a state of high expectation. It took a few minutes to explain, until Gillespie finally begged, 'Can we no' speir inside?'

Ash appraised the box without touching it, 'It was found in our house, so I think we can,' but he still made Wendy bring a clean linen tea-towel to place under it, in case it fell to bits and we had to explain things to the authorities.

The box was about 8 inches high, and about 11 inches long in the shape of a house or a chest, with a raised crest of metal along the top that had almost entirely corroded. The outside of the box was covered all over with enamel plaques of red and blue, with a running yellow ribbon weaving around it on which were words, but it would take some restoration to see what. The roofed top was hinged to the base. Carefully, Ash lifted it to see what was within, while I held the top firm.

Reaching inside, he drew forth a red silken cloth. Inside its wrappings was a small round disk, the size of a locket, in which was embedded a small sliver of what looked like bone. On a piece of vellum under it, in red ink was medieval script saying, 'de Sancta Margareta V.M.'

'I think this is a medieval relic of St Margaret of Antioch, hidden during the Reformation for safety under the floorboards,' Ash whispered in awe.

'What's the VM mean?' Wendy asked.

'Virgin Martyr,' said Ash and myself in one breath.

On the back of the disk was a wax seal and the remains of a ribbon we feared might crumble away. We shone a torch upon the seal, which Ash identified as that of Jupiter-Serapis.

It was an utter mystery to us why a Christian artefact and an Egyptian seal of the Ptolemaic period should be lodged together. We fetched the camera and took some good shots of everything in case nothing survived our examination. Then Ash phoned the authorities to report the find, saying to our fallen faces, 'If it is gold or silver, then it will be declared Treasure Trove, and will end up in a museum.' From his tone, we could all tell how much he would hate that.

The county archaeologist came round to collect the reliquary, for such it was, and to take pictures of the Sanctuary and look into the void where it had been discovered, saying he would send a team round to check the void expertly before the floorboards were put down.

All these things were done in due order, and when the archaeologists had gone, Ash and I looked at each other. He said, 'The spot where the reliquary was found is precisely where you told us to lay Ned down when we came back that day. Did you fathom there was something there?'

'Not really. It was just Harlequin's curling up place – you know how he is always trying to get in here. When I meditated on the Long Man, I might have let him in – he always gravitated to that spot.'

Ash laughed loudly, 'Well, it's none the worse a miracle for all that!'

There was a lot of humming and hawing about the reliquary, but the records established that the Beacon had once had its own chapel dedicated to St Margaret and that it clearly dated from the time of the reliquary, or at least the Sanctuary part did. The reliquary, being neither gold nor silver, and containing just a bit of bone, was not after all subject to the Treasure Trove Act, and so it was returned to us when the British Museum had finished restoring it. Ash paid for the restoration himself and though they begged for it to be deposited with them in their early medieval collection, he refused.

The cleaned-up reliquary was identified as a 13th century gilt-copper with enameled plaques of French workmanship, and that it housed a dubious relic of what most people believed to be an apocryphal saint, whose identity was quite plain.

Around the box were woven these words in Latin:

'Believe on St Margaret and God Almighty. Commemorate the holy virgin Margaret, giving alms for her sake, so that ye might overcome the power of all devils, and be received into heaven.'

The curious design on the seal accompanying the relic was identified as the actual seal of Boniface of Savoy, a 13th century Archbishop of Canterbury, who did indeed take the emblem of Jupiter Serapis for his device, though perhaps not fully understanding what it depicted.

Ash explained, 'The bishop's seal was the confirmation of the relic's authenticity, but he must have taken some Gnostic jewel with that Graeco-Egyptian mash-up divinity, Serapis, as his own device – though I doubt he knew anything about how Osiris and Jupiter were brought together to make the divinity, Serapis!' Afterwards, a researcher from Lambeth Palace came to write a monograph about our relic and its chest. Occasionally people apply to see the reliquary, which it stands on its own shelf under the trefoil window. But the ecclesiastical authorities will never be about to prove whether Ned's recovery to our world was a true miracle or - more likely in our view - just a put-up job between St Margaret of Antioch and the Long Man of Wilmington.

The restored Reliquary

It was only after this nine days' wonder that I remembered to ask Wendy what Ned's gift to Wilma consisted of.

She pressed her lips together in a smile, 'He made her a loveliest little felt book of eight pages, and on each of them, he attached little felt letters in the shape of each of the sacred sites they'd visited together. Every one of them read the same, "Sorry. I love you."'

'Now that was a miracle,' Ash said.

Case 3: OUT OF THE ASHES

The soul of sweet delight can never be defil'd.
William Blake – Marriage of Heaven & Hell

When I first came to work at the Beacon, my sister had somewhat pruriently asked after my employer's sexual orientation, implying that, since he was single, he must be gay. It wouldn't have mattered to me in the slightest as, for me, people are people. The case that underscored and confirmed my own observation of how the land lay came shortly after my arrival. It was one of those tiresome cases that you know is always going to be trouble – a woman who flings herself at anything in trousers.

Caroline Adkins might have been likeable enough, I suppose, but her propensity to come on to any man she addressed was pitiably alienating to us at the Beacon. Within a day of her arrival, I came into the art-room to find a wild-eyed Gillespie corralled against the far wall of the studio with a haunted expression on his face, as Caroline pressed up to him, blocking his escape by planting both hands either side of his chest against the wall. In my head, the scene frivolously translated itself into a cartoon, entitled 'The Highland Stag at Bay.'

Gillespie greeted my entrance with all the fervour of a drowning man being thrown a life belt. I peeled her off of him. Caroline's clutches escaped, he skipped youthfully out of the door in a trice. I addressed her in serious tones, 'Now, Caroline, you know that's not allowed, and you promised me to be good and leave the staff alone.'

I felt quite proof against her wiles, but when it came to Ash, Caroline became incandescent with passion. His response was often simply not to respond at all, except to pull her off, or set her aside, time after time, like a persistently clingy pet: an approach which I usually tried to follow, in a good-humoured way.

Wendy's thoughts on the matter were less tolerant. Once Caroline's flag was raised upon him, she determined to ensure that her husband was kept at as far a remove as possible. Banished to the kitchen and the garden, Gillespie managed to flee into his shed at Caroline's every approach, locking himself in, while singing the *Bonnie Banks of Airdrie* in as loud and menacing a way as possible.

"Wid ye be a rank robber's wife
Or wid ye dee by my penknife?"
"I'll no be a rank robber's wife
I'd raither dee by your penknife"

I only hope that she found his accent too obscure to understand.

Caroline was a referral from a Harley St colleague of Ash's. Just a few weeks previous, she had been in an East London mental hospital. She had come to us for Ash to sort out, as her family clearly didn't want to know. Caroline in her seductive phase was pitiable enough, but when her back story was broached, I was able to access compassion as well, for hers was a sad story. She had been living with an older man, as his lover since she was a teenager. Ian Dunch was a deeply repugnant fellow who seemed to have washed seldom, let us say. The house where she lived with him, was full of hoarded newspapers, and other detritus – none of which he allowed to be moved or cleared away. In the back garden, the fruit of similar hoarding, he kept bits of old cars from which he built Frankenstein-like vehicles from their constituent parts that were sold on to drag races, destined to be bashed to bits.

The property in which they lived had been condemned as unfit for human habitation and had been the site of a militant confrontation, with the bailiff and council officials dragging Caroline and her boyfriend out. Why anyone so vital should wish to stay in such circumstances with so unwashed and unwholesome a person was the mystery.

I know that the sun shines upon the just as well as the unjust, but when such aberrantly paired lovers like that come together, you feel that Puck has slipped them a magic philtre for a joke. Caroline herself was pretty in a child-like way. She was not unintelligent, but she lacked the ability to negotiate the world for herself. Her mother and stepfather seemed conventionally English enough to have brought her up to expect better. But they had shown little interest in her welfare, especially her mother, who had been very severe upon her. Caroline, at 23, had been at least 30 years Ian's junior. Seeing them together, which I eventually did, was like observing an embarrassing relationship between niece and dirty old uncle. I felt soiled witnessing them together - although, as it happens, he was not the villain in this case.

When the council had moved in to eject both Caroline and Ian, and repossess the council house they'd been living in as being 'unfit for human habitation,' Ian had gone to live in his filthy old van, while she was left to reluctantly return to the parental home, where she was not very welcome. Adrift without Ian, she had gotten herself into some awful scrapes with casual sexual encounters until her mother had thrown her out. Fortunately for Caroline, her attempt at suicide forestalled any descent into prostitution. Unable to support herself anymore, she had tried to throw herself under a bus. Fortunately, quick-witted bystanders pulled her back in time, but after she tried to end it all with a cocktail of aspirin and alcohol in a bar, she was picked up and taken to the hospital where, after assessment, she had been sectioned. She had been fortunate that, despite her lack of funds, she had been seen by Morris Fairchild, one of Ash's colleagues in the Guild of Ecumenical Psychology, as a pro-bono case. The Guild had arranged for Caroline to come to the Beacon for a couple of weeks, supported by a grant from their charitable fund, since her family refused to pay.

Ash and I discussed our strategy.

Passing back Caroline's meagre case notes to Ash, I said, 'You are not going to tell me that is a particularly mysterious case, now? Surely, this is a desperate case of unfortunate attachment and immaturity, compounded by rejection, and fuelled by a need for acceptance?'

'So everyone has thought, but no-one has so far no-one has plumbed the cause,' said Ash, levelly. We both knew it was common enough for young women to attach themselves to the first man who comes along, however unsuitable, with the understanding that they have found a solid partner. 'I don't think we can be content with just the conventional explanations here... Even Morris lost patience with her, in the end, I'm afraid. He's a good psychiatrist, but he knew he'd reached the limits of his competence with this one,' Ash didn't judge. His care for Caroline came first.

It remained unspoken, but during my time at the Beacon, Morris Fairchild had certainly referred a number of his cases in our direction, especially those that proved tedious to him. It was hard not to feel that, for Fairchild, the Beacon was a convenient dumping ground for the untidy cases that came his way.

I asked what I thought was a reasonable question, 'How are we best going to deal with her, then?'

Ash looked up from her case notes, his grey eyes boring into me, 'I think that has been the problem: Caroline has presented all her life as "someone to be dealt with," someone to be directed, rather than someone who has any story of her own. – I would like us to find out that story and help her recognise and remove the compulsions that have distorted it.'

Suitably chastened, I suggested, 'Perhaps starting from the beginning….?'

Ash nodded, 'Certainly, though the beginning may lie beyond her birth, and she will not be able to tell us much about it. The likelihood is we may have to discover the root by going behind appearances.'

He was speaking of the ancestral and reincarnation antecedents of the case, I realise now, but at the time, I was mostly innocent of these methods of diagnosis. In those early days, I retained a dubious attitude to such things.

We had an initial session with Caroline, who had made herself up for the occasion with the overkill of a model in fashion week rather than for an indifferent, cloudy morning on the South Downs. Eyeliner ringed her eyes so deeply that she resembled a panda, while her lips shouted in shockingly pink, pathetically reminding me of a little girl who had been in her mum's make-up box.

Fingering the chair-back, she asked archly, 'Is there no couch? - Morris always had a couch.'

With more than a glimmer of an inkling, I began to understand exactly why Morris Fairchild had referred Caroline conveniently out of his own practice into ours!

Ash replied, 'We use chairs here, Miss Adkins.'

'Oh, please call me Caro,' laying a seductive hand on Ash's outstretched ankle. The allure sat sadly upon her, like an unfledged teenager in socks playing at Pussy Galore.

Ash uncrossed his legs, dislodging her hand. He had purposely set out the chairs in a triad in the room but had neglected to put a table in between.

The session went on tediously in like fashion, with Caroline more interested in trying the limits of male endurance with her wiles, than in providing much information or background.

At one point, she answered Ash's perfectly standard question about her childhood, with a pulling down her top; leaning forward, she jiggled her breasts at him, 'Not a child now, though, am I?'

'No, you are not. But I wondering whether this session would go on more comfortably with another woman present?'

Immediately, the seduction routine was quickly packed away. Sulkily, Caroline flounced back into her chair, 'I don't need a nanny.'

'It was not for *your* benefit that I suggested it,' said Ash, neutrally. 'I was of the impression that Dr Rivers and myself might be better able to do our work if Wendy came and joined us.'

That arrested her. From her pout, it was clear that another woman would entirely cramp her style.

Ash stood up, hand on the door jamb, 'Shall we ask her to join us? - It is up to you, Caro. I sense that you want to find a new way forward, but maybe you would rather leave the Beacon?' Caroline looked between us both, confused, then burst into tears at the thought of being cast out. While he spoke kindly and sympathetically to her, it was not like Ash to make so stark an alternative, but we had to start somewhere.

We asked Wendy in anyway and both retired from the room while she comforted her. Caro had no experience of being with women as friends, it would seem, only as rivals; as we left, we could hear her attempts to reject Wendy's presence, and Wendy's gentle, unruffled response.

Stepping out into the garden for a breath of air, we took in the outline of the Downs magnificently defined against the sky; the long spring grass shifting in waves as the clouds cruised overhead, sending their massive shadows like galleons over the chalk hills.

I pointed out, 'She is used to having serial men on which to build her affections, I suspect. You are the next available man along, Ash.'

He grimaced ruefully, 'Myself, you, Gillespie, the milkman, any older man....'

'Have you done any exploratory investigation yet?' I referred to his method of looking at the case from the other side of reality, through meditation, exploring the things that human eyes cannot see.

'A little, but I want Caro to tell her own story first.'

Wendy came out to join us, shortly, 'She's calmed down a bit, now that she accepts I am not going to behave like her mother. I don't know what lies behind all this, but I would seriously begin with the mother. – Do you want me to sit in?'

'If she wants that, yes.'

We came back into the room. Caro stood in the window holding the vase of grape hyacinths between her hands, her face thrust into their blooms. At sight of Ash, she was poised to slip back into her seductive regime, but something made her stop. What halted her seemed to be Ash: he had raised his right hand in the Buddhist gesture of fearlessness, palm facing out and was regarding her steadfastly as if she were a trustworthy and balanced person. That one small thing settled her down: a small instance of how Ash inspired confidence in the people under his care. I saw how Caro gathered herself and began to look more hopeful.

'Shall we start again?' Ash asked.

Caro glanced at Wendy, nodded slowly, and sat down. The story began to piece together: after her father died when she was 9, her mother had taken a series of live-in lovers until she had settled on her present husband. It was clear that these lovers had sexually abused Caro systematically, and that this abuse had had the effect of normalising her sexualized behaviour around men. It was the only way she knew to relate to them.

Wendy asked quietly, 'Was your mother at all aware of what had happened to you?'

Caro looked away, out of the window, where the white clouds were scudding eastward, 'No... I don't know... Perhaps it helped her...'

Astoundingly, she went on to recount how her mother relied upon her in many ways, because she frequently suffered from some mysterious recurrent condition and was often too ill to even get up. 'I used to come home from school and make the dinner for her, and do the shopping.' She didn't have to say it, but we all understood: with the mother so often out of action, it sounded as if Caro had also taken over her mother's bedroom duties as well.

Wendy slipped her hand under Caro's.

'It was alright, really! I was used to it, you know?' she insisted, in response to our appalled reaction.

Ash said, 'It was never alright, Caro. You were still a child.'

Caro merely shrugged. 'Mum didn't like it when Dick started though.' Dick was her stepfather.

'What happened then?'

'She used to lock my door at night, to keep him out, so I used to shin down the creeper and went to hang out with friends down the estate.'

Still only 16 or so, Caro had given up going to school and started to live a semi-feral life with older, working friends who had their own crash-pad, and who allowed her to come and go in return for occasional domestic help, until they suddenly upped sticks while she was out, without warning. She had come back from the laundrette to find a locked door, and the prospect of living on the street. She had managed to live for a few days by sleeping in an old disused car to which she had the keys: it had acted as her 'room' where she sat when her friends wanted her out of the way.

It was at this point that she met up with Ian, who had - in her eyes - heroically rescued her from the street and given her a stability that she had not previously enjoyed, albeit in filthy and crowded conditions. It made a kind of sense.

'He was looking at the car to see if it could be scavenged, but he found me instead,' she reported, matter-of-factly.

'Were you happy with Ian?' I asked.

'He was my knight in shining armour,' she enthused. 'We did things together: car-boot sales, drag races, and steam fairs. He knew all about cars and stuff, and he showed me how to mend things for people. I had no money to spend for myself until then.'

It said a lot about her previous experience that a man like Ian Dunch could appear as a hero in her eyes still.

Ash asked, 'Do you still miss Ian?'

She nodded, unable to speak.

'And would you want to live with him again, if things worked out?' Ash asked carefully. It was always good to test the ground about relationships and their ongoing or concluded nature. It clarified how our work was to proceed, and also where Caro was to go after her time with us, though I hated the very thought of her returning to him.

Caro was unable to respond clearly. There was some conflict about where her affections might now be bestowed, and I wondered whether Ash and being at the Beacon had something to do with that.

'When you were evicted by the council, did no-one try and help you?' I could not help asking. 'Surely they had a duty to rehouse you?'

She looked at me, as if seeing me for the first time, and I realised the depth of the emptiness that she had experienced then, 'No-one lifted a finger,' she said bleakly. I realised then that, even despite the help of many organizations being available, she would not have known how to ask. Caro being over 18, the council officials would have had no legal necessity to shift themselves for her. She had been effectively rendered homeless.

The rest of the story we knew from Morris and her mental health assessment, though the extent of her abuse had not been fully disclosed in those reports. We didn't need to ask why she had tried to commit suicide, but we did need to ensure that she no longer had that compulsion.

Ash asked her, 'If our work together is successful, how would it change things for you? What would you like in your life, Caro?'

The openness of her longing look told us that Ash would do nicely for a start, but she reined herself back, saying, 'I would like to have a place of my own and a cat for company. And maybe learn some new things.'

'What kinds of things?' Wendy asked.

'How to drive properly. I think I could be good at that, and maybe more about how to make cars work when they break.' Her aspirations seemed largely shaped by Ian's own interests, but we did not gainsay them for all that. Any glimpse of our guest's further horizon was better than none, I always thought. If Caro could entertain the future with hopefulness, then her suicide attempts were likely to be the fruit of despair and homelessness, not long-standing depression.

Back in the kitchen, Gillespie was drinking a cup of strong tea, 'How is the young nymphette this morning?'

Wendy observed sweetly, to the air at large, 'Strange, isn't it, that when a woman enjoys sex, she becomes a nymphomaniac, but when it's a man, he's just "a bit of a lad?"'

Gillespie hurrumphed into his tea.

Ash said, 'Wendy is quite right, of course. We don't use those kinds of labels at the Beacon,' it was the nearest he came to a reproof. Gillespie rose, 'I beg your pardon,' he uttered, taking himself off to the garden like an offended giraffe.

'Nymphomaniac' was a designation long taken off the mental diagnostic index, to be replaced by 'hypersexuality' or 'sexual addiction.' Strong, even normal, sexual urges in women were historically linked to mental illness in the past, of course, causing many utterly innocent women to be incarcerated, surgically altered, or given barbarous treatments: everything from leeches in the uterine area, to blisters on the perineum, or even douches of borax – a substance we now use to clean drains! From the time of Aristotle onwards, even normal female sexual desire was seen as dangerous and unnatural - something that ladies should avoid enjoying.

Now that the depths of Caro's abuse and neglect were revealed, we began to proceed a lot easier. She still had lapses into her old behaviour, but she soon learned that what might have been winsome to abusers, was not at all welcome at the Beacon. She began slowly to turn from trying to seduce Ash into trying to please him by her efforts, which I hoped would not become a problem later.

Over the course of that first week, we came finally down to the question of her hyper-sexuality by a careful but frank route. It became clear that two of her abusers had introduced her to pornography: both words and images had burrowed into her, 'It's like an express train running through my mind all the time. I can't turn it off,' she admitted. It explained how her sexual come-ons had been learned: from the poses and open-mouthed gurning of porn-stars. For her, as for many men and women worldwide, pornography had become her first deplorable introduction to what passed as normal sexual behaviour.

In the world outside the Beacon, the usual methods for dealing with sex-addiction were chemical, psychological, behavioural, group therapy or support group, or spiritual – with the latter usually suppressing the addiction by a kind of Alcoholics Anonymous 12 step programme, whereby you gave yourself over to a higher power. I wondered where we might range at the Beacon.

'How many times a day does that train run? How often do you think about sex?' Ash asked.

'Probably every few minutes, unless I'm busy…' She stared at Ash with surmise, 'Are you going to derail it?'

'Would you like it derailed?'

Caro chewed her bottom lip, for a long while, 'Yes. It makes me do stupid things.' This was a big admission. The abuse had left Caro with a lack of emotional resources or a vocabulary of ordinary behaviour. The very first emotional satisfaction she had from any of the sexual encounters in her short life had been with Ian, who had given her shelter and some form of fellow-feeling, albeit not in the most healthy relationship that a young woman might expect to enjoy.

By beginning to keep a log of the impulses she was experiencing, the feelings that accompanied them, and the results that the impulse produced, Caro began to see for herself that things could be much better, that she could be in charge. But the scar of pornography had gone deep, and her exposure to it at a young age had clearly misshaped everything in her development. People think that it is just men who suffer from pornographic addiction, but that is not true. She was going to need on-going support with this when she left.

'How are we going to help her?'

Ash said, 'By replacing it with something else.

I raised my eyebrows in surmise, 'How on earth can we do that?'

'With any addiction, the well-worn path is most easy to slip into. Starting a new path is hardest. In Caro's case, harmful, unhallowed and unhealthy thought forms led by greed, depravity and polluting violence, have taken their hold. However, she is still young…. While her emotional immaturity can be developed, she will need our help to cleanse her imagination. These violent and sexualised fantasies are like pollution; they are degrading and clouding her imagination, and standing in the way of her developing consciousness. She needs a differently structured thought-form.'

'I understand, but I've no idea how we're going to achieve this. It seems a very tall order.'

'Caro needs something to do, something immersive so that the express train in her mind will have fewer stations to stop at. We also have to help her rebuild her image of herself, to restore it to her, so that she can go forward again. Find out from her what activity would give her something to live for and leave the cleansing part to me.'

But before we could build up, there were still some revelations to come and some things to clear away. The next morning, Ash led Caro into the Sanctuary, of whose existence she had no awareness. Awed into silence by its calm silence and beauty, she finally asked, 'Is that Mary?' pointing to the medieval wall painting to the right of the shrine, then slapped her hand quickly over her mouth as her voice came echoing back to her on the long acoustic.

'No,' said Ash, 'It's St Margaret.'

'Who was she? I don't know anything about her.'

'In ancient times, she was a beautiful young Christian girl who was desired by the governor of that country. He wanted her but she refused him, so he beat her with iron combs, and imprisoned her. The legend tells how a demon in the form of a dragon tried to swallow her up, but her prayers made the dragon burst: you can see it here...' Ash pointed to the dog-looking dragon straining at the leash of her chain, 'She tamed the dragon.'

'What happened to her in the end?' Caro asked in a hoarse whisper.

'She was martyred by being beheaded, but she prayed that if any woman was in labour, that they might call upon her and be helped in their time of need, so that they might be safely delivered...'

Caro broke down at this point, her miserable sobs pulsing around the chapel. She cast herself into Ash's arms and wailed, 'She wouldn't ever help me, then. - I did a terrible thing....'

He held her close and let her have her cry out, finally asking, 'Why would St Margaret not protect you, Caro?'

From the confines of his chest, she stammered out, 'Because I had - an abortion...'

The story tumbled out: how when her stepfather had started to abuse her, she got pregnant, how he had taken her to a clinic and paid for an abortion, pretending to take her to the seaside for the day, so that her mother had no notion. Nothing more had ever been said about it. She had been 14 at the time.

I had wondered about this aspect of her life, and how she had managed to avoid pregnancy all these years. Apparently, the abortion was badly done, leaving her infertile. In the Sanctuary, I'm afraid I wished all manner of ill upon the heads of her abusers, and on her stepfather in particular.

She sobbed, 'It would have been 10 years old now... I killed it...and now I'll never have another...'

Ash gave her his handkerchief, saying with compassion, 'I am very sorry to hear that you can't have a child of your own. Believe me when I say that you were not the person who is at fault here. You were not even old enough to be having a relationship, let alone a baby. We don't judge you, here. And the help of St Margaret is available for you and anyone at all. Like her, you can escape the dragon.'

Caro went very still, 'Do you really think I can?'

Ash said seriously, 'Yes, we do,' including me in these words.

Carol looked suspiciously between us, as if we might be in collusion to deceive her.

'Truly,' I assured her. 'I have never seen a better dragon-tamer.'

After that confession, it felt that we had all the background we needed to help Caro move forward, but there was still one challenge ahead of us.

Despite her exasperation over Gillespie's putative seduction by Caro, it was Wendy who ferreted out that it was Caro's birthday that week, and that she had never had a party thrown for her in her whole life.

I'm afraid my blank 'so what?' expression did not meet with Wendy's approval. Fixing me with a very female stare, she explained, 'Well, she is going to be 24 and it is a day we are going to mark in this young woman's life, whatever you think about it! At present we are all the family she has to support and celebrate with her so....'

Ash put down his cup and asked her, seriously, 'What do you think she would like?'

'Well, I don't think she's ever had a pleasant night out with friends of her own age where *she* was the centre of attention – not that going out on the town is possible or advisable at present, of course. But it strikes me that she has pitifully few female acquaintances of any kind. Not one woman seems to be for her, not least her mother.'

We had not been able to determine whether Caro's mother had been actively or passively collusive in her daughter's abuse; but she certainly had not taken any care of her.

I added, 'Well, it's an important developmental step, I agree. Caro doesn't seem to have evolved into any relationship more attractive than her last amour. It's like she's stuck. I think it would be a good idea, frankly. Anything that raises her self-esteem would be helpful right now.'

Ash looked thoughtful. 'Wendy, we will be led by you. You make the arrangements and we will fit in with them. If you need anything beyond the ordinary, then I expect the emergency fund can help.'

'The emergency fund' was a bottomless box in the shape of an appealing spaniel that stood in the hall – the relic of a now-defunct Edwardian animal charity started by Colonel Alexander Rydale, the father of our founder, Melanie - into which we threw our loose change or any small donations to the Beacon's work. All small children loved it, and would sit stroking it and talking to it whenever their parents were visiting guests. Several times a year, its contents were emptied, reckoned up, and changed into banknotes for any small improvements or necessities.

And so it was that Wendy stealthily became Caro's advocate. They spent a couple of evenings together looking into clothes catalogues and making plans which kept her gainfully employed in those evening hours that she found so difficult. The feminine chat and occasional giggles coming from the chimney corner sounded much healthier to my ears.

It was agreed that Wendy and Caro, helped by Myrtle, our Barbadian cleaner, with whom she'd struck up a happy friendship, would go into Christminster and acquire a few items, making a shopping afternoon under strict surveillance. 'She has just the two outfits and I think they came out of the charity box,' observed Wendy. It was true that I had not seen Caro in anything other than the same top and trousers since she arrived. 'It would help her self-esteem no end for her to have new clothes that she has chosen for herself. I'll take her to the hairdressers too, so she has a bit of a pampering.'

'By all means, let her chose something. But what about the party: there won't be any drinks? Considering the problems she's had....?

'No alcohol, just soft drinks,' Wendy assured us. But there was one problem, 'She is ok having Myrtle's friends over, but she wants someone else.'

'Can Ian come over, too?' Caro had asked.

Having gone to so much trouble to distance him from her, it was the last thing any of us wanted to have him back in her life, or so I thought.

We discussed it in the back kitchen.

'Let him come,' Ash observed, judiciously. 'In this setting she might be able to see him for what he is and make a better choice for herself. He is someone who played an important part in her life and, whatever we may think of him, he is still someone who may have well saved her from a worse fate. We have to admit that. Let her be the arbiter.'

'But Myrtle and her friends are coming over after work at 6.30pm!' Wendy protested, seeing all her hard-won efforts going to waste.

Ash thought, 'Then invite Ian over for mid-afternoon and make it clear it is just for tea, not for her party, which should not be mentioned.' We had both seen the photographs of the council house where Caro and Ian used to live; the Beacon with its beautiful furniture and calm setting was a million miles away from it. Perhaps Ash was right.

A letter was duly despatched to Ian Dunch's *post restante* address, and he was duly invited to tea at the Beacon, so that we might see him at close hand.

He sent no response but was seen arriving on the day by Gillespie who came through to the kitchen with, 'Well, quean,' he said to Wendy, 'you'll be needing your dust sheets for yon clarty yin! His van is brimming ower with stuff.'

Peering through the side window, Wendy exclaimed with dismay, 'His van looks like it just came through the Dustbowl era! And as for the man....' Words deserted her, clearly.

Ash went to the front door to greet our loathly guest, while I positioned myself in a chair in the living room where I could observe Ian's effect upon Caro.

Ian looked indeed as if someone had poured the dustpan over him.

His receding hair was lank, and his person innocent of any recent ablutions. Over his paunchy stomach, stretched what might once have been a dark green patterned shirt, but it was difficult to see which was pattern and which the remains of past meals he had eaten. His sulphur-coloured trousers sagged, while the outer thighs bore the unmistakable signs of having been used as an oil-rag substitute.

He came in beaming, his full lips curved in a grin, but his button-like eyes were wary until they lit upon Caro who was looking her very best, in a new pink cotton dress with a mauve pashmina, freshly made up, and with her hair beautifully styled and shining. With hastily-disguised horror, Wendy watched Ian lower himself into an armchair, but she poured him a cup of tea with a heroic hospitality that belied her misgivings about her furnishings. He shuffled to the very edge of the armchair, as if aware of how unclean he was, allowing Wendy to make all the small talk.

I watched Caro closely: how she didn't even rise when Ian came in; how her eyes slid from Ian to Ash and back again, contrasting the dishevelled, aging man with the lank hair, with the ageless, handsome Ash, sitting at ease in his cream linen shirt and blue waistcoat, the epitome of suave and sophisticated. I foresaw all the signs of a full-blown transference and wondered how we would be able to shift that once it developed.

'Nice place you got here,' Ian said to Ash, then, almost without a pause, 'Got any opening for a caretaker, like?' Even his voice sounded greasy.

'Thank you, but we already have one: Wendy's husband, Gillespie.' Ash spoke more calmly than I could have managed before such bare-faced cadging. I put my nose into my tea and professionally chewed my cake instead.

Ian appraised his surroundings, 'Nice stuff, really nice!' He nodded, as if adding up the room's worth like a rag and bone man, or calculating how he would fill the spaces between the furniture with his next stint of hoarding. He finally turned to Caro, 'You doin' alright, girl? How's my little Carolina?'

Caro didn't quite arch her neck, but embarrassment made her blush pink. Even with Wendy's hostesty skills deployed at full strength, this was going to be uphill work.

After about half an hour in which all small talk was eventually exhausted, Ash suggested, 'Why don't you take Ian into the garden, and show him about, Caro?'

Caro would clearly rather stick needles in her eyes than go anywhere with Ian, but she had invited him and now she must deal with it. She rose swiftly, going ahead so fast that Ian had to scramble to catch her up. We continued drinking tea in enforced silence until they had both gone outside.

'What *are* you doing?' Wendy protested in a loud whisper. 'The very last thing she needs is to be thrown together with that walking dustcart.'

Ash smiled enigmatically, 'Bear with me, there is method in my madness… After all your good work, I think Caro will have a few thoughts of her own on the matter.'

'Do you want me to tail them?' I asked.

'No. Just give them some time. If she doesn't come back in with him, we'll leave it there. But if he follows her back in, you can do your strong-arm doctor act and ask him to leave, so that Caro can rest.'

Gillespie was stationed in the garden raking the lawn, and by dint of Wendy taking out his tea and collecting his cup again, we got the relay of the events outside. Apparently, Caro kept up a good speed striding through the garden, with Ian having to exert himself to keep up, but she was sensibly keeping within sight of the house. Before long the McLain's relay reports became unnecessary as we could all hear the altercation from the back.

Caro's, 'No, I am *not* coming back!' echoed sharply right up to the top of Hartsworth Beacon, I should think. We ran out to the back garden and found them both in the Spinney where the lavender and rosemary bushes grew between informal ranks of birch and paper maple trees. Ian was now very close to her and Caro was fending him off with, 'Get off me!'

I inserted myself between them speedily, 'I think Caro needs a rest now, Mr Dunch, if you wouldn't mind leaving please!'

Caro seized me round the waist, keeping me between her and Ian.

Dunch looked me up and down with, 'So, that's how the land lies, is it?' insinuatingly, his eyes judging me.

He began to walk backwards down the path serenading her with, 'Nothing could be finer than to be in Carolina ….' in a vile, suggestive imitation of Dean Martin.

Narrowing his button eyes, he spun round to confront Ash who had followed me out, 'Nice kind of rest home this is! Got it well set up for yourselves, eh? I wonder what the council will think about your carry-on?'

Ash merely looked into him with those penetrating grey eyes, 'Goodbye, Mr Dunch,' holding open the garden gate for him.

Wendy came and pulled Caro from off me, and took her back to her room to get cleaned up. She went away wailing, 'He didn't even bring me a present!'

When the coast was clear, Gillespie joined me in the Spinney in silent solidarity, finally asking, 'Yous alright?'

I nodded, picking the top off a stem from the bush in front of me and raising to my nose, 'Nothing that a good sprig of rosemary won't alleviate!'

After the kind of day we had had, Ash and I walked up Hartworth Beacon to clear the air - men being banished from Caro's party, in any case - and to listen to the nightingales which had begun to sing just before twilight. We both wore jackets and sweaters as the evening wind was chilly. Settling down in a clump of birches, we soon rewarded with their unmistakable liquid song, fluting and calling, repeating and oscillating down the slopes to where we lay. It was good to let go of the atmosphere of justified anger that had held sway at the house.

I said, 'I do wish Caro could hear this. - But it will have to be Wendy who brings her up here, I think. It would be professional suicide for either of us!'

The nightingale underscored our thoughts with an almost ironic series of descending notes, *caroo, caroo, caroo,* and a final scolding *chew, chew chew chooo.*

I raised a question that had long perplexed me, 'Did you never want to marry, Ash?' It was the single most personal question I had ever asked him.

He smiled, 'I knew a long time ago that marriage wasn't for me. - Oh, I didn't think so when I was a young man, of course. I had a lot of girlfriends, but my time with Melanie made it clear enough. What she revealed to me helped me expand my capacity to understand many things.'

I was about to make some really inappropriate remark about him and Melanie, when he continued, 'I fell in love with the whole world, I think....'

I tried to envisage this, 'Like a monk, you mean?'

Ash squinted against the golden sunlight, 'Not really...I don't think I ever had that kind of vocation.'

'I don't think I understand. It's difficult enough getting through a medical training and practice without some companionship or sexual relief, but was there really no-one for you?'

The nightingale uttered a series of interrogative trills.

'The only woman who would have done was already engaged in her own work. She was my soul-mate, but never my partner, if that's what you are asking.'

Fortunately, the sunset camouflaged my blushes, 'I didn't mean to pry, really.'

'It's been burning holes in you since you arrived,' he observed percipiently.

I nodded, blurting out, 'My sister insisted you must be gay.'

'Your sister is, I'm afraid, utterly mistaken.' He stretched out on the grass, tilting his cap over his eyes. 'Ask the maidens of the Vale of Pewsey! Rick and myself were quite the lads back then.' He meant Rick Stevenage of the Viking

Metal band, *the Rune Wreckers*; he and Ash had been to school together, though there both the story and the resemblance ended.*

At that point in my life, I was still stewing in the no-man's-land that one enters after an acrimonious divorce. Amy and I had been a train wreck, and my dear Jane still a long way in the future. I missed having a partner of my own, but I knew I was not fit to be with anyone for a while. As long as that waiting time didn't stretch ahead too far, I thought, I might plunge in again. But the thought of Ash living his life without any kind of partner seemed a very bleak prospect to me. I was still none the wiser about how he could live without companionship.

The nightingales fortuitously covered any further speculations with their liquid song.

Despite the afternoon's alarms and excursions, Caro's 'girls' night in' party went pretty well, I gather. We came back to the sound of Bob Marley, vigorous dancing, and many giggles. Gillespie had remained staunchly in the back kitchen before inviting us to the pub, 'It's no the place for the likes of us the night, laddies.' And we agreed, taking ourselves off to the White Hart.

The next morning, Caroline was much more amenable. Over breakfast, we were regaled with her views on a variety of topics: the best kind of pashminas, reggae musicians in general, and cats in particular. We had never previously heard any of her opinions voiced so volubly. From Wendy's glance of guarded amusement, I gathered that these topics had been discussed last night, and thus were being mirrored back for our benefit. Top of the list of wonders were her presents, each of which was brought out for our admiration: a selection box of bath oils and a padded journal with pen from Myrtle's friends, a turquoise shawl printed with sunflowers from Myrtle, a chapbook of illustrated poetry from Ash, an African violet in a pot from myself, and a brooch in the shape of a phoenix from Wendy and Gillespie. This latter was her pride and joy and adorned her new tunic. 'No-one's ever bought me presents before.' Simple kindness and a return of beauty were making a different woman of her.

Later that morning, Gillespie came back from running his morning errands with a long face, 'Yon dust-heap is parked up down the lane. Do you want me to phone Farmer Jelley to tow him awa'? He's squatting in the neuk by the Goose Field.' The 'neuk' was a little lay-by off the narrow lane where vehicles could pass each other.

I'm afraid I swore loudly and rushed off to see Ash, 'Caro's dusty swain is apparently encamped in his half-timbered van down the lane, according to

*See *Odin and the Rune Wreckers* in *Diary of a Soul Doctor*.

Gillespie.'

Ash picked up the Chinese paperweight, examined it, and put it carefully down, 'Are we under siege, do you think?'

His deep unconcern riled me, 'I don't know, but that kind of man is out for anything that he can get, that's clear.'

He nodded to himself with a chuckle, 'Good! Then we will soon be driving our geese to market, I think.'

However, later that afternoon, a strange car drew up outside. We could hear Gillespie challenging the driver, 'It's a no-through road, madam. Best turn yourself around.'

'I have business at the house. I want to see your employer, please.'

The middle-aged woman in glasses who stepped out of the car came with a briefcase from which a clip-board poked out.

'Miriam Vaughan to see…' she looked down at her clip-board, 'Dr Ash?' She didn't sound very sure.

'You mean, Dr Richard Ashington, madam,' Gillespie enunciated very clearly, as if for the hard of understanding. 'And where shall I say you are from?'

'Social Services.'

Two words to strike fear into our hearts. A Social Services investigation could close us down, I knew.

Ash was summoned, and I rushed to stand by his side.

Rather than the living room or the office, we went into what we all thought of as the waiting room. Facing north-east, this was a like a traditional front room or morning room, rather more formally furnished than the living room. We used it less often because it was a bit chilly in the colder months.

Miriam Vaughan pulled her cardigan closer while Gillespie started a fire for us, as it was a windy spring day. She began, 'We have received a complaint of about the treatment of one of your patients, Dr Ashington: one Caroline Adkins who is currently under your care?'

Letting his feelings be felt, Gillespie clapped a spread of newspaper noisily to the chimney breast to help the fire draw, and turned his head to fix the woman with a monitory stare.

'Miss Adkins is here as a voluntary patient, at the expense of the Guild of Ecumenical Psychology,' Ash told her. 'What is the nature of the complaint, if I may ask?

The Social Services woman spoke crisply, 'This is an initial inspection, prior to a full investigation, if we believe it is warranted. I am the Investigation Officer for the county… A Mr. Dunch has reported that Miss Adkins is being systematically abused here by yourself and another doctor,' her eyes flashed from Ash to me, in cool appraisal.

I don't think I had ever wanted to hit anyone more than at that moment. No-one had ever accused me of such a thing, and as for Ash...

Gillespie snapped the newspaper shut, and strode out very stiffly, letting the door slam behind him as his Parthian shot.

'Mrs...' Ash scrutinized the card showing her official credentials and photo ID, and responded, '...Vaughan, I fear you have received a malicious complaint from this man. Ian Dunch was living with our patient until they were summarily evicted from his council house in Broomhampton some months back. Caroline Adkins is indeed from an abusive background, but is without any family support, as her notes will show. She asked to see Mr Dunch, who came here yesterday for a short visit, under supervision. Our patient is a vulnerable young woman, and she soon made it quite clear that she no longer felt comfortable in his presence: he is now parked half way down the lane you have just driven along, - we believe with every intention of making a nuisance of himself. He made it quite plain to myself and Dr Rivers that he meant to imply some unprofessional conduct on our part, so after he left, I spoke to my solicitor, Mr James Stenson, to swear a statement concerning the situation, and to get advice about Mr Dunch's avowed intent.'

We watched Mrs Vaughan stealthily recalibrate her approach, pursing her lips, 'Nevertheless, I will need to see Miss Adkins, to ascertain the truth of the matter. I will also require to interview you and any of your staff who have been involved in her care.'

'Certainly. Jack will you go and ask Miss Adkins to join us?'

I closed the door behind me, shaking all over with fury, and went to relay the news to the McLeans, 'She wants to talk to us all.'

Wendy bridled but went to fetch tea, while Gillespie drew back into himself like an unspent thunderbolt, 'Of all the slimy, lavvy-heided....' I left him to his cursing and fetched Caro, explaining to her what had happened.

As I spoke, her face seemed to close down. 'Ian's just jealous,' she said, finally.

'Yes, but he can still cause us a lot of trouble at the Beacon, so please tell the truth to Mrs Vaughan.'

She came down looking apprehensive, as well she might after her last experience of the council bailiff and his men. Hovering in the hall, she asked, 'Can Wendy come in with me?'

'I'm sure that will be alright,' and went to fetch her.

While Caro was being interviewed, Gillespie phoned Sergeant Hobbs to complain about the blockage to our lane.

Wendy came and fetched me after she emerged with Caro, saying, 'Caro spoke very cogently and clearly,' praising her.

Then Mrs Vaughan interviewed myself and Ash separately, coolly and professionally, followed by Wendy and Gillespie. I was seething throughout, but managed to keep my frustrated ire in check. She also looked over the Beacon from attic to cellar and was making her final notes on her clipboard when Sergeant Hobbs called to tell us that he had moved on the offending vehicle and its loathly occupant with a police caution. He nodded to Mrs Vaughan, recognizing her from the court, 'I hope there is no trouble here?' He explained what he had found.

'It would seem not,' said Mrs Vaughan, who realised that she had been conned. 'From my preliminary enquiries it would seem we have had a nuisance complaint.' Turning to Ash in a conciliatory way, she said, 'I am sure you realize that we have to follow up any complaints of this kind. I am satisfied that Miss Adkins is not at risk here.'

Ash courteously escorted her to her car, seemingly unfazed by this brazen attempt to stain our reputation.

As Mrs Vaughan got into her car, Wendy beckoned Sergeant Hobbs in for a cup of tea. He took off his cap, watching our faces as the car drove off, and gave a short laugh, 'Well, you all look pretty relieved! Nasty piece of work, that woman from the Social, though I shouldn't say so. - Don't worry! I'll keep an eye out for that van. If I see it again, I will detain him. He's been cautioned. The van's contravening several vehicular laws, not to mention the amount of dirt obscuring the number plates. He won't be on the road for long before someone nabs him. If he comes back, ring my personal number, and we'll get him.' He gave his card into Gillespie's hand.

We had a confab in the kitchen.

Wendy was scarlet with anger, 'For anyone to accuse either of you of such doings! How could he? That poor young woman…'

Ash laid a hand on her arm, 'It's alright, Wendy. No harm is done… Jack, could you go and see to Caro? I think she will be a bit shaken up.'

The McLains continued to vent their disgust with Ian Dunch, while I went in search of Caro, who I found in the kitchen garden on the bench, moodily twisting a clump of grass over and over between her fingers.

'May I join you?'

She nodded, looking miserable, 'How could Ian do something like that?'

'He wanted to make trouble for us – like you said, a mixture of things – jealousy, a sense of ownership….'

She spat angrily, 'Well, he doesn't own *me*!'

'No, he doesn't. You showed him that. – Wendy said that you spoke up really well. I am very proud of you.'

A little glimpse of the old Caro began to sparkle at my compliment, but I refused to reciprocate. She had never been successful in her attempts to engage me with her come-ons.

'I expect it's my fault for asking him to visit,' she observed, glumly.

This had been a puzzle, so I asked, 'Why *did* you invite him, Caro?' I thought it was worth testing the ground.

It took her a while to articulate a clear response, 'I wanted to check… to see if he was … to see if I… to check that there was no more "we."'

'And is there?'

She shook her head, 'Not anymore.' Caro turned to me, 'I felt nothing except disgust.' She turned to me, frowning, 'How can this be happening?… I should be really grateful to him, not feeling like…' she had no words.

'I expect you are coming back to yourself. You're catching up with the person you were always meant to be, and that means being able to make choices for yourself….'

It was a very sober young woman who interrupted, '…And not just taking the next thing that comes along?'

'No, indeed!'

She threw the clump of twisted grass to the ground, 'I always used to do that, you know – taking the next thing, whatever it was. I really want to start planning things that work out for me for a change. Can I… will I be able to do that?'

'I see no reason not. Sorting out what *you* want to do, especially when people around you want you to go along with what they want, is a big step forward. What happened to you in your home was not right because your consent was assumed, not given.'

Caro looked at the ground, 'I just wanted to please them, Mum's friends. I thought that was what women were supposed to do. I wanted to be grown up….'

My heart turned over for the girl she had once been, and the kinds of unsavoury inducements she had been exposed to. Very carefully, I said, 'It's not always easy to know how to say no, especially when people are being coercive – forcing you to do things they want instead, rather than checking what you want. But you're an adult now and the way your life unfolds will very much depend on how you give consent or withhold it.'

'Should I have said no to Ian?' I asked earnestly.

'You mean today?'

'No, back then, when he found me in the car.'

That was a hard one. 'I can't judge the rights and wrongs of it, but I know that you were vulnerable and that he took you in, offered you safety. At the time, I think, for you, that was an acceptable escape from something much worse. Whatever his motives, you are right to have a sense of gratitude to Ian, in my book, but whether it was good for you to stay with him in the long term... that's for you to say.'

She thought about that, 'I don't think I've ever thought far ahead. How do I start doing that?'

'Well, it's a great thing to cherish your heart's desire, to take it for a walk and see how you can walk with it. What is it you most wish for?'

She closed her eyes and took several deep breaths, looking into the future.

'To be free of all this. But most of all, to start again, to feel *clean* ... I feel so dirty – do you understand?'

Many women who've have been raped or abused, or just had terrible relationships had often spoken about that feeling: something I, as a man, could not entirely understand. To have the joy and freshness of your youth squeezed out of you was a terrible thing.

'Let's ask Ash, he'll know what to do.'

I had to admit that, for all his meddling that day, Ian Dunch had helped Caro's healing move into a higher gear, giving her more insight than I could have credited.

Since Ash had gone up to London directly after our alarms and excursions with the Social Services, to see some new clients, I had no chance to confer. Caro was coming near to the end of her time with us. We were all anxious about what came next. Wendy had already looked into the possibility of a half-way house situation for Caro, but wondered whether she was quite ready for that responsibility. 'Living in with a proper family would be a far better thing than some tiny flat in a housing association, all by herself, in my opinion - where she could have both a room of her own but also be part of other people's lives. She needs people with her who care for her, and who act as a responsible sounding board for what is normal, but she's unfortunately too old for a foster home.'

Caro herself was also dreading having to leave. With no clear path leading ahead, she began to get very clingy again. In her experience, any man was a port in a storm, an escape from destitution and prostitution. She badly needed other options: ones that she had instituted and had control over.

I was still wracking my brains to think of a way she could step back out into the world that afternoon. Taking advantage of the sunshine to clean the car out the front of the house, I saw Caro in the garden. She asked if she could help: I sent her in to change, so as not to dirty her new clothes. She came out in her old things, and helped polished the windows for me. Then, examining my rather elderly Peugeot saloon with a severe and expert eye, 'It's got a lot of rust on this side over the wheel.' She shook her head with all the gravity of a garage mechanic, 'It won't last long if you don't fix it. I could clean it up for you, if you like? Have you got any filler?'

Only Gillespie could tell us that, so we duly trotted off to his shed. He peered out cautiously from behind its well-defended door, still leery of Caro's approaches, 'Aye?'

We explained what we needed, and Gillespie duly supplied some fibreglass based filler, some sandpaper, and the tools for the job.

'Will she ken what to do?' he asked, coming out as Caro ran off with the stuff.

'Well, she certainly can't make it any worse,' I said. 'I was on the point of swapping it for a new one, anyway, the rust has got so bad.'

'Weel, there's only yourself to blame for that!' was his bald conclusion.

Later on, though, Gillespie came and checked on Caro's work. Apart from the replacement colour paint which I would have to pick up at the DIY emporium on the edge of Frisdon, the repair looked sound enough, 'Aye, she's made a decent job of it! I could nae do better!' was his assessment.

When Ash returned later from his consultations in London, I reported my conversation with Caro and her confirmation that indeed she was over Ian and that she wanted to move on. He was very struck by her need to feel clean again, 'I think we can help her. I've just been waiting for the sign that she was ready.'

I asked him, 'Ash, I understand why Caro clung to Ian in the first place, but what kept her with him? – Was it just insecurity or convenience? Did you find any good reason from your investigations?'

'I don't think it's the first time over their incarnations that they have been drawn together. They share experiences of alienation and obligation during times of crisis. But where Ian has remained sunk in what seems to him a safe condition, walled up in a womb of junk, Caro is like a bird trying to peck her way out now. Let's see if we can help her get free.'

He stopped Wendy after supper, 'Do you think Myrtle and her friends might come over again to help Caro?'

'What did you have in mind?'

'Just a short ceremony – something to recognize and cleanse her, to help her step into her place again.'

'Better make sure that the Social Services don't hear about then?' I observed darkly.

'Oh, don't be an old kill-joy!' said Wendy, picking up the phone to Myrtle.

Nothing could have prepared me for what Ash had in mind.

On the chosen evening, only Myrtle and Betony, her cousin by marriage, were available to come over. Ash thanked them for coming, explaining what he had in mind, 'The ceremony tonight is to support Caro and give her the strength and courage to start her new life, and to leave disappointments and sorrows behind. This is what we'll be doing...' He had spoken with Caro earlier and explained the ceremony. She was keen to go ahead, 'If it makes me feel clean again, I'd do anything.'

In the middle of the Sanctuary, Gillespie had already erected a low couch which he had surrounded with late spring flowers: many-coloured anemones, lily of the valley and bluebells from Hartsworth Beacon, all arranged with his best love. He himself bowed out of the ceremony, not wanting to intrude, 'It's a lassies' kind of thing, ye ken? I'll be awa' in the snug of the White Hart.' I would have liked to join him, but Ash decreed that I should be part of it.

The medieval chapel was bright with candles and the smell of fragrant incense. Only I was present when Ash consecrated the space for the ceremony, and I could feel the sense of gathering as he intoned and chanted in each direction. Fortunately, my job was merely to act as acolyte for the evening, which I reckoned I could do without too much effort. Myrtle and Betony were invited in, with Betony exclaiming like everyone did when they first entered, as it was such a surprise to find something so medieval hidden at the heart of the Beacon. Myrtle put a calming hand on Betony's arm and they took their places.

Ash rang the bell, which was the signal for Wendy to lead Caro in. Wearing her best dress, she came in with wondering eyes, taking in the scene. In front of the couch stood Myrtle and Betony beaming their welcoming smiles.

Ash stepped forward, holding out his hand, 'Dear Caro, welcome to this place of healing. Leave your sorrows at this threshold and enter this place of peace, knowing that all within this place are your friends. Come and be made glad in your soul!'

I asked, 'Who will stand by Caro and support her this night?'

'I will,' said Betony just a fraction before Myrtle.

The two young women, one white, one black, drew close, taking their places beside Caro.

Facing them, I asked that ancient question without which no healing can come, 'Caro, is it your will and desire to be healed and made whole?'

Caro nodded her head, 'Oh, yes please!'

Then Ash asked her his question, 'Is there a spiritual power on which you'd like to call for help?' We had discussed this earlier with her, and Caro had made her decision. While she didn't have a particular faith, she had fastened upon the story of St Margaret of Antioch as her talismanic helper: 'I want to blast that dragon to bits, just like her,' she'd said.

Now, in the candlelight, Caro regarded the image of the saint upon the Sanctuary walls with trust. 'I want the help of St Margaret.'

'Then come to the place of healing and rest in the presence of St Margaret!' said Ash, leading the way to the couch with its banks of flowers.

Her sponsors, led her to the couch and helped her lie upon it, moving to kneel at her head and foot and hold her head and feet supportively.

Wendy came to stand on her right, while Ash and myself stood on her left, where I could fetch and carry, as his acolyte.

Ash took up the censer and wafted the smoke across Caro's body, saying, 'With burning herbs I cleanse you; with sweet smelling incense, I drive pain and hurt from you,' he made sharp passes through the smoke, as if casting something aside. Then with gentler hands led the smoke downwards, 'With scented smoke, I hallow you.'

Completely wrapped in the enclosing smoke, Caro peered up at me, a little frightened. I nodded encouragement and she calmed down.

Mixing water and salt in a silver bowl, Ash sprinkled it upon her forehead, smoothing the liquid tenderly down her cheeks with the blade of his thumb, saying, 'With sweet water, I cleanse you and wash away the tears of pain and sorrow.' Caro's eyes were not the only ones beginning to well up.

Sprinkling her body, legs and feet, he continued, 'With salt I cleanse you and make you pure and sacred once again.'

Then I brought him the chalice of spring water. Ash held it up over Caro's body, letting it sink nearer to her as he spoke each phrase, 'Ever holy and inviolate, blessed St Margaret, we ask you to renew and reconsecrate the sacred centre of this woman. Make her clean and holy once more. Help make her conscious of her womanhood as a thing of joy and beauty. Restore to her the image of herself as child, seeker, woman, and wise one.'

Like a priest bringing down the vessel of consecration, he gently rested the chalice upon her, saying, 'What is filled with light above shall be filled with light below. What is perfect in the upper realms shall be made perfect in the lower.'

Then he passed the chalice to me to hold until it was needed.

Ash spoke again, facing first the wall painting and then Wendy, 'I call upon St Margaret of Antioch. Blessed St Margaret, I ask you to come into the body of your oracle, Wendy, and speak words of comfort, healing and wisdom to Caro.'

Wendy folded her shawl closer around her, eyes closed, seeming to tune in. At first nothing happened. Betony stared up at Wendy, eyes wondering, while Myrtle kept her focus upon Caro, patiently waiting, solid and still. Caro lay with eyes closed, as if floating between heaven and earth. The silence in the Sanctuary seemed to be in-gathering, like the breath of a swimmer between strokes across a wide sea.

When the oracle spoke, it had Wendy's voice, but with a deeper tone. It was fetched from the depths of the dragon that had once attempted to envelope St Margaret, who was undoubtedly with us, using Wendy's voice. She was speaking exclusively to Caro, 'Dear one, I have heard your voice calling upon me. You have been heard and witnessed. I will keep a watch upon your heart and be beside you as you make your life anew. The days that are past have been burnt up. The dragon's skin has burst in pieces. It holds no power over you anymore. Go forward and be at peace!'

Caro's arms thrust urgently up towards the voice, and the oracle caught her hands between hers, 'Fear not! You will walk with a blessing, wherever you go.' Then the oracle gently let Caro's hands go again, 'When days are dark, remember this night. I shall be always with you.'

The resonance of the voice was all that was left behind in the silence. After a moment, Wendy shifted and began to breathe in a different rhythm. Ash touched her lightly upon the shoulders, 'We thank St Margaret for these words of wisdom. Leave now the garment of your servant, that she may know herself again.'

I passed Ash the oil. He anointed Caro, making circles of oil on brow, breast, belly, hands and feet, saying, 'Fortified by these words, made holy are your thoughts and all your dreams. Made holy is the heart within you. Made holy is your womanhood. Your hands shall heal the hurts of others and your feet shall walk forever in the light.'

In that moment, it seemed to me that Caro was sucking in all the goodness, like a cat lying in the sun.

Ash nodded at Betony who helped Caro to sit up. Taking from me the chalice, Ash set it to her lips with, 'Drink from the cup of life.' Her eyes came open as she drank, fixing upon Myrtle who took her hand, leading Caro around the couch. With her clear, carrying voice, and with the dignity of all her West African ancestors, Myrtle said, 'I lead you back to your birt'-right and your blessing. I lead you back to your own country which is your womanhood and to your true holiness.' Myrtle made a dance of it, in which Betony and Wendy joined. Caro began to laugh and cry at the same time. As Betony let loose a mighty ululation, it felt like we had crashed the sound barrier.

Then we seemed naturally to come together into a circle, as Myrtle said in a loud joyful voice, 'Behold your sistah, renewed in body, heart and soul!'

Caro came to each of us to be congratulated and hugged. Wendy took her in her arms, saying, 'Caro, never doubt that you are now cleansed. You are made whole and holy. Never forget it!' They clung together in a strong, fierce hug.

Ash kissed her hand, 'Caro, may you go out into the world again and walk with pride in your womanhood!'

I held both her hands at arm's length to appraise her, nodding, 'Welcome back to the circle of life, Caro!'

Gillespie came back from the White Hart with a suggestion. As the chair of the local folk club, he'd been meeting with the other southern regional chairs to plan a folk festival. One of these, Helen Frasier, a fellow Scot, owned a garage off the Frisdon ring road where she lived with her husband, Rob, and their three children.

He told us, 'Helen's looking for some help. She said she'd give Caro a two-week trial. She's offering bed and board in return for work, and a wee stipend during the trial period. If it works oot, she'll take her on, and she'll be on regular pay.'

We put our heads together.

'Will she have to handle money?' Wendy worried about the temptations.

'Nae troubles! She'll be helping oot the back, with the mechanics. She'll have Helen's family around,' Gillespie added. 'The two girls are aboot 15 and 17, and the boy is jist 11. They have a granny flat behind the hoose.'

'Before we get ahead of ourselves, does Caro want to do it?' Ash asked.

'I know it's late, but let's ask her!'

Caro, Myrtle and Betony were still drinking hot chocolate in the living room. Wendy sat down with them and told Caro the good news, asking her, 'Is this something that will work for you?'

'I don't want to leave here, but I wouldn't be far away, would I?

Myrtle told her that the buses that ran from Frisdon on Sea, where she lived, passed the garage and had a stop up on the main road near the Beacon.

'Can we go and see?'
'We'll go tomorrow,' Wendy promised.

A few days later, Caro went with myself and Wendy into Christminster to get the weekly shop, and to pick up some last bits and pieces for her trial fortnight at the garage. She started on Monday next. The set-up at the garage was ideal for her and Caro got on well with Helen and her family: the granny flat was somewhere of her own and, while it wasn't a permanent solution, it meant she would have a chance to get on her feet, grow in confidence and earn her own money. To ensure that everything went smoothly, Ash contacted the local Social Services and arranged for a case-worker to be assigned to Caro. I had also discovered the nearest sex-addicts group and accompanied her to a preliminary meeting. We had set up a big safety net and could do no more for the moment. Time would have to tell.

I watched her as we went around the Thursday market, enjoying the home-made produce, sampling cheese, smelling the hand-made soaps. Ash's ceremony of healing had brought her peace and a better resilience, I thought, as she giggled over the second-hand book stall with Wendy. The year was heating up and she had acquired clothes more suitable for the summer – I suspect Wendy had paid for them as well as the new pair of sandals that Caro was wearing.

On our way back to the carpark, Caro stopped short outside the RAF recruitment offices. I walked back to see what had engaged her attention. The window display was pretty plain – just a photo of a couple of young women on deployment somewhere in the Middle East, driving a refuelling vehicle.

'Can we go in?' she asked, strangely agitated.

'Of course.' I called to Wendy who was walking ahead, 'We'll meet you in the carpark.'

Inside, the female recruiting sergeant welcomed us, 'And which of you is interested in joining us?' she smiled.

I nodded to Caro who stood uncertainly, eyes slewing around the office. At first, I thought it was the sight of several fit young men flying planes or on parade in the advertising posters, so I was entirely unprepared for her, 'I saw the picture in the window. Can I really become an air-force driver?'

The sergeant indicated a seat, 'Let's see, shall we?' She swiftly outlined the requirements for the job of RAF driver, 'If you get through the application process, then you will get to operate many vehicle types, from cars and minibuses to cranes, coaches, articulated trucks and refuelling vehicles. Not only that, but you would need to know how to make sure they are in working order.'

Caro's eyes gleamed.

The sergeant asked Caro a few questions about herself, took some details, and enquired about her qualifications. Caro hung her head, 'I don't have any, but I do know about cars. My boyfr... I used to know someone who showed me all about cars and things.' With a small boast, she added, '*And* I am working in a garage.'

'Do you have a driving licence?'

'No, but I do know how to drive. I used to do it on the fields where we did the car-boots.'

'Well, you would need a driving licence before you apply.'

Caro seemed initially dismayed, then looked to me, wordless, pleadingly. I had a good sense of what it was to be a father in that moment.

I replied, 'I'm sure you could take the test and pass easily.'

The sergeant was clearly trying to work out whether I was Caro's father or a very much older brother. Seeing Caro's uncertainty, she added, 'If you had your driving licence, and got through the application procedure, we would also need to know that you are fit enough to do the work – there is a physical test that you would have to do; if all went well, then you might be offered an apprenticeship.'

I came out of the recruitment office with a completely different Caro. Clutching leaflets in her hand, she took one last lingering look at the photo in the window display, and turned decisively, 'I'm going to try. I know I have to work at the garage first and prove I can do it. But do you think I can?'

The services can be a fine place for young people to learn in community, but Caro was still many steps from joining the RAF. Her vulnerability needed the support that Helen and Rob could hopefully provide. If her mental health report was not to count against her, she would have to make a good showing, but I hadn't the heart to cavil, so I said, 'Concentrate on your work, earn some money and save it, do some driving lessons, and let's see.'

After Caro had gone to upstairs, I reported the recruitment office visit, 'She said she was interested in becoming an air-force driver.'

'I wonder what happened to having a place of her own and a cat?' Wendy wondered.

Ash said, 'That was what she wanted when she first came: now she is moving on, spreading her wings. At this stage, I think we should regard that as good evidence of healing.'

'Then it's down to your cracking ritual,' I said. 'I was never in such a ceremony before, but I can see how it's helped her put her old life behind her.'

On the following Monday, the household were up early to wave her 'bon voyage,' in her new venture. Clutching an old suitcase of Gillespie's, she hugged us all, 'Thank you. I shall miss you all terribly. You all have to come and fill up at my garage, now!' We promised.

Looking at her with a US baseball cap wedged over her brown head,

it was hard to remember the old Caro who had attempted to vamp us all. The phoenix brooch that Wendy and Gillespie was pinned onto it.

As we waved her off, Ash said, 'A phoenix from the ashes indeed!'

We heard from Caro regularly. She passed her fortnight's trial and started to earn money. Then, some weeks down the line, Helen phoned us late one night to say that Ian Dunch had finally tracked her down and had attempted to invade her flat. The police had been called. It ended with the Social Services helping Caro to obtain a protection order against him for harassment: he was forbidden from coming within three miles of her flat, and threatened with legal action if he attempted to approach her in any way. Our anxiety was allayed when Sergeant Hobbs reported that Ian *had* finally prosecuted, though for driving an unlicensed van, not for harassment. It was his lack of transport that had finally seen him off.

Wendy kept in touch with Caro, while Betony and Myrtle still met up with her, finally giving her a proper girl's night out on the town at Frisdon's funfair.

I was several cases down the line when Gillespie and myself ran into Caro on her day-off on Frisdon sea-front, where we had gone for a breath of air after Gillespie's essential half-year visit to the dentist.

The children had all gone back to school, so it was quiet, but the intense summer heat still lingered on. There was Caro swinging along in a bright full-skirted sundress, arm in arm with Betony. I bought ice creams for all, except for poor Gillespie whose jaw was still frozen into post-anaesthetic stiffness, and so we sat on the front for a while trying to consume our cones before they melted away.

'How are things, Caro?'

'I have my RAF test next week, so think of me on Tuesday!'

'And are you going to try for the air force if you pass?'

Licking her cone with a long pink tongue, she nodded vigorously.

Betony told us, 'She's got all the forms to apply ready.'

We chatted inconsequentially for a while before they took off.

With just a scandalizing tincture of the old Caro, she turned, 'How do you like the outfit, Gillespie?' twirling round on the spot so that her full circle skirt did the classic Marilyn-Monroe-over-the-grating trick, grinning over her shoulder at him.

It was measure of our success that Gillespie could say, 'I like it real fine, lassie,' and mean it.

Case 4: AN OLD MASTER

Assist a man in raising a burden; but do not assist him in laying it down
Pythagoras

How many times does a gift turn out to have strings? I wondered, as I watched our latest guest in the art room, standing helpless and defeated before the canvas, pastel stick in reluctant hand, like a man who would rather be put down than ever paint again. He had come to us via one of the Ash's colleagues in the Guild of Ecumenical Psychology. The letter of referral simply said, 'I think this one is more up your street than mine.'

Alan Ansgar was a young-looking 30 year old with the loose body of a 22 year old youth. The first impression of his character was that he was weak and undeveloped. You couldn't image a beard ever sprouting upon that face, but then you caught the down-tilt of the head and the stubborn under-lip, which bespoke a man a decade his senior, someone inured to life's calamities. After a breakdown, Alan was still in the need of care.

His worried parents brought him in after a painful interview in the London consulting rooms, where his deaf father gave us the second degree, while his wife sat with down-cast eyes, holding her grown-up son's hand quietly. Every time Mr Ansgar shouted at Ash, Alan would flinch, I noted.

'I don't want no nonsense. If he's harmed by drugs or the likes, his mother will be right grieved.'

Alan was, or had been, an art student, but had gone off the rails after a spectacular burning of his entire *oeuvre*. Unlike some notorious celebrity artists, whose only goal was to make a holocaust of their work for the purposes of an installation, Alan's burning seemed to come from a place of genuine valediction. He truly wanted to relinquish his work forever, or so the firemen who had found him seemed to think.

Having heaped all his sketches, studies and canvases onto the family barbeque on the brick patio, he had then dowsed them in lighter fluid and set a match to the lot. Found hunched over a badly burned hand by an alarmed neighbour who'd spotted the flames from his garden, Alan had been crying without any tears. Such was his distress, after his burns had been treated, that he ended up in therapy, but it had been to no avail. The decision to section him finally arose when he made a more serious attempt to harm himself in a similar fashion to his own artwork. Fortunately, that time the lighter had been out of fuel, and his father had intervened before a box of matches and some olive oil finished the job.

Alan arrived heavily medicated, lethargic and unfocused. Ash and I discussed cutting back the dosage, since our guest had been given some of the more heavy-duty anti-psychotics which only aided the suicidal ideation. Even after we knocked back the dosage, he remained utterly subdued and without energy.

The weather didn't help. In London, the pavements were sour. A prevailing southerly wind had turned the city from balmy to sultry, but it had stayed in the southern quarter without let up for several weeks until we were driven mad with the lack of moisture. Even the Downs themselves looked parched and dry as we drove south. But it was still a joy to be away from the confinement of city and back in the countryside.

Following Ash's 'watch and observe' routine, we left Alan to get settled in. After a few days of mainly sleeping or slumping, he began to explore, notably shunning the art room. In the smouldering heat, he lay about in the garden smoking - apparently a habit he had picked up while he was hospitalised from the other inmates. His mother assured us that he had been far too fastidious to smoke when he lived at home.

When we got to the story, it was more bizarre than I could have imagined.

'I've never been an artist, only a fraud,' Alan insisted.

'Why a fraud?'

'Because I am.'

Ash listening intently to the unforthcoming silence, tried another tack: 'When did you begin painting?'

Alan's responses were mostly monosyllabic, with long sporadic pauses between question and answer. Each answer was prised painfully out.

'Six. At school.'

'Was it always a pleasure?'

'Then, yes.'

'And now?'

'No.'

'What changed?'

'I had a dream ..... you already know this!... *Everybody* knows this....' he spat with disgust.

'Neither myself nor my colleague know of your dream,' Ash assured him.

With great impatience Alan told us, 'I dreamed a man came to me with a brush in his hand. He stared into me, like someone looking into an interior.

Then he blew the pigment from the palette onto me till my hands and face were speckled all over with colour.'

I could not restrain my question, 'And when you woke....?'

His answer was matter of fact, with the barely concealed patience of someone explaining to a simpleton, 'I could paint like *him* – the man in the dream – but not like me anymore.'

'How old were you?'

'Fifteen.' Alan responded flatly. 'Can I smoke?'

'Not here, no,' Ash said, softly, but without offence.

Alan's mouth twitched into a series of grimaces at being thwarted, and I thought we would have a nasty episode, but he controlled himself.

'What was your own style like before the dream?'

He shrugged, 'An average school kid's effort.'

'And afterwards?'

'You've seen the pictures?'

Ash nodded. Having come in late to the case, I had not yet seen pictures of the full *oeuvre*, so I had little idea of how different those styles might have been. Alan became very restless and uncooperative, so we left it there for that day.

The story sounded very like that of the Edwardian artist, Augustus John; he had gone swimming off the Pembrokeshire coast at the end of the 19th century and hit his head on a rock. Ever afterwards everyone believed - so changed was his behaviour and artistic style after his encounter with the said rock - that he had been transmogrified by this craggy experience into an artistic genius. Alan, on the other hand, looked merely defeated, sounding quite fed up with the whole circus that had attended his dream.

In the cool of the summer house down in the Wilderness, Ash and I conferred. A couple more abortive sessions had ensued, making it clear that Alan did not intend to cooperate much further.

'We need to hear more about that dream,' I said.

Ash opened the shutter to the summer house to allow in whatever residual breeze might alleviate the oppressive heat. Even down here in the shade of the Wilderness, it felt as hot as northern Australia.

He nodded, 'Certainly. Whoever that was in his dream acted as a trigger to Alan's art style.'

'Like Augustus John and his rock?'

Ash shook his head, 'No, I don't think so. Augustus John's diving accident seems to have triggered the turning on of a native talent. Alan's dream is of a very different order, don't you think? Pigment is sprayed upon his flesh, especially his hands and face. It is more like an artistic sacrament, a transfer or initiation into something.'

He threw back his head to allow the infant breeze to blow about his neck. It barely lifted his hair. 'We need some more back story.'

'Well, his parents don't seem to have a clue about it, that's true.' Mrs Ansgar had spoken quietly about her son's love of art as a small boy, seeming to us strangely incurious about his suddenly-accelerated talent. For Mr Ansgar, who inhabited a world devoid of culture, art was evidently some weird activity that only loopy people pursued: whatever insights he might have had seemed negligible.

'Heredity seems to play no part in this case, indeed! I imagine there are no long-lost artists lurking in the Ansgar family line....' Ash smiled. 'But his parents are paying for his treatment here, and we must do our best.'

He leant against the door frame, staring up at Hartsworth Beacon, 'I know it's something we don't do often, but I would like you to visit the Minster Barton Art School and speak to Alan's tutor.'

Ash believed in client-led treatment, and it was rare for him to explore the client's background behind his back like this, but Alan's failure to cooperate was not helping.

'Won't he resent it?'

'Perhaps, but we are not making good progress. The Ansgars haven't the money for a long stay, I think. If Alan were in a more stable condition... but since he clearly does not give his consent.... I would like an opportunity to gain that, at least, so let's see if a little provocation will help.'

I eventually tracked down Alan's tutor, Werner Lentz, at the Minster Barton School of Art in Leddenham, Suffolk, and made an appointment to meet up.

Lentz met me in the car-park and walked me to the canteen where we drank some excellent coffee.

'Was Alan's work considered good?' I asked, naively, as you never know what counts as excellence in the world of modern art today – and I speak as the Philistine who once complained loudly about a set of mops and breeze blocks being left in the middle of a gallery, unknowing that they constituted part of an exhibition!

Lentz looked long at me, more in sorrow than in anger, '*Good?*' He went on in the hushed tones of homage that normally accompany the recently decease of a great artist, 'Oh yes – Alan Ansgar really didn't need my tutoring at all – it was as if an Old Master had arrived in my class fully-formed. His was an eye that saw through the centuries.' He shook his head in self-deprecation, 'No, my main job was to support his progress, and help him find his place in the art market. Despite his genius, he was still an inexperienced human being. Not only did he lack confidence, but he carried a *weltanschaung* that was very heavy for one so young.'

I made no more note of that last remark until a little later.

'Are there any friends of his who might be prepared to speak to me? We are trying to help him as best we can, since he returned from the hospital, and a little background would be most helpful.'

'Kumar and Nancy spent more time with him than anyone else; they both looked out for him when some others were jealous. If you wait here, I'll send them down to see you. Please take my card and contact me again if you have need.'

Kumar proved to be a solid young Asian man with chunky thick-lensed glasses. He seemed the very antithesis of the pale, waif-like Nancy, whose hair had recently encountered a non-too steady razor in the last week, though you could tell from the stubble that it had previously been dyed some shade of pinky-purple. She came twirling in like a dancer, Kumar following her more like a tame bear. Both were very sweet about having to meet an old medic like me. Their concern for their fellow student was touching, 'How's Alan doing?'

'Not so well, though we've been able to knock back the medication he was on under section, so it's a step forward.'

Nancy sucked her bottom lip with anxiety, 'Alan hated anything to do with drugs.'

I asked them to tell me what they could so we might help restore Alan to health.

Kumar looked deeply into me, 'Did you ever see any of his work in the flesh?'

'No, only photos.'

'Then you need to see in person.' He was insistant.

'I thought he'd burned the lot?' I said to Nancy, who was pulling me up excitedly.

Kumar stood, 'Follow me... It's the only thing that Alan couldn't actually destroy because of where it was.'

Kumar led me into the foyer of the exhibition hall and looked up. The four walls of the foyer tapered to vaulted ceiling whereon were murals of the most delicate and detailed kind. I exclaimed at their beauty, then looked to Kumar for confirmation, 'Alan did *these*?'

He nodded, tears in his eyes, 'They are the only thing left, we think.'

I finally found my voice again, 'But...but... they look like something from

Renaissance Italy.'

These egg tempera murals could have easily come from within any palazzo or church in Northern Italy, and it was impossible for me to conceive that someone from the 20th century could have painted them. These were not pastiche, but the real thing: the topic was Noah's Ark: the animals were processing up the walls towards the centre of the vault, in perfect pairs – rhinos, giraffes, lions, peacocks - only they were rendered as a 15th century man would have seen and drawn them. Each animal had its own dignity; there was no sign of any modern self-indulgence or self-awareness, and not a trace of the knowingness or cynicism that mars modern art. A lad from West Yorkshire simply didn't have the ability to create these wonders, I knew.

Nancy let go my arm as I gawped up, saying to Kumar, in a confiding voice, 'Now he's sees it too, he'll do his very best for Alan.' She seemed touchingly sure of my abilities to heal her friend.

I knew that Ash had to see these murals, for they were proof positive of something far beyond ordinary causation, 'Are there any photos?'

Nancy dragged me to the desk and picked out a packet of postcards from the rack of goods for sale. Placing them in my hands like an offering, she turned swiftly and pressed coins into the honesty box, brushing aside my proffered banknote, 'No, no, we want you to have them,' she said vigorously.

Kumar excused himself, 'I just need to get something, Nancy. Take Dr Rivers into the garden.' Nancy drew me out to the enclosed garden at the heart of the school, which surrounded it all sides, where we sought shade under a spinney of aspen trees. The heat was surging like an animal about to pounce, but Nancy looked as fresh as a daisy. She told me about her own work in textile design while we waited for Kumar to return, which he soon did, bringing us a jug of water with lemon slices in it.

'But how can he have painted like that?' I mouthed, peering at the postcards, still struggling to understand.

Kumar looked grave, 'He didn't like it, you know. He wanted very badly to paint like himself.'

'It was as though he didn't feel worthy of them, at first… well, I thought so…' Nancy said, sucking the end of her rainbow scarf.

'Of course, he had been living with this style for few years before he came to the Minster,' Kumar went on. 'We three came together naturally because we each work in a representational style…. Although neither of us was as good as Alan.'

'Your tutor said something about jealous students…?'

Nancy and Kumar looked at each other, and then over their shoulders, in case anyone was listening. Through narrowed eyes, Kumar said, 'A few of the students in Fine Art really resented him, especially Tako – Takihito Miura – he was great at ceramics but streets behind Alan's natural skill in painting. He could be really spiteful. They were all jealous, some of his skill - which was effortless - but mostly because of his sudden art market cachet.'

'Were there any serious incidents between them?'

'Apart from a fist fight one night in the bar, it was all water off Alan's back.'

From the Yorkshire stubbornness we ourselves had already encountered, I could understand how Alan might get under the skin of a sensitive young rival. I asked if Alan had had any girlfriend.

Kumar shook his head, 'I don't think there was any room for anyone intimate. He was really wedded to his art.'

Nancy tugged his arm, whispering something, 'Go on, tell him! You know it's important.'

Kumar looked very reluctant to vouchsafe whatever it was, so Nancy told me, 'It was the week before the 2nd year show. Everyone was getting in a state, and both of us were behind. But Alan seemed very... well, relaxed... like he had let go of everything... and when we asked what he was working on, it was pretty clear he had prepared nothing. Mind you, almost anything he had made *could* have gone into the show, of course.' She sucked her lip again. 'Well, he asked us to come and witness him do something the night before... and so we both came because we thought it was something he was making for the show, but ....'

She became very distressed and couldn't go on, so Kumar continued, 'We thought maybe he had some document for us to witness or something or we would never have gone, of course. When we got to his room, it was dark, lit only by candles. Everything was set up like for a *puja* – a ritual of some kind. We both thought it was about the show still. Then he told us, "I want you to witness me sending the artist away."'

Nancy ceased her sobbing and said, 'It was just awful! He wanted us to watch him send away the one thing that gave him his creative genius... It was like being asked to watch someone kill themselves!... I couldn't do it. I just couldn't stay....' She started sobbing again.

'Do you mean he thought all his talent came from this artist – the one from his dream?'

'Yes,' said Kumar. 'Without it, he would have no skill worth speaking about, he said. Well, we all knew the story about his dream - it was a very badly kept secret - unfortunately some art dealer had got hold of it and wrote something about Alan, and so soon the whole art world knew. It invested him in this massive mystique, but *he* felt this knowledge utterly devalued everything that he did.'

Well, Alan had tried to kill himself after having made two good attempts to remove himself from the artist's presence, even though it was the one thing that made his art commercial. I could see how there would be very little left for Alan.

I praised his friends for their devotion and promised them that I would contact them as soon as I had any news. Nancy planted a faery kiss on my cheek before running back to her class, while I returned once more to the foyer to view the murals with Kumar, who answered some more questions.

I couldn't help asking, 'I know you may not have any notion, but just how did Alan plan to send away his genius?'

Kumar shifted his glasses back up his nose, 'He had a palette of pigments and he wanted us to spray those onto his face and hands, and then to transfer his image onto a linen cloth.... Then I think he intended to burn it.... I don't really understand how he thought that would possibly work. But I'm still glad we refused to help him do it.'

'I hope that the whole world will be in your debt for it!' I said, and clapped him on the back.

From his back pocket, Kumar produced something in a fold of material: 'Please would you give it to Alan? I painted it for him when he... when he tried... but I've had no means of giving it to him.'

I received it, asking, 'Any message with it?'

With unshed tears in his eyes, Kumar said, 'Tell him, "I'm not sorry. I just hope you will remember our friendship."'

On my return to the Beacon, I reported to Ash, telling him about the intended ritual, 'The very thought of it upset his close friends so much they refused to cooperate.'

Ash looked very relieved, 'It shows that Alan was trying to find the ground of his own being again, and to me it confirms that this is a case of over-shadowing.'

'Over-shadowing?' No matter how many years I spent at the Beacon, it seemed that I would remain as clueless as when I first arrived.

Taking pity upon me, he said, 'It's when a person is joined by another personality which dictates its own terms.'

'You mean a sub-personality?' This was the kind of thing I was familiar with, I thought, when dormant aspects of the psyche emerge to behave in aberrant, childish, or dominant ways. It can be controlled by medication initially, and then it needs a lot of therapy to build up the main personality again.

Ash calmly disagreed, 'No, I mean a completely separate being or entity that steps into the person. Sometimes the interface is total, and it signals a complete change of behaviour; most often, it is an intermittent interface, such as Alan has had, though the subject in question may not have much control over it. His attempt to make the other being go away was unsuccessful, so he burned all the art that the overshadowing had produced – like a sit-down strike, in effect. But it sent him over the edge because he still couldn't wrestle back control.'

'Well it sounds like a sub-personality disorder to me. Alan is a perfect candidate: a young man insecure in his own personality.'

He held up the postcards of the murals, 'Yes, but *this* kind of painting?'

I could not explain that, admittedly. Thinking back to their impact upon me, I said, 'Yes. Someone who can paint that well must have some outside help, if it wasn't there before.'

At that point, I think I finally understood that why the case had been referred to Ash. Employing my usual strategy of 'if you don't understand it, act as if it were true,' which usually stood me in good stead with Ash, I asked, 'What triggered the step-in, do you think?'

'That's what we need to find out. Whoever it was came into him during that dream has his own agenda, and I don't think that it is the same as Alan's.'

'Well it seems to me that the article about his dream – the one that brought the art market down on his back – was likely to have been the last straw, from what his friends said. How can anyone have been that crass?'

'The writer clearly didn't understand what's it like to be over-shadowed, nor what's it's like to become public property.'

On my way to the garden to find Alan, I ran into Wendy carrying a platter piled high with shredded beef fat.

In dismay, I cried, 'Not more beef, please say it's not for us?'

Our last client had been a butcher's wife, and her husband had shown his gratitude by gifting us with a massive piece of beef that could have fed a whole Oxford college. We had done our best with it, but even Gillespie couldn't stomach another beef-based meal. He had sternly refused any more beef sandwiches at lunch earlier that week, and uncharacteristically demanded a salad, causing us all much mirth, for he had hitherto sworn that, as a Highland Scot, rabbit food could not pass his lips without risk of serious injury.

Wendy nodded, 'I'm afraid so! It was very kind of Mr Barnard, but in this crushing heat, no-one is wanting any. I thought I would take the fat out for the birds. At least the rooks would be grateful for it.' Her airy tone implied we were ungrateful wastrels to turn up her good food, so I wisely said nothing.

Alan was sitting down the Wilderness, having pulled a deckchair under the shade of the plum trees, near the bird table. I hesitated suddenly at sight of him, wondering about the wisdom of giving him Kumar's gift, which I had forgotten to mention to Ash. If I handed it over now, he would surely know that I had been to the Minster, that we had been asking about him. I knew I could tell a white lie and say that Kumar had sent it, but I thrust it back into my pocket, intending to ask Ash what was best. I didn't want to prematurely trigger anything, as I didn't know his plan.

I nodded to him, and watched Wendy loading the bird table with the beef fat that she'd shredded. She retired to the shade of the summerhouse and flapped herself with a tea-towel.

A detachment of rooks soon came down, noisily pulling at it the fat, sating their appetites with squabbling ferocity. Quite a lot had fallen on the ground, and pair of green woodpeckers flew down to feed more delicately. After such a long time working in cities, it still felt like a great privilege for me to see these beautiful birds, so I melted back into the plum trees to watch them for a while.

Without any greeting, Alan said softly to me, so as not to disturb their feeding, 'It's like they are on casters – they seem to have no feet when they walk.'

'It must come from spiralling up and down trees, I suppose,' for I had also watched them.

'I wonder where they nest?' There was a heartening note of curiosity in his voice.

Wendy thrust her head through the summerhouse window, saying in a stage whisper, 'They usually nest up the hill, in the oak trees over the first rise.'

In the ensuing wildlife talk, it became apparent to me that Alan still had the same natural eye for animals as he had shown in his murals, and that this was part of his own wisdom, not that of the painter who overshadowed him. While the painter may have portrayed animals in his own style, Alan had a naturalist's eye that informed him also.

Wendy joined in, contributing her extensive knowledge of the area.

'When is the best time to see them?' Alan asked.

'Usually mid-morning down here,' she said, 'And up on the Beacon in the early evening.'

Somewhere south of us, the dull retort of a gamekeeper's rifle shattered the peace of the afternoon, and the green woodpeckers took flight up to Hartsworth

Beacon.

Taking up the garden hose with a sigh, Wendy tried to fill up the bird-bath that the rooks had emptied in their splashing about. A mere trickle of water came out. 'It must have a bend in it somewhere...' and she went off to investigate.

I asked Alan, 'Would you like to walk up there tonight and see if we can see them?'

'Yes.'

It felt like a great step forward, to get even this much cooperation, so I determined not to spoil it.

That evening, as the sun westered, Alan and I took our way up the private path that ran between us and Hartsworth Beacon. Melanie had been able to retain it as a private right of way from the house, despite the protest of the Ramblers Association who wanted all access to be public, but I was very grateful for it. The evening was beautifully quiet. Having been broken on the anvil of the unfading sunlight all day, few people wanted to spend their evenings up here, except for the usual dog-walkers.

Alan seemed to make short work of the slope, being younger and in better condition than myself, but he had less stamina since his many trials, and I was soon pulling him up over the first rise as he began to tire. We stopped on the first rise to catch our breath, turning to look over the incomparable view south. From up here, you could even discern the sparkle of the sea in the far distance, and the land that stretched out for miles, right down to the chain of beacon hills that marked the Downs.

We found the stand of oaks to which Wendy had directed us and settled down to observe. After about twenty minutes, we heard the distinctive peal of laughter that gave the green woodpecker its country name of 'Yaffle.' Alan's keener eyes spotted it first. Following the line of his finger, I refocused to make out the female feeding on the tree, looking for ants in the bark. It was soon joined by the moustached male who flew in under the oaks with short gliding bursts of flight, like a paper airplane, wings held to his sides. He searched the grass thoroughly and called up to his mate, but the female was wary and soon climbed round to the other side of the tree, out of our line of view.

'It's almost as if she knew she was being watched,' I whispered to Alan.

'I know how she feels,' he said, feelingly, with a sideways glance.

'What? Do you feel we are watching you?'

Alan gave a wry, lop-sided smile, 'Not really. It's just I've been under surveillance for a long time, you know.'

Then, fortunately for his sharp eyes, he caught sight of something in the undergrowth and picked up the little fabric parcel that had fallen out of my back pocket as we squatted in the bushes. 'Is this yours?' He handed it towards me, but I shook my head, 'No, it's actually yours. Kumar … sent it for you. Your tutor knew you were here, you see, and he sent it on,' I said, lying fluently.

With patient fingers, he undid the knot in the ribbon that held the fabric in place. Out of its wrappings fell a small, flat object secured in tissue paper. Alan shook it out and drew in his breath as he gazed down in the light of the sunset. It was a square miniature, only four inches tall and wide, but it was the subject that made us both gasp: a pair of beautiful green woodpeckers, one foreground, the other in the background, painted by Kumar in a Rajasthani style.

The coincidence was extraordinary. I could not have found a more opportune time to give it to him than now, and was congratulating myself on my cleverness, utterly forgetting that the gift came with a verbal message that I couldn't really deliver without spilling the beans.

I watched Alan's expression slide from amazement into suspicion, 'Did you know what was inside?'

'No, not at all. I'd just forgot it was still in my pocket. I was going to give you it you earlier, but I…'

He assessed me again, clearly spotting the lie: 'You've been there… to the Minster?' he accused.

To my shame, I had to tell him. The hunch of his shoulder towards me showed I had probably lost his trust for all time. But I ploughed on and gave him Kumar's message: 'He said, "I'm not sorry. I just hope you will remember our friendship."'

'Was that all?' his voice had a curious wobble in it.

'Yes. He and Nancy are good friends to you. They care for you very much, you know.'

He looked down at the miniature. For one awful moment, I thought he was going to pitch the beautiful thing over the Beacon, but instead he clutched it close and followed me down the slope without another word, behaving as if I didn't exist.

Once I'd sluiced my face under the tap, I knocked on Ash's door with a heavy heart and made my confession, keeping my face turned away with shame. His silence was so long that I looked up, expecting to receive my quittance and a month's pay in lieu of notice, but he was beaming all over his face, trying to repress the laughter that was bursting out of him, 'Oh, Jack, you've done the very best job! I shall name you my agent provocateur, first class!'

'But I thought you were trying to handle this case discreetly? I've absolutely blown it now!'

'Not at all. We've shown our hand and that will have the effect of inviting him in and enabling him to get really angry at us.'

'That's a *good* thing?' I asked in tones of such bewilderment that Ash collapsed into unrestrained laughter again. When he had composed himself, 'Wait and see!'

True to his word, Ash went straight for the jugular in the next session. He made me sit in, though I kept a low profile. Ignoring the surliness which had returned fourfold since last night, he asked Alan, 'Are you curious at all about *why* you have been over-shadowed by this painter?'

Alan looked innocently baffled by the question, 'You mean there might be some rhyme or reason to it?... I thought it was just my bad luck.'

A torrent of emotions played upon him; to hide his confusion, he rose and restlessly paced the room. Then he turned on Ash demanding, 'You've had other people who were ... over-shadowed?'

Ash nodded, 'Indeed I have seen many cases where people have worked out their over-shadowings under a kind of compulsion, but they were largely unconscious and bewildered by it... I think yours was not quite like that?'

For answer, Alan bit the side of his fist.

Ash allowed the silence to gather, then asked, 'What did you call him?'

'He calls himself Giovanni: *I* didn't name him.'

The change of tense immediately made the hair on my neck stand on end.

'He is a person in his own right,' Alan explained, reasonably.

'Is he here, now?' asked Ash, making me suddenly swallow, for this was an invitation you never extended to delusional clients.

As a rookie doctor, I had once foolishly asked a similar question of a perfectly pleasant middle-aged man with some personality problems, who had promptly screwed up his face, and with ghastly distorted tones bawled back at me, 'Yes, I am the Devil incarnate!' That session had not ended well, I fear.

Into the silence, Ash asked Alan again, 'Is he here, now?'

'Si,' said Alan, only it wasn't Alan who answered him nor, I think, was it any sub-personality. The man standing before us now had a lift in his chin, a direct gaze, and a compact body: the loose-limbed Yorkshireman was utterly transformed. Resolution sat upon his mouth, which was no longer surly or turned down, and there was a light in his eye that would not be gainsayed.

Ash stood, nodding with respect, 'I am addressing the painter Giovanni... forgive me, signor, but I do not know your place of birth?'

'Giovanni di Pontassievi - a volte, Giovanni da Piamonte.'

Ash never turned his gaze from the painter, but with his left hand gestured urgently to me to take notes.

In attempting to record the dialogue that ensued, I still havered as to whether such a polished performance could be just that, or whether we really had a sub-personality who had just stepped in. I still felt my view was justified. A rapier-quick interchange between artist and soul-doctor was soon beyond my powers to record, as it was conducted in Italian, and since my Italian is confined solely to football, music, and gastronomy, I gave up trying to record it, fascinated by the interplay between Giovanni and Ash, and by the rapid change from sullen young man to confident, even somewhat petulant, Renaissance artist. It was impossible to understand how Alan could do this: he was no actor and I am pretty certain did not know this much Italian, for the interchange was fluent.

Without ceasing the conversation between them, Ash cunningly opened the inner door and invited our guest to accompany him into the Sanctuary, the enclosed heart of the original medieval house around which the Beacon was built.

We stepped into what had once been the chapel. Ash was evidently showing Giovanni the walls of the chapel, the partially erased medieval wall paintings that Tudor reformers under Edward VI had once white-washed over. Like a patron informing an artist of his needs, Ash was instructing the Renaissance artist with a commission, I understood that much. Giovanni examined the wall paintings with distain, stretching out one finger to feel the quality of the mural and the surface of the wall. He evidently asked some short questions about how it had happened to become so damaged, gesturing at the faded St Margaret on the right hand of what had once been the altar. Then Ash led him back through his room and downstairs, with me following on. I guessed where he might be leading. On their approach to the art-room, Gillespie spied that something was up and swiftly went on before, opening the door for us. Our guest did not even acknowledge this courtesy but, taking it as his right, stepped into the studio where the easel was set up with a ready-gessoed wooden panel. I then realised that Ash must have anticipated the outcome of this session, for he had also left a palette charged with colours, and some chalk pastels.

Gillespie and I watched open-eyed as the artist considered the panel for a second before selecting a pastel stick and making a fine preliminary outline sketch, working fluently. He turned to Ash for confirmation, who responded. 'Si, maestro!'

The artist continued to work without reference to us whatever. Gillespie sank down into a chair looking up at me and back to the easel in wonderment.

Tacitly, we kept silence, so as not to break the moment. During the next hour, we were treated to the most extraordinary masterclass.

The formation of the subject on the board was a St Margaret of Antioch complete with dragon. Even as a sketch, it was a more fully rendered image than the partial medieval remains in the sanctuary upstairs. Swiftly the artist filled in his sketch with pastels. St Margaret was now dressed as a Renaissance woman, with a red under-gown and a white pleated over-gown, her long golden hair shook loose in waves down her back, with a neat gilt crown perched upon her head. From her hands hung a delicate chain which wound about the dragon's neck. The dragon himself was particularly ferocious while still managing to resemble an exotically elegant form of Italian hound. The artist turned to see if his work was approved. Ash nodded.

Then everything went suddenly into slow motion. Giovanni was not there anymore, only a very bemused Alan who was staring down at the pastel stick and up to the panel with a disgust bordering on horror. As realization sank in, he folded up like a piece of crushed cardboard, falling forwards into Ash's arms.

Gillespie and I helped carry the unconscious Alan into the living room and laid him on the settee. His pulse soon settled down and we decided to let him sleep where he was. But Wendy was despatched to bring us some lemon drizzle cake and a large pot of tea, while we opened the windows to enjoy the breeze that had begun to tease the dried-up trees. Gillespie took Wendy off to the studio so she could see the newly painted image. She returned with saucer eyes to peer at our genius, lying crumpled on the cushions, 'Poor lad! What a wonder he is! – will he be alright now?'

'We're not sure yet.' While Ash looked after him, I ran upstairs to look in Alan's room, where I had not yet been. I wanted to check something. Sure enough, under the window, in pride of place on the desk, the green woodpecker miniature had been propped up. Alan had also set a small posy of flowers in the empty inkwell beside it. It confirmed to me that his heart was in the right place and that friendship was one of the most important medicines for him.

About seven, Alan began to stir. Ash threw away the medical abstract he'd been reading and sat alert.

Our guest passed a hand of his eyes as he awoke then, realizing that he was in the wrong place, sat up and saw he was in the living room. His body relaxed and it was clear that we had Alan back among us again, without his Italian overlay. On seeing his colour-streaked fingers, he began to swear, 'Jesus Christ, it's happened again!'

'Not quite the same, I think,' Ash countered.

Alan frowned, struggling to remember the sequence of events, 'I was in your room, the one with the convex mirror like the Arnolfini Marriage... how did I get here?' Holding up his chalk-streaked hands, 'And what has *he* perpetrated now?'

'Did you want to see?' Ash offered.

Alan stomped off to the studio, baulking at the door at sight of the panel on the easel, hands covering his mouth and nose in dismayed denial. He turned violently on Ash, 'I thought I was supposed to be here to get well, not to be sent back to stew in my own juice?' His balled fist was ready to punch and I tried to get between them, but Ash parried the blow before I could do so.

Mildly and with great sympathy he said, 'Being an ambassador or mediator is never an easy task.'

That took the wind out of Alan's sails, 'What do you mean?'

'The artist who's been moving through you is a great artist, but the burden of his ambition has fallen upon you: you have been his honest mediator. Our task now is to treat him, and restore your own juice to yourself, rather than have you mix yours with his. - I'm not sorry that we had to invite him to come forward, so that we could begin sorting this out.'

Alan wailed, 'I've been trying to do that for so long!'

'I know, and you had very good instincts about the method. The pressure must have been very difficult.'

In that moment, Alan knew he had been witnessed. His limbs began to tremble, as if a great weight had been lifted from him, 'What do we do now?'

Ash regarded him, solemnly, 'Well, Jack is going to help you back to the living room...' and with a sparkle, 'And we are all going to have a large pot of tea. - Tomorrow will be time enough.'

I half carried Alan back to the settee, as his legs were too wobbly to be trusted. Ash returned with a brimming teapot and the largest cup we possessed. Alan drank his tea virtually milk-less but with two full spoons of sugar, downing cup after cup until the pot was spent and I had to go and top it up. After this emergency hydration, he fell upon the remains of the lemon drizzle cake, poking it urgently into his mouth. 'By God, I needed that!' He sounded very like his father. He later went on to put away a double helping of Wendy's fish pie and half a pineapple. Tacitly, we didn't discuss things anymore but let him eat and then sleep.

After we had got Alan settled, Ash ransacked his *Dictionary of Art and Artists* to no avail, 'There is no entry for him; our painter is just not there. Giovanni will need to discovered, I think.'

So, I phoned Werner Lenz for clarification, on the off-chance that he would be about, as his card included his home number. He was fortunately in that evening.

I explained, 'We are on the verge of a breakthrough with Alan, Professor Lenz, but we need some help. Can you tell us anything about the Italian artist...' I squinted at my notes 'Giovanni di Pontassievi or possibly Giovanni da Piamonte?'

The name rang no bells to him but he promised to check for us.

After a few minutes, he phoned back, 'Giovanni da Piamonte was a pupil from the workshop of Piero della Francesca who designed a set of murals on the *History of the True Cross* for the Bacci Chapel, in the Basilica of San Francesco in Arezzo, but he delegated some of the actual painting to his assistants. It's thought that Giovanni da Piamonte worked on the *Torture of the Jew, the Meeting of Solomon and the Queen of Sheba,* and the *Burial of the Holy Wood.*'

I scribbled down notes as best I could, 'Did Giovanni do anything of his own?'

'By all accounts, very little of his own work seems to have survived, only the *Virgin and Child with Saints* of 1456 at Castello, a couple of prophets, a fragmentary San Bernardino, and a mural of the risen Christ with Angels. No-one knows when he was born nor when he died... Is this helpful? How is poor Alan?'

I assured him, 'That's very helpful. We are beginning to get somewhere at last, though Alan is still rather upheaved by it all.' Then I had a brainwave, 'Professor, one more thing. Could you please check out the art style of Giovanni and have another look at Alan's murals? Just let me know please if there is any stylistic correlation.'

Going back up to Ash's study, I enquired, 'So are you going to interpret for me? My Italian note-taking was a bit of a non-starter.'

'Well, Giovanni was keen to do some work, so I gave him a commission, which he has started upon, as you see.'

'Nice ruse! Employing possessed clients to get your chapel redecorated!'

He chuckled, 'Well, I don't expect it to go much further than today, but it's evident that Giovanni is the one we have to treat; then we can help Alan.'

'But won't that affect Alan's art – maybe his whole life?'

'Possibly, but you saw that he cannot sustain the overlay of Giovanni any longer without loss of integrity and possibly his health. That artist is a frustrated man with a fine opinion of himself: Alan's native skill, his youth and his unformed character were the perfect stamping ground for Giovanni to continue his own career, but it's been at the expense of Alan's life.'

'So, you are going to do the same thing that his friends were too alarmed to witness?'

'I don't know what we'll do yet. I want Alan to help us get to the bottom of what Giovanni's intentions are, then I'll know how to act.'

On my way to bed late that evening, I heard the phone go downstairs. It was Gillespie who answered. Ascerbically he called up to me, 'Tell yer man to ring at civilized hours.'

It was an apologetic Werner Lentz, 'Sorry to call so late, but I didn't know how vital it might be. I had to do a lot of research, and speak to colleagues in Italy to get pictures faxed to me, but you are right – the styles of Giovanni da Piamonte and Alan's murals are almost identical. How did you know?' His voice was full of wonder and surmise.

'I really can't say right now, but please keep this under your hat until we see how the treatment works out. It's most important that Alan is not embroiled in another international art exposé.'

'Of course. I will fax some images through tomorrow for you to see.'

True to his word, we came into the office the next morning to find a long trail of paper hanging from the fax machine. Werner sent through the images of the Bacci Chapel and the Virgin and Child. He must have been up all night working on this for us. On the last page, he also sent a personal message, 'I know you didn't ask for this, but it struck me that you might not have seen this article.'

It was the five-page exposé of Alan in *Fine Art Quarterly,* written by Dolon Michelson of the Courtauld Institute, entitled *Lure of the Old Masters: A Charming Spook?* The side-bar photo of Alan was too revealing altogether: like a shy horse, frightened by the camera. The article carried some good photos of Alan's paintings that no longer existed. Even though they were in black and white on the grainy fax paper, my heart mourned for them. The tone of Michelson's writing was full of the most massive condescension and off-key mockery, as if Alan and his work were a circus side-show. It made for a good article for the writer, of course, who came over as so clever to have discovered this old/new painter, but I saw immediately how Alan's retiringly modest Yorkshire soul would have been mortified. Notoriety in the art world tends to run from the oddball maverick to the downright deviant, but Alan's reputation, based on the strength of this piece, looked to be set permanently on 'fey.' The images of his lost paintings struck me again like lost old masters recently discovered and conserved, and my fellow feeling for him deepened.

Alan still seemed to be in a very deep sleep, Wendy reported. After showing Werner's findings to Ash, whose eyes widened with interest, I finally knocked at Alan's door at 11am and brought in a tray of breakfast. He tucked into Wendy's pile of crêpes, pouring on maple syrup with a will, while I finished my coffee.

'I don't remember ever being this hungry,' he said, finally pushing away the tray. With an unaccustomed levity, he looked enquiring, 'What's on today's agenda? The Sistine Ceiling? Goya's Black Paintings? The Banqueting Hall at Whitehall?'

'You sound ready for anything! No, I don't think so. I expect Ash would be glad to talk with you, when you feel up to it.'

It seemed to me that the residue of his medication was beginning to finally leave his system, which I took as a good sign. His returning appetite also seemed to have been accompanied with a less cynical zest for life.

Ash was in his room. He had clearly digested the import of the faxes and was peering from the original paintings to the sadly-destroyed images in the article with keen interest. He looked up, 'All well?'

'Yes, he's got a roaring appetite and the will to live is beginning to shine through.'

He nodded, 'Good. – Do you have Werner's number to hand. I just wanted to thank him and to ask a question.'

Werner's card was still in my pocket. As he dialled, Ash indicated the spread-out faxes, 'Take a look again – can you see it?'

I scanned at the images without a clue, until half way through his conversation with Werner, Ash asked one of his great unlocking questions, 'So, Professor, how would you equate the work of Giovanni and the work of Alan? Would you say there had been a notable progression?'

He had turned on the speaker, so I could hear both sides of the conversation. Werner paused, then said, 'They are definitely by the same hand, but Giovanni's work is …well, less experienced than Alan's painting. It is also as if…'

'… they are continuations of each other?'

Werner's silence was telling, 'But that's impossible, of course… How could a dead 15th century painter progress in style? It doesn't make sense.'

'Quite a lot of our work doesn't make sense to the world we live in, Professor, but it soon falls into place when you consider what lies beneath it,' said Ash. 'As the underpainting of an image prefigures what is laid over it, so Giovanni's painting prefigures Alan's, I think. Thank you for confirming that and for helping us out.'

I looked at the poorly reproduced images again, and saw what Ash and now Werner were seeing, 'What does it all mean?'

'It means that Alan has been right all along: he has been made use of, and resents it.'

Ash's dictum that the body's owner was often the keenest diagnostician, had never been seen so clearly demonstrated.

'But how....?'

Ash stacked the faxes neatly in his out-box, 'Let's see if he is willing to take the next step.'

Our next session with Alan that afternoon proceeded much more satisfactorily, if a little dramatically. Ash's ability to go to straight to the point was often more than my poor nerves could take, yet it seemed Alan was up for it. Outside, the sky was becoming overcast, though the heat was no less oppressive. Hartsworth Beacon seem to grow ominously in the shadow of the sky.

Ash asked him, 'Do you understand or have any notion why Giovanni overshadowed you?'

Alan shook his head, 'I really don't know. Only that I am alive and he is....'

The word hung in the air, unspoken.

Ash nodded, 'So, are you game to find out?'

'What will that mean...?' Then he caught Ash's drift, 'Oh! You mean... allow Giovanni to come forward again?'

'Yes. – I know it's a big thing to ask you, and I understand that you might not want that.'

Alan's body language showed how much the thought of this upheaved him, but finally the light of resolution shone in his eyes, 'Well, if it will mean he finally walks out for good and I can shut the door on him, then yes, I will do it... What do I do?'

'Just talk to me, as you did last time. Myself and Jack will be with you the whole time and we will ensure that you are supported throughout.'

'Will it mean draughting something again?'

Ash said, 'Possibly. We don't know until we see how.'

Alan straightened himself, then gathering his limbs together, as if to jump. Watching the process was rather as I imagined time-travel should be, only without any Wellsian machine: a mere stepping from one shore onto another.

Ash started speaking quietly and persistently in Italian to Alan, evidently talking to Giovanni. Soon enough, I saw the change happen: loose-limbed Alan was gathered up into the taut body of Giovanni, with his direct glance. I have seen actors take on a character between one breath and another, but there, it is with craft, and I would swear this was not. Giovanni flowed into Alan, as water runs into a jug. Alan was almost drowned in that overshadowing: something I had not properly noticed till now.

After the first courteous exchanges, and some general chat whose import I couldn't follow, Ash had evidently asked a question that Giovanni baulked at answering. His chin rose and he refused to answer. Ash spoke again, made some apologetic gesture and invited him to come downstairs to the studio. Giovanni appeared to be mollified, rose and stood on the threshold uncertainly, finally coming downstairs, with me following. It was as well that I was so close.

Ash had already gone ahead to the studio door, opening it on the easel with its half-sketched St Margaret, but Giovanni was undergoing some kind of emotional turmoil and stopped dead in the hall. Because of the humidity in the house, Wendy had propped the front door open with a doorstop, hoping to get some flow of air circulating inside.

Following closely behind him, I saw how Giovanni had caught the scent of danger. Instinctively, I picked up on it: for him, the studio was like a kind of trap into which we were herding him. Pride and fear together fought a battle in that moment, and fear won, propelling him straight out of the open front door.

I called urgently for Ash, and dashed out just in time to catch the mother and father of a downpour. Torrential stair-rods of rain made it impossible to see more than a few yards ahead. Of Giovanni/Alan, there was no sign whatever. I told myself that there were only two ways he could go – down the lane, or up onto the Beacon. Ash joined me and I shouted over the rolling thunder that deafened the Downs, for him to go one way, and I another. We both knew that with Giovanni on board, Alan would be vulnerable.

Ash took the lane, and so I ran towards the Hartsworth Beacon path, slipping around in the mud caused by the great pelting torrents that splashed up the earth. Soon I was half clambering, half-climbing, cursing that I had I not maintained more than a passing acquaintance with the Italian language all these years – for how would I be able to talk to Giovanni? It took twice the usual time to climb the first steep ascent. If there had been any footprints – Alan was wearing just sandals – the downpour had eliminated them. The Beacon was vast and I would have to decide which way to go soon.

Calling upon what divine powers and animal instincts I could muster, I tried to intuit the way. All that came was an image of the oak-grove where Alan and I had gone to see the woodpeckers, and so I headed over the rise, climbing towards the left. Today there was no view to behold, only huge dark clouds so low that they seemed tacked to the horizon; the sky looked bruised and broken.

I made a quick scan of the area, finding nothing, then, a flash of something. Thank goodness Alan had put on a red t-shirt that morning! Standing under one of the great oak trees he was there, his hair darkly plastered with rain, his fingers gouging and raking the bark, like a man on a precipice, seeking for handholds, his head turned at an alarming angle.

I approached cautiously. As Ash had called Giovanni by speaking Italian, so I called for Alan to show himself. I don't think he could possibly have heard me over the combination of rain and the thunder that seemed just about overhead. Closer, I saw the terror in Giovanni's eyes. It was not Alan that I had to deal with, I realised with sinking heart.

'Calma, signore, calma! Tranquilo…. Sono Gianni. – Alan, it's me. It's ok. Just a storm overhead.'

I don't think he either saw or understood me. His eyes were opened upon some other scenario, and it was not now or here. Like a sleepwalker in the grip of a nightmare, he held to the tree. His fingers were alarmingly lacerated by his continual grasping at the bark, his nails shredded. And then I understood from his fearful looking down, that he believed himself to be about to fall.

'Stand back, Jack! Let him fall!' Ash joined me, scrambling up on the rise, pulling me back as I was about to go catch him.

It seemed the cruellest thing to me, but I obeyed him. We watched as Giovanni finally broke his grip from the tree and fell with a terrible shriek that went on and on, even though the actual fall was just a few feet into the leaf-mould and wet grass just in front of him. His body pitched and twisted, just a body would in immense agony after a fall from a great height. Then it lay horribly still.

Only then did Ash step forward, turn over the prone body, and close its eyes with gentle fingers, saying, 'Giovanni da Piemonte, proficiscere, anima christiana, de hoc mundo, in nomine Dei Patris qui te creavit…'

It was the 'Go forth, O Christian soul, out of this world,' the prayer made by the priest over the dying, but I was struck with horror, for there really seemed no signs of life in Alan. I stepped forward as if to check his pulse, but fell back at one sharp glance from Ash.

He continued to compose the limbs, as if laying out the body, praying in Latin, the prayer of the commendation, 'Commendo te omnipotenti Deo, carissime frater, Giovanni, et ei, cuius es creature, committo; ut, cum humanitatis debitum morte interveniente persoveris, ad auctorem tuum qui te de limo terrae formaverat revertaris.'

I had enough Latin from my classics classes to follow this, 'I commend thee, dear brother to Almighty God and commit thee to His mercy, whose creature thou art; that, having paid the debt of humanity by surrendering your soul, thou mayest return to thy Maker, who made thee out of earth.'

I responded, 'Requiem æternam dona ei Domine; et lux perpetua luceat ei. Requiescat in pace.' 'Eternal rest grant to him, Lord, and let light perpetual shine upon him. Rest in peace.'

And we both said, 'Amen.'

The whole sky seemed to be coming down on us now, as the rain abruptly ceased. Forked lightning was making vivid streaks across the horizon and an ominous rolling set the Downs reverberating. The sky turned a nasty shade of yellow bruise.

'Lift him up, Jack. We need to get him out of this, quick.'

Together, we lifted either arm over our shoulders and attempted to carry him, but dead weight is hard enough to manoeuvre in ordinary circumstances and the conditions up here on the Beacon were atrocious. We had just reached the edge of the rise, where we realized we would have to carry his body in a different way, when a streak of lightning struck one of the oak trees behind us, illuminating the whole tree with white electricity, before one of its chief branches fell – it was just where Alan had been lying. We had had a lucky escape. Electricity shivered the air of the grove.

Suddenly, in our arms, Alan began to come round, to my great relief.

'Why am I so wet?' his muffled voice complained from the confines of my shoulder.

We set him upright, and Ash gave him a quick examination, 'It is just a storm. We are all very wet. Let's get down into shelter now.'

The storm moved off even as made our slippery way down the slope to the house, and a brightness appeared from the south, as the dark horizon-clinging clouds made their way northwards.

Gillespie had seen us descending and was there to lift Alan and bring him into the living room, while Wendy distributed towels to us all, tutting and fussing in the most mother-hen fashion, but we gratefully received the help, even as she scolded us, 'Going up there in this storm, you could have been killed. What were you thinking of?' she up-braided Ash forthrightly, before turning to me, 'I thought *you* had better sense.' Ash grinned from ear to ear, accepting the huge mug of tea that Gillespie handed him.

Wendy and Gillespie efficiently set about cleaning up Alan's hands which were fit for nothing. Wendy used her tweezers to ease out splinters from under his nails and Gillespie cleaned the wounds before they were bandaged up.

After a few swigs of tea, held to his mouth by Wendy, Alan asked, 'So, is that it?'

Ash nodded, 'Yes, Giovanni really is dead and gone.'

Alan was silent, examining his bandaged hands, 'It hurts, but it's a good hurt.' He wriggled his shoulders, as if feeling the fit of his own skin, 'I can't feel him anymore.'

'Good?' I asked, cautiously.

'Good that he's finally gone,' said Alan, in his most Yorkshire accent.

I turned to Ash, 'What did you ask Giovanni, up there in your room?'

'I asked why he felt it necessary to take over the life of a young man who wanted nothing more than his own life back.'

'And what did he say?'

'Nothing. The question drove him back to the moment when he knew his life was coming to its end. He died by falling from a scaffold in a church in Arezzo, as far as I can work out. It was just between the moment of fall and the moment of landing that part of his soul vacated before his body dropped.'

Alan frowned, 'You mean that part of his soul survived the fall?'

'Yes. By whatever means, it came to overshadow you.'

I interrupted, 'But what about the great gap in time between then and now?'

'There is no time in the otherworld,' said Ash, calmly. 'That soul part, sent out of Giovanni's body at a point of trauma, just abided until the time was ripe…'

'…and stepped in to continue his painting and even improve his own style, at the cost of Alan's own?'

'Yes.'

Just as calmly as Ash, Alan said, 'I will never paint like him again, then,' as if that settled everything.

Which is how at the Beacon we come to have the only 20th century sketch of an obscure old 15th century Italian Master hanging in Ash's study. While many have exclaimed over its beauty, and a few have longed to know its provenance, we have decided, following Alan's own wish, that this extraordinary study of St Margaret, matron of holy intervention in times of childbirth, shall remain mysterious: proof to us of a different kind of miraculous deliverance.

Alan's story is still unfolding. After a visit from Kumar and Nancy, and an even more incredulous one from Werner Lentz – who has seen the St Margaret for himself and recognizes an unprovenanced Giovanni da Piamonte when he sees one – Alan went home to recover and do some very ordinary things for a while. The new direction of his art, as a wild life illustrator, has taken him all over the world, and his mural for the new Wildlife and Nature Conservation building in Stockholm is now famous worldwide. Free to develop his style in his own way, Alan's art has come home to itself. And if his critics mourn the loss of Giovanni's hand, Alan himself does not.

Case 5: THE GHOST OF SHOTLEY MOOR

For you perhaps, if as I hope and wish you will live long after me, there will follow a better age. When the darkness is dispelled, our descendants will be able to walk back, into the pure radiance of the past.
Petrarch – *Africa IX*

Shotley Moor is one of those barren heaths that typify the north of the county. It has necessarily become the stamping ground of the army, being neither flat enough for habitation, nor drained enough for agriculture. I daresay many a young squaddy has had cause to loathe its isolation. Its nearest small town, Sollingshot, boasts three pubs, a pool hall, a tattoo parlour, and a thriving brothel, but no cinema.

You might think that, with so many young men thrown into each other's company, there would be more of a problem of unruly behaviour off the parade ground than the need for psychic investigation, but you would be wrong. It appears that two recruits had committed suicide in the last few months and the army, sensitive to accusations of bullying and military intimidation in its barracks, due to the inflammatory media attention given to camps elsewhere, moved swiftly and discreetly to allay any further publicity. Alongside their own internal investigators, they approached Ash to provide an independent psychological assessment of their personnel's morale, but it seemed to me that they really wanted him to work his special magic, and no questions asked, with that official mindset that refuses the possibility of unseen things, but wants them cleared speedily away, all the same.

The road to Sollingshot is a kind of drive that even the Sunday motorist speeds through with as little sightseeing as possible, for there is frankly nothing much on which to rest the eye in the north of the county. On the day we drove north, the drab summer-dry heath was unrelieved except by the bright swatches of gorse that merely accentuated the sulky, unpromising heath-scape. To add to the lowering aspect, there yet remained huge tracts of post-war forestry pine fringing the heath, planted in an attempt to grow telegraph poles. The steep upland rim of the heathland was still stained with their darkening gloom, re-enforcing a sense of restrictive enclosure. Whatever the government was thinking of in those hungry post-war years, it was certainly not with an eye to the improvement of the landscape.

'The Forestry Commission has a lot to answer for, to my mind,' I remarked, eyeing the gloomy swathe of blackish-green foliage cladding the uplands.

Ash, who had been humming quietly to himself, broke into a bluesy chorus of:

> 'In the pines, in the pines,
> Where the sun never shines.
> And we shiver the whole night through.'

This eerie little song didn't make me feel any better about our errand across this blasted heath – to visit the Ghost of Shotley Moor.

It had begun, first with a phone-call, then followed by a visit from Captain William Toibin, chaplain to the 2nd Battalion of the Prince's Hampshire Regiment, stationed at Shotley Moor. Capt. Toibin was a rubicund Irishman, sweating slightly in his uniform, 'I've interviewed the companions of the two soldiers who committed suicide, and what they have told me in confidence is something that goes beyond the findings of an official enquiry. I have the approval of Lieutenant Colonel Franklin to consult you unofficially, to avoid publicity, and to get to the bottom of things. If you are willing to investigate the matter, with discretion, you would be the guest of the regiment for as long as is necessary. The Lt. Colonel is keen to get this cleared up without fuss.'

'What exactly has been happening?' Ash asked.

'Apart from the recent suicides, there have been reports of "phenomena," I suppose you would call it, from several soldiers of company B.' He sounded embarrassed to even mention this.

'What kind of phenomena?'

'Well, were I back at home, they'd call it a *taibhse* – a ghost or spirit. Things have been moved about - furniture, shoes, anything not screwed down.'

'How and when does it manifest?'

'The men say it tends to show itself when there has been any unpleasantness in the camp – that could be someone being dressed down for some misdemeanour, or an unpopular general order, like being confined to barracks preparatory to some planned manoeuvres. Apart from the disruptive casting about of objects and furniture, I would say that it is not something that anyone *sees* so much, but it rather *heard*.'

I asked frivolously, 'A talking ghost?'

Toibin turned to me, nodding vigorously, 'Indeed! But the words that it utters are usually the most disconcerting thing.'

'Have you heard it yourself?' Ash asked.

'I have not, so, but there are plenty of the lads that have. They thoroughly demoralize the lads, I tell you. I've had to take prayers in the barrack block B every night for the last month, since no-one will lay down their heads without a blessing - and these lads are usually the spiritually uncommitted, if you take my meaning: obedient to church parade but strangers to prayer or a Bible. If the Ghost of Shotley Moor is walking, then no-one will sleep without some reassurance.'

'So, is the ghost place-specific? Does it only appear in that block?'

'No, but it seems the activity has been widespread across the camp over the years, from well before my time, but now it is targeting B company's block.'

'Is there any good reason for that?' Ash had asked.

'Well, the two suicides were in that block.'

'Are the men who've witnessed this phenomenon willing to assist in our enquiries?'

Toibin smiled broadly, 'Sure, you would be doing them the best service in the world if you rid us of this unholy thing: of course, they are willing! But you will have to speak with each of them separately, in case the fear gets contagious. That was the one thing that Lt. Col. Franklin was insistent on.'

I looked at Ash questioningly. 'Then we will come and see what we can discover,' he said.

Which is how we came to be driving across the blasted heath towards the army camp. It suddenly struck me, as I thought back to that interview, 'Ash, Capt. Toiben didn't report what the ghost was supposed to have said, did he?'

'He did not. But I daresay that we will find out soon enough.'

I now fully understood why Shakespeare had set his Scottish Play on such a heath as Shotley Moor. As in Ash's bluesy number, it was a place of loneliness and potential hallucination. Even as I entertained this thought, so did little curls of mist begin to play over the tops of the bracken. Within ten minutes, it had begun to thicken. Any stray witches could easily have made their convenient appearance from out of the mist-strewn moor.

Ash had been driving fast and smoothly. But now he curbed his speed and snapped the fog-lights on, not a moment too soon, as a succession of slow-moving army trucks lumbered out of the mist onto the road from a spinney of larch on the bend ahead of us, causing us to first brake, and then follow them at a limping 18 miles per hour.

They say that it is a sign of old age when you think policemen look too young to you, but it was evident that several of the young men in their military camouflage perched on their transports *were* actually teenagers, in this case.

'They look impossibly young to be deployed in the theatre of war,' I said. 'Why would any of them commit suicide?'

'Post-traumatic stress disorder, especially if they have been on successive tours of duty, or any of the stresses experienced by young men away from their homes. Suicides call other suicides,' Ash said, gravely. 'When people live together within an institution like a barracks, a university or a prison, a group soul builds up. When one commits suicide, those near to them are like people standing right on the edge of the platform when the high-speed train goes through: it is liable to drag them onto the rails and into the wake of the one who has departed.'

I had never thought of things this way, but it made a kind of sense to me, 'So, you mean, suicide is like a door left open, through which unsuspecting others might inadvertently fall through?'

He nodded, 'We may be plugging up the hole, or looking backwards to the source of the disturbance, we don't yet know. One thing is certain, we will not be so free to operate as at the Beacon.'

His prophecy was immediately fulfilled as we were finally halted at the checkpoint of the Shotley Moor camp, while the trucks ahead of us were ushered in. Our visit did not start well. We duly presented our credentials, only to be met with the stymying that only extreme officialdom can provide. One soldier from the guard post went to and fro many times between gate and office before we were granted access to the base.

We finally passed muster and were waved through, to be met by Capt. Toibin, who loomed anxiously out of the mist, peering into our car window, 'Sorry about all that nonsense! I'll guide you round to where you can park,' and he got into the backseat. He informed us that our lack of welcome was due to impending manoeuvres, which meant the camp was on lock-down, 'Civilians like yourselves get treated to the full security treatment, I'm afraid. Pull over here. Now, if you will just leave your things here for a bit, Lt. Colonel Franklin would like to greet you first.'

Capt. Toibin led us into the main building upstairs. From the balustrade hung the battalion colours, bearing the same device which appeared on the cap badge: the Prince of Wales feathers bounded by a mailed arm with an upraised sword, and the motto, *Acta non verba* - 'Deeds, not words.' Various military honours adorned the colours, with embroidered memorials of conflicts as historically far distant as Malplaquet and Sebastobal, and as recently as Suez and the Falklands.

We were admitted on a knock. Lt. Col. Franklin, the Battalion's Commander in Chief was a lean faced man of about 50, with the relaxed drawl of a public-school education, and an even, ice-blue stare. He was brisk and brief with us, 'Gentlemen, thank you for coming: I'm afraid you join us at a time of manoeuvres, prior to deployment, so I hope you have time for your investigations. Capt. Toibin assures me that you are men of discretion and that you will conduct your enquiries without alarm or disquiet to the men under my care. Please liaise with him should you require anything. I want it clearly understood that you will have to work around our schedules in this busy week. I hope that you will be able to bring these affairs to a satisfactory conclusion. Now please excuse me, as I have a full timetable.' He extended his hand.

He could have been instructing the vermin operative about exterminating an infestation of rats, I thought, he was so dismissive.

Ash shook the outstretched hand on both our behalves, 'You can be assured that we will do our work discreetly, but we will need access to the places and men affected in this affair, and possibly to relevant records of any past occurrences.'

Franklin's expression did not alter, but his eyelids flicked like a snake's. In a voice several degrees chillier than before, he pronounced, 'There are no such records.'

'Yet there are accounts of this disturbance over several generations,' Ash persisted.

'Nevertheless, this battalion holds no such records. You are here to assess the psychological state of the men under my charge, not to lead any séances. Gentlemen, you must excuse me.' And so, we were dismissed.

Capt. Toibin kept his face averted until we were downstairs, when he apologized, 'I'm afraid you did not get much change from the C. in C. He finds the whole incident a profound embarrassment. Metaphysical things are just not in his remit of understanding. Your best thanks will come from the men who are suffering from this'

'Clearly!' I breathed.

Capt. Toibin showed us to our room where a pair of beds demonstrated that we were expected to share. The appointments were as spartan as only an army camp could provide, but with the added benefit of a small en-suite cubical rammed into the corner of the room in which it was just possible for a single man to brush his teeth, but not much more. The slatted blind over the window hung crookedly.

'When you're ready, just join me out front,' he said.

We threw our bags down on the single narrow cots and looked at each other. Ash seemed remarkably sanguine after his dressing down.

I said, 'Well, if we get to the bottom of all this, it won't be with the help of the C. in C!'

'Umm, well it looks as if Franklin is using the upcoming manoeuvres to cover our presence here,' Ash observed, trying to right the blind without success, peering through the small window at the scurrying of men without. 'Optimum mayhem to cover maximum embarrassment.'

Outside, Ash asked Toibin, 'Can we see B block first?'

Both Ash and I understood that suicides in such institutions are usually the result of poor welfare and, in the case of the army, hazing and bullying. You cannot put a platoon of squaddies down in a benighted spot like Shotley Moor and not expect some indiscipline or over-discipline. It was my first question, what kind of bullying had there been?

Capt. Toibin told us as we tramped over the parade ground that the Shotley Moor Camp had once had a very poor reputation. Back in the 1950-60s, there had been instances of extreme hazing, as well as outright abuse, with recruits hung naked out of the window by their heels, sexual assault with broom handles, and the like. We were assured that all such initiation rituals were now utterly forbidden, and only the 'Crossing the Line' ceremony, done when troops crossed the Equator on secondment, now downgraded to non-obligatory, still remained on the books. Toibin was not aware of any infractions to this new regulation, 'But you never know! When young men are confined together, something bizarre comes over them, I know. My wife calls it, "One boy, one brain: two boys, half a brain syndrome."'

As to the abuse, he told us that, in times past on this very parade ground, one particular staff sergeant had imposed harsh punishments 'in order to toughen up' the recruits, who were frequently ordered to roll around in the mud and then reprimanded for being disorderly, made to run naked around the parade ground until exhaustion or hyperthermia set in, mocked in front of their fellows, or subjected to all kinds of abuse. Even local residents knew the kinds of things that went on. The staff sergeant in question was finally court-marshalled and dismissed, subject to a civilian justice. 'The abuses of past eras may once have been given the blind eye, but the army has had to clean up its act pretty fast today,' he assured us.

'But some of the old reputation still remains....?' I asked.

Capt. Toibin wriggled his shoulders uncomfortably, 'You could well be right. Here we are...' He opened the swing door of B block and led us to the dormitory where a row of beds ranged against either length of the wall interspersed with bedside tables and hanging space, with foot lockers under each bed. The odour of male sweat, feet, and Brasso assaulted our noses, but very little else. It was spotlessly clean and orderly, devoid of anything other than institutional presence. A portrait of the Her Majesty the Queen hung on the far wall.

While Toibin and myself remained near the door, Ash walked into the centre of the dormitory and stood silently, tuning into the atmosphere, before ranging about the space, stopping once or twice as if to look at something I couldn't see. Stretching out his hand over the corner bed, he swiftly withdrew it. Uttering a series of bell-like tones, still with outstretched hands, he seemed to be mapping a route from the corner bed to a part of the wall three beds down on the other side.

'Was there another building here before?' he asked.

'This block replaced a Nissen hut. You know – the prefabricated war-time sort of thing - to my best knowledge, but that was before my time. What are you finding?'

'Which beds were occupied by the men who committed suicide?'

'The corner bed, where you were, and this one to your right.'

'And does anyone occupy either bed now?'

Toibin's wiry eyebrows shot up, 'Lord bless you! Wild horses would not compel any of them to sleep there, I tell you.'

'Good! Now can you show us where we will be doing our interviewing? Is there any particular order of men we should see?'

'I took the liberty of asking Lt. Speed, the Assisting Officer who was brought in to help in both cases. He's waiting in my office.' Toibin told us Lieutenant Matthew Speed, who had been seconded from the Army Volunteer Reserve Force had investigated the two cases, and would be able to furnish us with the backgrounds of both men.

Toibin's office was off the hall leading to the chapel. Lt. Speed was a mature reservist with a firm handshake and down to earth manner. 'I am very glad to meet you both. Thank goodness we have some expert help on this at last! Military discipline and petty misdemeanours are one thing, but hauntings like this are beyond my skill.'

'Please tell us about the two men who committed suicide,' Ash asked, as I realized at no point prior to this had their names been mentioned.

'Corporal Christopher Dyson was the first to go. He had been on night guard duty for most of the preceding week. He shot himself with a semi-automatic pistol which he had illicitly retained. Pte. Antony Clarke followed him out by a fortnight. He was found hanging in stores.'

'Was there anything in either of their backgrounds to provide any reason for their suicides? Or any other factors?' I asked.

'Dyson was the older of the two at 27. He was back at the base after three tours of duty in Afghanistan and was on his way to promotion to sergeant. He was a steady kind of fellow, but his calm may have been covering an undiagnosed PTSD, we'll never know. Clarke and a few of the younger lads hero-worshipped him, so it was a great shock to them all when he was found shot. Nobby Clarke was just 19, from a troubled background. In addition, his elder brother had been in the Navy and was lost in an action fought against drug runners near Gibraltar.'

Ash digested this and asked, 'Were either of the men particularly close to any of the others in their platoon? And do you have concerns about them?'

Toibin and Speed exchanged troubled glances. Toibin said, 'We both feel that Pte. Andrews is particularly vulnerable. He is also young and was very close to Clarke. After his suicide, Andrews went and got a tattoo in Sollingshot: it reads, "Nobby and Chris, RIP my best mates." There was some talk of redeploying him to C Platoon, but he opted to stay with his mates, and I'm afraid that no-one has taken further action about it, hence our concern.'

It was the turn of Ash and I to exchange horrified glances: engraving what amounted to a memorial plaque on your own flesh seemed tantamount to declaring an intention to join dead comrades.

'And how much information do we have about the phenomena and its part in these suicides?' Ash asked.

Speed levelled his brown eyes, saying, 'When I investigated, there was a general reluctance at first to mention the ghost, but it turned out to be one of the most salient and repeated anecdotes that emerged: that the ghost had been busying itself and that it was responsible for their suicides. I'm sorry if that's short on detail, but they were most reluctant to share what had happened. In the official report, such things would automatically be left off, you see, so we were not obliged to dig deeper.'

Ash then asked to see any maps or plans of previous occupation, and to be given a list of the men we were to interview. Toibin pushed a piece of paper over the desk, 'Here's the list. I will try and secure these men, but probably not in this order. Use my office as your own while you are here: I may need to fetch a few things from it, but I'll be in and out in a jiffy.' Lt. Speed promised to look out any plans, after he had taken us to the Officer's Mess for lunch.

We began the interviews after lunch, managing to assemble fourteen of the possible twenty men on the list: the others, including Andrews, were all required on duty.

A succession of faces scrubby or with acne; lads tall and short, laid back or tensely wound up, the young men all told the same tale: for them the Ghost of Shotley Moor was a living presence, a nightmare that threatened their wellbeing and stole away the lives of their fellows. Because we were outsiders, and possibly primed by Toibin, they were inclined to be more confessional with us.

Of all the men we saw that day, a young man McDermot was the most spooked. He sat, clammed up in the face of Ash's gentle questioning, until I offered him a swig of non-regulation whiskey that I had secreted in my backpack, 'Would this help?'

Looking swiftly round to ensure no officer was about, he ducked his red head and took a long pull, handing it me back under the desk, 'Thanks, mate. Capt. Toiben says you'll get rid of the...' He jerked his head, '... you know, the ....' He was clearly unwilling to even mention its name.

'...the phenomenon?' suggested Ash.

McDermot nodded, grateful that we could use a neutral word for the terror, his glass-blue eyes fixed on Ash.

'We will do our very best to track it down and stop its activities,' Ash said, 'But we need your help to track and trap it. What's been your experience of it?'

Twisting his cap in his hand, he told us, 'It's always after dark that I get it. It starts to talk to me, close to my ear,' he scrubbed at his right ear, shaking his head as if it were full of pollution.

'What does the voice sound like? Is it the voice of anyone you know?'

'No, no-one I've ever known but, like, it knows me and what's in my head. It knows what I know, that's the bugger of it... It speaks low, kind of whispering, but like it's sneering as well.'

'What does it say?'

McDermot looked towards the office window where a truck was being loaded, 'It suggests things to me. "Why don't you bloody..." only it doesn't say bloody, you know... it uses the C and F words a lot.' He shook himself, 'It tells me to do filthy things, you know, with the other men. Pervy things. It shows things to me in my head: my mates lying dead, the bodies of animals and civilians blasted to bits. Horrible things. They go round and round like a spin dryer in my mind.'

Ash spoke with him a little more and then sent him away, 'Poor chap! Psychic as only a red-head could be.'

I was inclined to think that the subconscious fears of McDermot and the others were likely to be nearer the surface that usual, but I reserved my opinion until I'd heard a few more reports. It soon became clear that the men feared the ghost more than any deployment.

Young Private Protheroe said, 'We can't wait to be sent away, to be honest. We'd rather face action in Afghanistan than lie in the dark waiting for that old bastard to pay us a visit.'

I sat carefully taking notes and making five-bar gates on my pad of any repeated features in the reports. By the end of the day, I had a list of occurrences and their frequencies:

> Objects thrown or moved after dark x 7
> Objects thrown or moved in the day x 2
> Vocal threats x 5
> Vile smells x 4
> Bedclothes lifted or thrown off x 6
> Areas of extreme cold in B Block x 10
> Broken sleep x 14
> Nightmares x 12

Ash concluded at the end of the day, 'Did you note which men had been threatened or who heard the voice?'

I read back the list, ' Savile, Jones, McDermot, Paston and Bryant.'

'Those are the ones we will have to monitor more closely. Did you notice what a horror they each had at hearing the ghost? And the dismay among those whose mates had heard it?'

Davenport had been the most fluent talker. He was clearly the fixer of B Block. He told us, 'It's like Russian roulette: it leaves some alone, while others it persecutes. I don't get it myself, but the boys all feel that if they hear the ghost's voice, they are kind of marked out for demolition, like trees with a white cross on them.'

After we finished the interviews, Lt. Speed brought us the plans of the earlier camp, which we both poured over, but without finding much. The camp had certainly been remodeled from its post-war shape, with some buildings reoriented, but the earlier Nissen hut had stood where B Block now was.

'I will have to go into Sollishot for any further information, and probably into Andover to the local museum to see if there are any archaeological or historical reports on the camp,' Ash said, sounding tired.

It had been a grueling day, trying to get blood from a stone in most instances, and coaxing reluctant admissions from many the others. Once most of the men had realized we were not the usual kind of trick-cyclists trying to fob them off with rational explanations that it was 'all in their heads', but seriously trying to get to the bottom of their ghost, they would open up a bit more.

After dark, the camp had a completely different aspect. The purposeful business of the day over, the whole camp seemed to gather into itself. After dinner, I strolled to the perimeter fence to watch a murmuration of starlings rise into the air over the moor and begin their aerial, group-formation dance before twilight faded to night. But I noticed that, no matter how many figures and formation clouds the starlings shaped themselves into, that not one of them overflew the camp itself. Over successive days, I checked for movement of wildlife, discovering that the place was as free of birds as the proverbial volcanic fields of Avernus. Distantly, I could discern buzzards and other birds, and at night, you could hear owls, but nothing came within the purlieu of the camp. I forgot to mention this to Ash, until later.

As dark fell, I began to experience again the menace that I had picked up on the moor itself. After our interviews of the day, I now had a better sense of what was to be expected. It felt as if the whole camp was waiting, fearfully. Amid the laughter and bonhomie of the officers' mess, Ash and I exchanged glances, wondering how the men of B Block were faring that night.

Back in our room, I speculated, 'Toibin mentioned years, but just how long has the Ghost of Shotley Moor been in existence, I wonder?'

'My thought entirely! Let's find out tomorrow.' Ash snapped out the overhead light. He turned over and went into a deep sleep within minutes. For myself, I listened to the periodic crunch of the night patrol on the gravel, and watched the triangle of light left by the crooked blind, where the spotlights from the perimeter fence shone into our room, for a very long time before sleep claimed me.

I did not sleep long, however. An urgent knocking on our door, followed by the entrance of Pte. Savile who shook us awake, 'Sorry, but Capt. Toibin says to come at once. It's the ghost!'

As we hurried into our clothes, an ashen Savile told us, 'We heard a noise coming from the storeroom, and Keith, Pte. Andrews, that is, he went to look, the bloody fool!' He seemed near to tears.

He led us to B Block and to the storeroom which lay next door to the dormitory. I laid a hand on Savile's arm, 'Is this where Nobby Clarke hanged himself?'

Savile nodded, unable to speak with terror.

Ash said to him, 'Regardless of orders, please would you stay outside?'

He saluted Ash gratefully, but I don't think he knew what he was doing at that point, as he sank the floor, crouching against the wall opposite.

The storeroom was about twenty-foot long and sectioned into differently sized compartments down one side, like a stable, with four bins which had lift-out partitions nearest the door. Capt. Toibin was crouched beside one of the bins on the let. He laid a finger on his lips and we listened. The light was much dimmer here than in the corridor, I noticed, and there was a strange, clammy coldness that seemed to extend to my ears, not just my skin. Of Andrews, there was no sign. I signaled with my hands and Toibin pointed at the bin.

Then the whispering began again. I realise now that this was what I had been hearing when we entered the storeroom. Ash stood stock still, listening, but there were no words to hear, only a sibilant susurration, as if a snake were drawing closer.

Ash indicated to Captain Toibin, and he lifted aside the partition in one silent movement. Inside, still holding his flashlight, Pte. Andrews was pressed against the far wall, the sweat beading his brow, unable even to pray. The beam of his torch held in his shaking hand raked the darkened space, giving it the intensity of a spotlight.

Without the partition, the whispering became more distinct. It was of a nature that I shrink to record here, but, in the interests of veracity, I give a brief verbatim account. The whispered words were squeezed out in a manner that brought to mind a foul-mouthed sergeant backing up one of his young recruits into a private corner, some distance from the parade ground, 'You feeble little bastard. Call yourself a fucking soldier? I've seen better material squashed flat under a lorry. I could lay hands on your lily-white body in ways you'd never believe. I could make you do things that would get you put on a charge, my son....' It is impossible to convey the relentless, toneless onslaught nor the violence implicit in the smutty, insinuating whispers that wrapped their way round your consciousness, like a black and greasy hand caressing your limbs with erotic intent.

Ash took one look at poor Private Andrews, and drew the flashlight from his shaking hands. He nodded to me, 'Help him out!' I was never so grateful as for that order of quittance. Getting Andrews out of the store-bin into the night was like dragging the tin-man out of a cupboard without benefit of oil-can. His limbs were stiff as boiled leather and his eyes started from his head as if he were about to suffer strangulation. We staggered into the yard, breathing the clean air in great gulps as if it had been previously rationed. Savile came out into the yard with us, 'You alright, Keith?'

Andrews seemed to be trying to loosen himself inside his skin. He dragged his tie off and undid his shirt, quite contrary to regulations, I'm sure, 'Christ! Did you hear that?'

I nodded vigorously, still drawing the clammy night air into my lungs, 'Yes, indeed, I did. You are not alone in hearing it. It was truly awful!'

Andrews' anxiety subsided a few notches, glad to have some confirmation of his experience. Savile took Keith's arm over his shoulder and led him away to sick-bay.

I returned to the storeroom. Without Andrews, and just in the presence of just us older men, the stores looked and felt normal. Capt. Toibin was shaken, but able to function.

Ash asked him, 'Was this room cleansed and blessed after Clarke's hanging?'

Toibin shook his head, 'No, heaven forgive me! I should have attended to that.'

'Then let's do it together now. Jack, you go and tell the men in the dormitory that it's over for the night. Then go and look out for Andrews.'

So, I left them to it.

Later that morning, we received distinctly more cheerful greetings from several the men who passed us on the way to the mess. Clearly, we had become visible over the camp radar. Over breakfast, we discussed the events of the night with Toibin.

'It's my first time hearing it. It sounded like the kind of abusive drill sergeant from the old days.'

'Nevertheless, I think we have something more complex on our hands than that. I think that's just one strand of the problem,' Ash said.

'Well, thank you for not judging me for my incompetence last night. It was good to give the storeroom a good going over with you. What do you make of it?'

'Whatever it is, wherever it emanated, it is persecuting the younger and more impressionable men.'

'Can the men be moved from B Block to other sleeping quarters?' I asked.

Toibin sighed, with a sideways look at the top table, 'It has been suggested but no-one thinks it worthwhile to disrupt the order of the camp...'

'...despite the order of the camp being disrupted?' I continued. 'How is Andrews this morning?'

'I got him off duties this morning, but I think he wants to be with his mates so, if you consider him fit for duty, then he will rejoin them.'

I promised to look in on him.

Ash asked him, 'I know the C. in C. said there was nothing, but are there any verbatim or eye-witness reports from before this present time that we can access, in addition to the men's testimony?'

Wiping a smear of egg from his mouth, Toibin said, 'Ah, I already made enquiries through the Friends of the Hampshires, and found a couple of retired servicemen who would be willing to talk to you. Major James, who is a lot more sympathetic to your cause than his commander, authorized me to alert them that the honour of the regiment was on the line, but they don't know yet what it's about. I will get the addresses for you on your desk after lunch, and see about arranging some meetings.'

But not half of the morning had expired when all our interviews were called off due to more manoeuvres. Suddenly, none of the men from B Block were available. Capt Toibin bustled into his office, 'Sorry, but this in normal procedure before deployment: a surprise set of manoeuvres to keep the men on their toes. - Look, since the camp is so upheaved today and tomorrow, I wondered whether you would like to pursue your enquiries with the retired servicemen, until the lads are back in camp.'

So, over the course of that and the next day, we managed to speak to a couple of retired soldiers who had been through the Shotley Moor camp back in the 50s, each of whom was aware of its reputation. Ash went to see Malcolm Donaldson, who lived locally still, as well as to explore the museum records and local Sollingshot gossip, while I took the train into south London to see Evan Howells. Major James had paved the way for us, merely asking that the retired men speak to us for the sake of the regiment, so they had no idea of what we had come to ask.

In a pub off the wrong end of Fulham Rd, I sat with Even Howells, a massively built barrel of a man, still formidable in his seventies.

'So is the Ghost of Shotley Moor still walking?' asked Howells, supping his pint.

'It seems it is,' I said. 'How did you come to know about it?'

In a rich South Wales accent he said, 'When I was sent to the glass house for bunking off to see my girlfriend without a pass. Nasty old thing that ghost, near drove me do-lally. I thought it was me mates making all those suggestions outside, but it wasn't.'

'So, it's not a recent ghost, then?'

Evan stared at me in wonder, 'Boyo, that ghost was old when I was a young squaddy. The locals in Sollingshot all knew about it, you ask them. No, it got inside you, that voice.'

'What did it sound like to you?... I mean, did it have an accent? Could you work out what it was after?'

Peering into his beer, Evan concluded, 'It sounded happy making people unhappy. But it was an English voice, from the South, I would say. God knows what it wanted. Nasty, evil thing it was. Wanted me to shit my pants, I daresay, throw in the towel, give up. But I wasn't haven't any of it, no! I stuck it out. I was even glad to be sent to Aden, in the end, and that was one arid hole in the ground.'

He chucked back the rest of the pint, 'So it's been scaring the lads again, then?' Then, in a lower voice, 'It's not made any more of them top themselves has it?'

'Two of them recently. How many in your time?'

'I'd say five, but the official report would say otherwise.'

'Then they're not in the record…'

'Ah! The Official Secrets Act can cover up anything it wants that way: died in action, you know… So, are you doing an article for the newspapers, or what? The Major wouldn't be giving you my address for that, I would think.'

'No, we're going to try and get rid of the thing, me and my partner.'

He didn't laugh, 'You've heard it too, haven't you?'

'Yes, last night. It was terrorizing a young squaddy.'

With a dead straight face, he poked his forefinger into my arm, 'You mind you get it good and proper now! And remember Sykes, Chalky, MacPhee, Albright and Pitkin: I blame that ghost for scaring them to death. Let's have no more of its tricks, now!' He made a fist, 'See this 'ere? Twenty-three years I was in the boxing ring. You don't get it, call on me, and I'll hit it to kingdom bloody come!'

Ash returned with a similar report from Malcolm Donaldson, 'He provided a different piece of phenomenon. Apparently, in his hut, writing appeared on the wall. It was put down to purposeful mischief-making at the time, but Donaldson swears that none of his mates put it there.'

'What did it say?'

' "Riley gets it next"… And yes, Riley got crushed by a tank when it went over a void in an area in the Peak District which had a cave system under it. It should have been marked on the map but the tank driver had been somehow issued with an older map. Donaldson swears that they all had it mapped on their instructions. It was a fatality put down to human error, rather than laid at the ghost's door, but all his mates knew what had caused it.'

I told him what Evan Howells had said about the ghost. And the number of its victims.

'It is clearly an old inhabitant, as I learned from Sollingshot. I spoke to the landlord of the Royal Oak. He's older than either of us and his father remembers it making itself a nuisance back in the thirties and forties.'

'Was there a camp there that early?'

'There had been various camps on the site, from the Napoleonic wars onwards. It was just a transit camp before the First World War: at a suitable distance from the coast, I suppose. It wasn't until the war was over that it became the Hampshire's main base: a lot of national servicemen had cause to regret it, I gather.'

'Did you find anything in the museum records?'

'Well, yes I did. The very helpful archivist showed me a newspaper report from the *Hampshire Herald*, of a Zeppelin raid in March 1917. It had intended to bomb a local benzol plant but dropped its load instead on the northern end of the camp, killing 49 soldiers who were on their way to the Western Front. A local vicar reported,

"We were aware of a bright golden finger, quite small, high in the sky towards twilight. Then there was flashes near the ground and a great shaking noise. It was like something from Milton's war in heaven, only visited upon the unfortunate earth of our county. I cannot get over it, the bursting shells falling upon the innocent soldiers about to serve their King and Country at the Front. May God have mercy upon them."

A later report goes on to relate that the size of the crater of the two bombs that had fallen one after the other was so big that it took a party of agricultural labourers and local people three weeks to level again.'

'But how does it connect with the ghost?'

'Well, not only do we have a quantity of military fatalities of the Hampshires, but we have an explosion whose aural resonance alone would alter the signature of this camp. People would have never heard anything louder than a thunder storm or a factory before World War One, remember: such an explosion could well have set up a traumatic memory which may be part of what is going on here.'

'Well, we don't have anything else to go on, until we get back to the interviews. So, what exactly is it? I know we've all been calling it a ghost, but what is it really?'

Ash pulled off his shirt wearily and sat on the bed, 'It's not easy to say. It is certainly not a ghost pure and simple – not just the residue of a long-dead person locked into a repetitive cycle of appearances. This one has malicious intent, it goes out of its way to inculcate fear and loathing. Apart from that, it has a telekinetic power to move things. All in all, I would say it is an entity that is composed of fear itself. It's been boosted over the years by the uncertainty and routine boredom of army-life, not to mention an institutional history of abuse, and it feeds off the fear and vital energy of the young. Have you noticed how it doesn't seem to affect or be experienced by anyone older than their late 20s?'

I went to the window to try and make the wretched blind hang straight for the tenth time, only succeeding in pulling the cord to bits. As the slats of the blind finally settled in their proper place on a permanent basis, I suddenly remembered, 'I don't know whether it's important or not, but have you missed anything since you've been here?'

Ash put both hands behind his head and considered, 'A fine oloroso, the grand piano, our dear friends at the Beacon?'

'Of course, but something else? Since we've been in residence, I've been watching the wildlife. Is it significant that it's all staying outside the camp? I've not heard one bird singing, nor seen any bird landing anywhere within the perimeter.' I told him about the starlings.

He sat up, 'Oh, my goodness, yes! That is indeed significant! Well done, Jack! The Ghost of Shotley Moor has an exclusion zone. It may be persecuting the men in B-Block at the present, but it has a much wider frame of reference. It could indeed have something to do with that bomb.'

'They say that no birds sing at Auschwitz,' I pointed out.

He nodded, 'So they do say!'

In the middle of the night, I was aware of Ash moving about, and grunted, 'What are you doing? Has something happened?'

'Get dressed, Jack. The Ghost has called again.'

I had completely missed the knock on the door, being so deeply down. I threw on some clothes and followed Ash.

When we arrived, all the lights were on in dormitory and the men, their eyes wide in terror, were huddled near the door. Capt. Toibin had his jacket on over his pyjamas and was praying aloud from his prayer book.

Looking beyond him, my eyes searched for what had frightened the men so badly. I didn't believe what I was seeing. A metal foot-locker was being somehow held aloft, just below the ceiling, but by no agency that could be discerned. Beneath it, with his back to us, stood McDermot frozen to the spot.

Ash indicated that we should go forward. As we did so, I seemed to step into a pool of intensely cold air, like stepping into the icy water of the sea. Goose-flesh raised on my naked arms and I slowed down.

'Grab him, Jack!' Ash commanded, as he circled round to face McDermot from the other side.

I threw both arms around the petrified soldier and pulled him back, just in time as the foot locker crashed down where he had been standing. The lights began to flick on and off intermittently, and an intensive smell of sewage began to pervade the room. Coughing and spluttering, I pulled McDermot back to the door, getting him to safety. We stepped back, out of the intense cold into the doorway: all the men were now the other side of the open door, but, in the strobe of the flickering lights, Ash was still circling, still within the thing's range.

I took a few foolish steps back into the maelstrom, as bedclothes and small, unattached objects from around the room – boots, clothes, alarm clocks, and books - detached themselves from gravity, beginning to lift and swirl. Fear incarnate reached its hand into me. Ash barked at me, 'Stay back!'

But he himself remained in the eye of the storm, a lone figure in the furore of whirling, angry power. The propelled objects drew closer together and fused, forming together into a looming, amorphous shape that stood over Ash. The ghost was really angry now. You could hear a shifting range of vocalizations – reminding me of the rapid turning of the dial on an old radio as it picked up different stations. The changing voices accelerated and grew in volume, but still Ash stood stock still, somehow making his own exclusion zone that remained unaffected.

The sound of the voices was now so loud, the whole camp must have been raised from sleep. The men were now the other side of the door with Toibin, and only he remained to witness what happened. I stuck in the doorway, my fingers white on the doorframe, desperate to help Ash but knowing myself utterly unfit to enter that unholy assembly. All I could do was pray to support him. Then the lights went out completely, and the separate voices began to overlap, accumulating into one vocal fury that struck dread into my heart. The snarl of a single voice coordinated all the fearful voices into one utterance, 'You will die.'

It was answered calmly by Ash, 'To those who have already died the death of the once-born, there is no death.'

At this, the great voice scattered into shards, some skipping away like ball-bearings, with a metallic swirl, others like jagged fragments of a mirror. Some of the voices echoed Ash's words in amazement, while others, like random hecklers within a crowd, hissed in fury.

His clear voice continued, calmly and compassionately, 'I speak to those who have been pulled into the maw of fear and despair of this thing: the way lies clear for you, behold the light!'

In the utter darkness of B Block, a small pulsing blue light formed into an egg. And I, who never see such things with my physical eyes, clearly saw it. It shed light into the darkness and seemed at first puny in the face of the whirling fury, but the blue egg grew larger and clearer: it was a sight on which to rest the eyes and its presence one to soothe the troubled heart. As it grew, it became like a ring around the moon, only at its centre, at the inside of the ring was a landscape into which you yearned to go.

The blue, light-ring's traction was irresistible. The greater reality of its presence began to rapidly destabilize the assembly of objects that had built up. One by one they began to fall to the ground, leaving the giant assemblage with significant holes in it. Power went out of the shape that it had made. The voices had gone, leaving only a vast void of despair that had nowhere to hide.

The overhead lights began to flicker once more. Under their strobing pulse, Ash stood with blood pouring from hand and head where some of the objects had slammed down past him. But he was not yet finished.

The ring contracted once more to a blue egg, then to a point of light that receded. Then standing clear of where the blue light had been, there dawned a more intense area, clear amethyst in colour. This new egg seemed facetted, like a jewel. From its heart flowed forth a fragrance and beauty that completely enveloped the despairing void of despair and anger. The despairing miasma flooded through that amethyst void like an unstoppable neep tide swamping the sands of a beach. The smell of sewage retreated, and the lights came back on fully and steadily.

All around, the floor was littered with broken objects, boots, and blankets that had subsided to the ground like the deflated remnants of a blow-up giant. In the midst of the carnage, Ash fell to his knees. Crunching over the rubble of broken watches, alarm clocks, shattered cups, and other personal accessories, I raised him up and carried him to the nearest bed, kicking off the detritus before laying him down.

'Ash, are you alright?'

His eyes were closed. I swiftly examined him, finding only the wounds over his brow and on his left hand, where he had raised it to fend things off the falling objects. His pulse was that of a child asleep, but I wondered about his blood pressure.

Then Capt. Toibin was at my side, and a pair of military policemen with bright torches, 'Is he injured?'

'Superficially, but he has just rid you of the Ghost of Shotley Moor for good, so treat him gently,' I urged, as the military policemen helped the paramedics load Ash onto a stretcher.

Lt. Col. Franklin and Major James stood back to allow the stretcher party to pass, then came uncertainly to stand in the doorway of the room, surveying the carnage with disbelief.

Franklin recovered first, 'Capt. Toibin, assign a work party to clear this mess up. I expect your full report by tomorrow afternoon.'

At this point, I could not forebear giving the C. in C. a very hard stare indeed, for I was very worried about Ash. At least he had the grace to lower his eyes, in homage of an heroic deed done on this field of battle.

We both knew who had really been in charge of the camp this night.

Back in sick-bay, Ash's head-wound had been sewn up and properly dressed, but he had still not awakened.

'His vitals seem ok, so I'm not worried,' said the camp doctor, reading my concern. 'After the kind of night he's had, I daresay a good sleep is the best cure.'

I sat beside Ash during what remained of the early morning hours, anxiously wondering when he would come back to us. He had done battle right enough.

When the orderlies had set things to rights and left us alone, I whispered to Ash, 'Whatever you learned in Nepal, or wherever you went, I hope they taught you how to how to recover from the kind of thing you did tonight.'

He did not respond. Of all the things I had seen him handle, that entity was bigger than most. If he looked as if he had gone nine rounds in the boxing ring, it was not surprising: he couldn't have come off worse.

I watched his breathing and monitored his vital signs until my own eyes closed. Consumed, like him, with the events of the night, I'm afraid I slumped speedily into a deep sleep, only to be awakened by an unfamiliar sound.

The unmistakable, liquid song of the blackbird was being poured out upon me.

I opened my eyes to see through the window a lone blackbird perched on the arm of the signpost outside sick-bay, singing its glorious song in the dawn light.

Ash still lay flat, as he had done since he was laid down the night before, unmoving and pale as the dead. I felt for his pulse, in alarm, to be reassured by a steady and regular beat. Tears came unbidden, dripping upon his arm.

He stirred, asking 'Is it raining?'

'No, it's a fine day. And the blackbird is singing.'

He smiled, opening his eyes, 'Then our work here is done.'

We sat in Capt. Toibin's office as he struggled to create a report that could go into military records.

'How does this sound?' he appealed to us. 'During the night of 16th August, at about 03.05, B Block dormitory was the object of a localized kinaesthetic disturbance, that caused damage to both personal property and dormitory fittings and furniture. No-one was hurt in the incident save Dr Richard Ashington who sustained impact wounds from the flying objects: he was treated by the camp doctor and discharged at 10.30 of the same day. After repairs were made, the dormitory has been pronounced fit for use by myself, etc.'

'I particularly like the use of the word "kinaesthetic,"' Ash complemented him. 'But I doubt that any insurer will care to cover the losses that the men sustained, on this evidence.'

I added, 'You might also want to drop "flying objects" and replace it with 'glancing objects.'

Toibin scribbled on his draft report, 'Good, then I'll get it typed up and see if the C. in C. will run it up his flagpole… What about your report?'

Ash said, 'It will go something like… the morale of the men of B section, of the 2nd Battalion Prince's Hampshire Regiment, has been severely shaken by the two recent suicides, but it is my considered opinion that with good psychological support, they will be fit for duty in the near future. – Which is what I think he wishes to hear?'

'Indeed, he does, since – it's no secret from you – we will be departing for a destination overseas in the next week or so. I can't say where, of course.'

'Then I would add a clause saying: it is my earnest recommendation that recruits under the age of 21 years who have recently lost a comrade by suicide, should immediately be given personal assessments, and if necessary therapy, by a professional psychologist.'

'Thank you, and God bless you for that! – I wish I had half your tricks in my armoury. That was no mean enemy you fought last night!'

Ash was cautioned by the medics to stay for another day, but we had received a call from the Beacon to announce two new cases needing his attention, and he was disinclined to remain, so we prepared to pack up. There was just one more task to perform. The men who had been touched by the deaths of their comrades were invited to come together and remember them in their own way. Later there might be a parade and a memorial but, after roll-call, Ash spoke to them all, with Captain Toibin beside him: 'I invite you to perform your own ritual of remembrance and committal for your companions. We have been given the sports hall. Bring whatever you think you might need - myself, Dr Rivers, Captain Toibin and myself will be available in the captain's office, if you want to ask anything. We will assemble for the remembrance at …' he looked to Toibin for confirmation.

'Eleven hundred hours,' said Capt. Toibin.

A small deputation made up of Savile, McDermot and Davenport came immediately to the office to find us. Davenport saluted us smartly, 'The boys want to ask you, is the ghost really gone, sir?'

Ash responded with a smile, 'Gone for good. – How does Block B feel now you've cleared up?'

'Clean as a whistle, sir, just a few breakages to account for,' said Savile. The others nodded, 'But Major James says they will be written off and all losses made good.' Well, that was good of him, I suppose.

'And how is Andrews?' I asked.

'He's doing alright. Doc says he will be fine to be deployed with us – we didn't want to leave him behind.'

They made no attempt to leave, so Ash asked them, 'Anything else you want to ask?'

Davenport asked, 'What *was* that thing? Can you explain it – just so as we can tell the lads?'

Ash phrased it like this, 'It was an entity, which is just an energy form that had built up over the years out of many factors - like a rolling snowball that builds up as it rolls down hill: the loneliness of the moor, the lack of good support for the men who trained here, all their fearful thoughts and their uncertainty. The energy form was also boosted by the bullying that many soldiers endured here back in the 50s and 60s. I think that was the voice that it tended to assume with you in B Block.'

The men looked at one another, as if they had suspected something like it.

Then he told them about the Zeppelin raid in the First World War and its likely psychic imprint upon the place, and they listened and tried to understand, but they had nothing like it in their short experience of life to compare with what happened the night before.

McDermot said, 'But you stood up to it - that thing. Capt. Toibin said you separated the lads who had topped themselves from out of it. Is that true?'

Ash nodded, 'Not just them, but the ones who took their lives before you were born, and the men who had been killed in the raid. They were able to take their way out of it and go free.'

The men regarded him with a certain awe. Davenport broke the solemnity by saying, 'You're what we call "special ops," you know!'

'Our secret weapon...' breathed Savile, running with the joke.

'Those super galactic light balls you spun...We could do with some of those tricks where we're going...' said McDermot, slapping his hand over his mouth, 'If you want to come along...'

It was their best complement to Ash, that he had stood to defend them when they were in a narrow place.

In a short, relaxed gathering, the companions of the dead soldiers remembered the men who had not been equal to the Ghost of Shotley Moor. Disciplined to respond in war, they were also versed in celebrating the peace that had come to their camp and to their comrades, bidding farewell to their comrades with reminiscences, songs, and a prayer led by Capt. Toibin. At the conclusion, every one of them insisted on shaking us by the hand.

Our leaving of Shotley Moor Camp was the very reverse of our coming: B Battalion lined the way to the gate and waved us off with a formal salute and cheers. But no officer more senior than Toibin and Speed was present.

'Will Toibin's report be acceptable to the C. in C?' I wondered aloud, as I drove back over the moor, demanding that Ash rest.

'I imagine it will be edited into a form that he would regard as "suitable to be filed," and then it will be conveniently lost. All he will have to account for is the destruction of personal and damage to army property,' said Ash.

The heat-haze over the moor began to lift as we drove, revealing the first purple beginnings of the autumn heather.

'It will be as if we had never been there to Lt. Col. Franklin,' I said, feeling badly that Ash's work had not been recognized.

'That's fine by me,' said Ash, 'If we are ever needed again, *we* have the option of going back, but some of those men we saw today may never be able to.'

He leaned forward, turning up the radio, as it played the chorus of *Over the Hills and Far Away*:

'Now, courage, boys, 'tis one to ten,
But we return all gentlemen,
While conquering colours we display,
Over the hills and far away.

And we joined in the chorus together:

'Over the Hills and O'er the Main,
To Flanders, Portugal and Spain,
The queen commands and we'll obey
Over the Hills and far away.'

Case 6: THE COMPANION

Neither man nor animal can be influenced by anything but suggestion.
Mikhail Bulgakov – Heart of a Dog

The young woman shown into Ash's consulting room that Spring day was stylish in a fashion that had gone out with Virginia Wolfe or the post-war opulence of Balmain. A large black chapeau elegantly framed a gamine face, shading a bright red helmet of hair. The rest of her was clad in elegant black. I experienced a sense of time-slip, for she looked like an actress strayed in from the set of some 1930s historical drama.

'My friend said that you might be able to help me,' her accent was from New England. Closer to, it was clear to me that, despite the sophisticated message her clothing sent, she was both very young and very frightened.

Ash drew out the chair for her to sit down, in an equally elegant show of manners, 'Please tell me how I can help, Miss Miller.'

'Please call me Bethany.'

'My assistant Jack will sit in, if that is alright, Bethany?'

She acknowledged my presence with an elegant bowing of her head, drawing off the gloves that encased her from forearm to finger. Her small hand pressed my fingers, and she launched into her account.

'I am employed as the companion of El... a lady who is well known in the world of the arts. Madame is elderly, and I act as her amanuensis and companion, accompanying her whenever she goes out to events. I write letters for her and take work to the post. She provides everything I need...' Her account lurched to a halt, to be followed by a more modest, 'I know I have been very fortunate to be chosen, but ... I live in her large house.... Over the last few weeks, I've been aware of something not right in the house.'

'What has been happening?'

Bethany looked down at her elegantly crossed knees, providing us with the optimum view of her profile. It was like watching a Daphne du Maurier heroine vainly trying to compose herself, 'I have been having such terrible dreams. They are very frightening. I've tried all sorts of remedies: staying up later, staying up and not sleeping at all, sleeping tablets, even alcohol. The dreams keep coming.'

'Tell us about the them, if you can.'

'Well, I am wandering about in a huge rambling house, somewhere in the country. I just know something is stalking me and is going to find me. I walk through a series of rooms that open out of each other until I come to a small crowded room. It is full of furniture that has been stored there and there is almost no place to stand up, there are so many things.' She stopped to get her breath and take a pace back from the fear pursuing her. 'It is very like the tomb of Tutankhamun when Howard Carter discovered it, with things all piled up. I know that if I stay there…' She halted again, passing a hand over her mouth, unable to speak what might befall her.

'Whoever is following is coming close. I look all around the room to get out, but the windows are barred and the only door is the one I entered by. Just before the thing comes for me, I see a small mirror….'

She pronounced it 'mirr', making it a one syllable word. As she said it, her pale smooth face became paler still. Gasping, she went on, 'The thing goes to lay its hands on me, only they are claws, not hands…. And then I wake up.'

Ash received her account silently, then asked, 'Why do you feel it is the house that is causing this?'

'Things have been tense recently, but … No, no-one has harmed me, really. What else can it be?'

'How long have these dreams been going on?'

'For about three weeks now.'

Ash digested this, leaving a space before saying, 'Has anything changed in the house since just before these dreams started?'

'No…Well, not unless you count my employer's old friend coming to stay.'

'Tell us about it.'

'Gaston is my employer's … well, he is some kind of distant relative of Madam's by marriage, I think. He is not a very pleasant man, but she enjoys having him around. He flatters her and jumps to serve her, when he is not up in the gallery drinking her brandy.'

'Is he staying long?'

'I don't know, but probably. He was thrown out of Venezuela for some kind of irregularity in his documents, so he has no-where else to go. I caught him going through her papers; he pretended to be looking for something for her, but I think he is short of money and is looking for something of hers to sell.'

'How is he with you?'

'He is perfectly polite when we dine together or when we go to events, but I don't care for him. He stands too close when are alone and he makes remarks… they are not threatening as such, but he just makes my flesh creep.'

'Does your employer know about how you feel?'

'I've tried to tell her that I think he's taking her for a ride, but she just dismisses it.' She stared at her hands in dismay. 'She doesn't see there's anything wrong.'

She sounded so forlorn, I couldn't hold back, 'May I ask, if you have friends or relatives in this country?' I was concerned that she should have some other source of emotional support other than this weird ménage.

'My parents are in the States, when they're not travelling in Europe. But, yes, I have many acquaintances in the art world: we meet up for lunch every Wednesday, if I am not wanted.'

But I bet you have no really close friend, no confidant, I thought to myself, as I observed her curious mixture of sophistication, pride, and fear.

The interview was hard to keep on track after that, and I blamed myself for introducing the topic of family before Ash had followed his own line of enquiry. Bethany suddenly stood up, like someone whose hour was up – though we were not in a particular hurry. Drawing on her gloves, she asked, 'May I come again next week?' She could have been a society hostess paying a call.

Ash didn't blink, 'Of course. Please speak to the receptionist and she'll arrange it.'

After Bethany had gone, I was on the verge of apologizing for interrupting untimely. but Ash looked quizzically at me, 'Well?'

'Something is not right in that house, alright, but I suspect the roots of the problem were already sprouting before the evil Gaston came on the scene.'

He nodded, 'Yes, I agree. Bethany wanted to speak about the apparent evil in her dream, but she doesn't want to look too closely at the evil that already festers. There are so many questions – the family situation sounds unsupportive, and the set-up at her employer's house…well, far from ideal'

'Those black clothes! They make her look like a dowager from the 1930s. How old do you think she really is?'

'According to the form she gave Maggie, she is 24. The clothes may be her disguise, her way of keeping up with this unreasonable person on whom she is dancing attendance.'

'It's like something from a book,' I ventured. 'I don't think she is a particularly poor girl, and she is certainly not an ignorant or unintelligent one, but whatever bonds she is under, it feels like some very old-fashioned kind of indentured servitude she is working through.'

Ash nodded, 'Exactly! I think you have put your finger on it.' Making a few notes for next time, he said, 'She feels under obligation to her employer. – Did you notice how she feels "lucky to have been chosen" by this celebrated artist. She feels both fortunate and unfortunate, both included and excluded from the magic circle of intimacy. She is the most un-at-home companion I've ever met.

I also doubt that she spends very much time out of her mistress's presence and is hurrying back to her even now, to appease her.'

'You think she is on a short leash?'

'I sense she just picked up the tug on the leash, yes! That's why she left so suddenly.'

'Will we be able to help her? If she is poised on the edge of flight all the time, it doesn't give us much to play with. Will she commit to coming to the Beacon?'

Ash shook his head, 'Oh no, we are not going to make much more headway until she is a lot more frightened, I'm suspect.'

By the next week when Bethany came to see us, things had evidently accelerated. Gaston had made further inroads into her employer's good books, ingratiating himself and becoming invaluable in ways that only a man intent on gain can be, becoming the old woman's escort to events, and generally elbowing Bethany out of the way. Despite all this, Bethany reported in a weary voice, 'Yet my employer seems to need me even more. She has me brush her hair every evening now, and help her get into bed. She wants me to read to her to help her sleep. She needs my help when she gets up, as well.' Seeing our faces, she added in mitigation, 'My employer is quite elderly now, and she really does need me.'

It sounded as if she now had two taskmasters; in addition to her companioning duties, she was rapidly being turned into a nurse. Bethany herself looked thinner and much paler, her black clothes seeming to diminish her further. Apart from the helmet of red hair, there was no spot of colour about her, including in her face, except for her red lipstick. Had I been a Yorkshireman, I would have termed her 'thrawn.'

As she spoke about her situation and her increasingly frightening dreams, my sense that she was like a girl in a folk story, set to perform some impossible task for a tyrant - like sewing seven shirts in a night, or spinning straw into gold – hardened. I had always practically wondered why folk heroines felt obliged to enter into such contracts, giving up their will, submitting to deadlines and abusive relationships from which their labours offered no escape, and now I was in the presence of one.

I realised too, that though I knew next to nothing about her employer, I had already cast her in the wicked stepmother role, and tried to catch myself back: we did not yet know enough about the set up or background.

Bethany's dreams were coming at an accelerated rate, several times a week, and she was reluctant to discuss them in any detail, as if reiteration caused them to grow in power. We got the impression that the clawed hand was getting closer. Her everyday life seemed to have been even more curtailed, and she reported that she had stopped writing poetry entirely. This seemed to worry her more than anything else, and Ash agreed with her that it was not a good sign of her spiritual health.

He asked again about the house and how it felt to her, trying to confirm exactly what she was suffering from, articulating the hinge of the issue, 'Is the problem *within* the house or just *the house* itself?"

'I am sure that there is something wrong with the house,' she persisted. 'It feels very fraught...'

.... and airless and isolating, I continued in my head. It was pretty clear to me that Bethany spent far too much time indoors, except when walking to the post. She badly needed a holiday and time out of that house, its inhabitants and all their circumscriptions.

'Has anything unusual happened in the house? Something out of the ordinary this last week?'

She began to shake her head automatically, then halted, 'Well... I don't know – it was a trivial kind of thing...'

Ash cocked his head encouragingly, 'So?'

'Just that one of the maids reported me to the housekeeper. The first I knew of it was when I was called to Madame. It was the strangest thing! Madame accused me of smoking in my room, but I don't smoke, I never have. She said the maid found some tobacco leaves under my pillow. They left a black stain on the pillow-case that she couldn't get out. I swore I didn't put it there.'

Ash and I exchanged alarmed glances.

I asked, 'Did she believe you?'

'I don't think so. She said she had employed me on the strength of my dedication to the arts and that she trusted me to act like a lady. It was most humiliating!'

Ash said quietly, 'We believe you, Bethany. Now, I would like you to search your room for anything unusual – things or substances that you have not put there and, if you can, come back here with anything you find – invent an appointment with the dentist if you have to.'

I didn't think it was possible for Bethany to go any paler than she already was, 'You think someone's getting at me?'

'Quite possibly. Try not to handle anything with your skin – wear gloves, and –' he firkled in the desk drawer, to bring out a plastic ziplock bag, 'put anything you find in here.'

'What am I looking for?'

'Something quite small. Possibly organic matter, or maybe some token or talisman.'

As we watched her leave, I asked, 'You think this is about witchcraft?'

'Witchcraft and the power of suggestion, yes.'

Maggie was instructed to show her right in. Bethany was back within the hour in a taxi. She burst in with the bag flourished in her hand, 'I found this. What does it mean?'

Ash took the plastic bag from her and tipped it out upon the steel thali tray that he'd brought from the kitchen. It was some dark looking stuff, coagulated like pressed dates, almost paste-like. 'Where did you find it?' he asked, bringing it up to his nose and cautiously sniffing it. Then he separated it with a knife, investigating it with the tip.

'There was some under each of the legs of my bed.' Bethany said very gravely, with a tremor in her voice, 'And some more at the back of a drawer.'

'But how did you find it then?' I asked.

'I happened to move my bed to look behind a cupboard in the corner, and there it was, under each leg.'

'Well that didn't get there accidentally!' Ash said.

'What is it?' I said, smelling it for myself. It smelt a bit like burnt cereal, with a deep musky hint to it.

'I'm pretty certain at base it's some kind of chimó – an alkalized tobacco that's chewed, smoked, eaten or used as snuff in Venezuala and Guyana. But there's something else in it too.' Ash sniffed again, then lit a match and let some burn on the thali tray. The smoke rose, smelling like caramelized cherry with vanilla and at all not unpleasant. Then something else happened. I began to pick up another odour beneath it that went straight to my frontal cortex, making me feel momentarily confused. The same thing was happening to Ash, who swiftly removed the tray to the kitchen, upending a bowl over it.

Bethany looked between us anxiously, 'What was in that stuff?'

'Chimó tobacco flavoured with Tonka Bean, but there's something else I can't identify, save by what it does. It will need analysis.' Ash looked at us both, 'I assume you also experienced the effect of the smoke?'

'I felt confused and don't know what would have happened if you'd not taken it out ...' I confirmed.

Bethany's face fell, 'Is this what is causing my dreams?'

'I imagine that this is at least partially the cause.'

'But who would do such a ... Gaston?'

'Well, you did say he had been in Venezuela!'

'But why?' she cried.

'We need to look deeper into that, I think. Could it be that he is trying to push you out of Madame' favour?'

Bethany looked bewildered, 'I suppose! But she would never throw me out. She needs me too much. Gaston himself is far too lazy to do half the things I have to do.'

'What now, Ash?' I asked.

Ash said, 'I am wondering how we might check whether the rest of the house or your room has been tampered with in the same way? You have said that he might be also trying to defraud your employer?'

'Oh, I hadn't thought of that. Poor Madame! You think he is trying to do something like that to her too?'

'Until we investigate further, it is hard to say.'

'Are you permitted to bring friends round?' I asked, wondering how we would be able to investigate the situation in the house at closer quarters.

She wrinkled her face, 'Madame has always asked me to entertain friends outside her house. She is an intensely private person and only invites those she knows into her inner circle.'

The household sounded impenetrable, staffed by a cook, a butler, a housekeeper, and two maids to fetch, carry and clean. The difficulty of understanding what exactly was going on was not going to be easily solved. But in our conversation, Bethany had already dropped the fact that her employer had monthly salons at her house

'Is it possible to gain an invitation to one of your employer's salons?' Ash asked, striving to create an opening in this impasse.

Bethany became very still, regarding us both doubtfully, 'Do you have an artistic skill in any discipline? You see, anyone who comes to the salon is required to present something.'

'Well, Ash plays the piano like a professional,' I observed. 'And while I have no skills in that department, I can read music and turn pages, if required.'

It was clear, from her severe look, that this would have to be ascertained by an audition, so Ash went to his upright piano, launching into a fiendishly difficult piece in 5 sharps by Liszt that took him from the top to the bottom of the keyboard. It was a brilliant encore piece that made it look like the pianist had 48 fingers.

Bethany was quietly impressed, 'Bravo! But the problem is that my employer only invites people into her salons who have been previously introduced to her.'

It was sounding like Catch 22 already. I was beginning to feel really uncomfortable with the thought of Bethany returning to so severe a captivity.

'How might we solve that?' Ash asked.

She thought long, saying, 'She goes to the opera every month. It might be possible to accidentally run into you at Covent Garden... She takes her interval drink in the Champagne Bar. We have tickets for the new production of Gluck's *Orpheo* this month.'

'Let us know the date and we will acquire some tickets,' Ash said, making a note.

Bethany gave him the date but then drew back into herself. With faint horror, she asked, 'But how will I introduce you to her? I can't say you are anything to do with the medical profession... she will not even talk about illness.'

'You can tell her quite honestly that we are both Harley Street consultants in "wellbeing and mindfulness,"' Ash calmly replied. He opened the drawer of his desk, passing her a card I did not recognize. 'You can truthfully speak of us as "friends of your family," since we have its well-being in our hearts.'

After she was gone, I asked, 'What was on that card that you gave her? It's not your usual one.'

'No indeed. Just one I keep for times when another persona might be handy,' he brought out one for my inspection. 'Special issue, only to be used in emergencies.'

It read 'Richard Ashington, Wellbeing Consultant' and the Harley Street address. At the bottom was a running logo of interlocked spirals and under it, the legend, 'Keeping your soul secure.'

'I won't even ask about this,' I thrust it back to him, astounded and disgusted. 'Are we really going to go to these fantastical lengths to find out what we already suspect – that it is not the house so much as its inhabitants that are causing all this?'

Gravely he said, 'That young woman is slowly losing the will to live, and it's our task to stop that, if we can. Without a proper exposure to her employer and the situation in that house, we can't tell what is going on. An inside perspective will show us more than we are able to garner here. Also, we need to do this soon. My sense is that time is running out for her. Whatever Gaston is about, it may not be only Bethany who is in danger here.'

The Royal Opera House, Covent Garden, is not a venue with which I have much acquaintance. I have never had to wear evening dress in my life but, since Ash said it would make a good impression, I went into Christminster and duly hired a penguin suit. Ash had one already, of course, but of a much better cut than the jacket I was wearing which. In order to accommodate the width of my shoulders, the hirers only had a jacket one size larger than I needed. It was my usual night for phoning Jane, so I called her before we went out. Taking a long look at me in my finery, she declared dryly that looked like a well-dressed gorilla. So much for marital support!

The crush at the opera was unspeakable, as this was just the second night of the new production. On the tube, I felt horribly overdressed, but at the opera house, I was glad to see that I was not so sartorially out of place, after all, as I'd feared. Most people were in evening dress but there were plenty of business suits, and some bizarre outfits, including a woman seated in front of us, with what I think is called 'a fascinator' strapped to her head, laden with plastic macaroons and a teapot.

It all reminded me of George Bernard Shaw's 1905 letter to *the Times* about sartorial standards at an opera night, where he had taken issue with a lady who 'had stuck over her right ear the pitiable corpse of a large white bird which looked exactly as it someone had killed it by stamping on the beast, and then nailed it to the lady's temple, which was presumably of sufficient solidity to bear the operation. I am not, I hope, a morbidly squeamish person; but the spectacle sickened me. I presume that if I had presented myself at the doors with a dead snake round my neck, a collection of black beetles pinned to my shirtfront, and a grouse in my hair, I should have been refused admission.'

Teapot-hat woman right in front of me had clearly decided to dress on theme with her headwear, for the production had been mounted by someone with a bizarre sense of design. Orpheo had to go to the underworld clutching a zither, attired in a pink smock, while both male and female furies were clad in black leather crinolines for no apparently good reason. The set resembled a biscuit box that had been kicked over, and the steps to Hades were ginger nuts and bourbon cremes. It looked to my untutored eyes more like Offenbach than Gluck. Only the sublime music made it worthwhile. I closed my eyes most of the time, attending to the singing, although Ash reported that I was actually sleeping through a great deal of the first half.

We made our way at the interval to the Champagne Bar, as arranged with Bethany, craning our heads over the thirsty throng to find her. Ash had fortunately pre-ordered our drinks and canapés or we would never have been reached the bar, which was already six deep. I located our order while Ash went in search of Bethany. She and her employer were sitting at a reserved table. Bethany's red hair was our beacon in the throng: she was wearing a harlequin checkered black and white evening gown over which she wore a black shawl beset with icy sparkles. She indicated that we should approach. Her employer was a small elderly woman, seated with her back towards us, attired in red brocade, with dyed black hair piled on top of her head.

Clutching his champagne, Ash stepped forward to greet Bethany like an old acquaintance. She coolly pecked him on the cheek and turned to the woman beside her.

'Madame, allow me to introduce to you Richard Ashington, a friend of my family. Mr Ashington, I have the honour of introducing you to Elizaveta Zakharova.'

Instead of shaking hands, Ash bent and kissed the older woman's hand, 'Madame, I am a great admirer of your *Camelias in the Mist*.'

As he spoke, the penny dropped; Elizaveta Zakharova was a world-renown Franco-Russian artist and poet who was reported to be semi-retired. I remembered little more about her life and work other than the fact that she was reputed to be temperamental. As a younger woman, she had been a patrician beauty, but now she was just a shriveled-up dame in a brocade evening gown. Beneath the glitter of a diamond tiara band, her face and neck were a network of imploding lines, and her gold-ringed hands were twisted with severe arthritis. Her hooded eyes regarded Ash's homage as but her due. All in all, I did not take to her one bit. This was a woman who required the whole world to jump to her command.

I was less formally introduced as the companion of Ash, which made me sound like his live-in lover, especially since La Zakharova's appraising glance put me in the 'bit of rough' category. It felt very awkward to be ogled by a woman of her advanced age, but Ash stepped into the breach by engaging her in discussion of the production, showing he had been more attentive than myself.

They were getting on very well when a deeply tanned man of about 52 with what can only be described as a ruined face came to the table with a fresh bottle of champagne. Madame's friend, Gaston Lucas, was introduced to us by Bethany, whose careful description of him as a relative of Madame's was vagueness itself. His handshake was offensively wet and his smile all teeth, like the Wolf in Red Riding Hood. His effusive bonhomie towards us was masking a wariness that I read as, 'Keep your hands off! This is my patch,' warning off any other man. I wouldn't have bought a second-hand car from this roué, I must say. The weakness of his mouth, and the narrow distance between his eyes did not inspire confidence, despite his 'man of the world' air. I had no doubt that, for whatever reasons he was thrown out of Venezuela, it was a well-advised decision, and that any dodgy documents would have been the least of it.

As though catching the backwash of this dynamic, La Zakharova became suddenly very fussy, snapping at Bethany to pass the canapés with unnecessary sharpness, raising her jewel-headed cane and stamping it down, causing heads to turn. Bethany meekly offered the plate like a waitress, her bright hair hiding her expression, but I felt for her petty humiliation before this unpleasant pair, watching how Gaston's nostrils flared in superiority. How on earth had she fallen into their clutches? And why did she remain?

My attempts to draw Bethany into a separate conversation didn't go down well: clearly Madame alone was allowed to shine as the jewel in any gathering, and we were all the mere setting for her unique lustre. Bethany's eyes warned me to back off and be biddable, so I copied her mien, setting my face to be that of an attentive listener. Any incipient pity I had harboured for La Zakharova as a poor old woman about to be fleeced by her nasty cousin was speedily evaporating.

The cacophony in the Champagne Bar was almost too much for any conversation, but Bethany skillfully steered it from *Orpheo* back to music at large, mentioning that Ash was a pianist.

'Professional?' Zakharova's deep, gravelly voice enquired. It still sounded more Russian than French, despite her upbringing outside Paris.

'Merely a talented amateur, Madame,' Ash modestly replied.

She regarded him again, reappraising her estimate, 'You must come to my next salon and play' she commanded. Her saurian neck swung to me again, and those serpent eyes glittered, 'Oh, and bring your big friend. - What does he do?'

'What he is told, Madame,' Ash replied with a flash of wit that made her smile and Gaston snigger.

I seethed inside my oversized jacket, but took a leaf out of Bethany's book, determining not to show how humiliated I felt.

When the bell rang for the end of the interval, we did the polite once more, Ash swapping cards with La Zakharova, skillfully turning over her hand to peer in her palm.

'Ah, do you read hands, Richart?' she addressed him in the French way. The greedy manner of her questioning was the only weakness she had revealed.

'Hands and cards, both, Madame.'

Her eyes gleamed, but there was no time for Ash to oblige with either as the bar was emptying, 'Then, I shall expect you both next Thursday at 8 o'clock. Bring your tarot cards with you! À bientôt!'

As we returned to our seats, Ash muttered, 'Always leave them wanting more!' Then he apologized, 'Sorry about that, Jack. Just a little window-dressing to set up our grand appearance.'

'I'm sure you will find a good use for me,' I replied, ironically, 'But, oh my God! What a pair!' I exclaimed, as soon as we were safely back in our seats.

I was unable to sleep in the second half, and took in little of the opera as I considered poor Bethany's plight. Not even the sight of Eurydice being cracked out of her underworldly black corset and attired in an Elysian smock of baby blue that matched Orpheo's pink one could distract me. It seemed to me that Bethany was not only condemned to spin flax into gold in this awful old woman's household but she was also living in the house of a vampire who was drawing upon her youth and power in order to prolong her own miserable life. Ash agreed with me.

On the way back home on the tube, we discussed the weird ménage that Bethany had to endure. 'Why does she stay, if it's that bad?' I asked.

'It may be the money, but I suspect it is more to do with being in a position of trust and honour. Bethany is a little too young to be able to just walk out. The early 20s are not a good age for young people: old enough to be adult but not experienced enough to know how to deal with the likes of Zakharova and her ilk. Never underestimate the stubborn pride of a 24 year old!'

As we returned to the Harley St flat, I voiced my concerns about our coming invitation, 'They won't expect *me* to do anything, will they? I don't think my comic *Albert and the Lion* monologue will be quite suitable!' Ash told me to learn a poem that I liked, saying that it was never out of place to present your party piece.

In the eventuality, I didn't need it, even though I did prepare a small selection of John Clare poems, on the understanding that someone who had been carted off to the madhouse might surely bring some sanity to the proposed evening. In the end, I was extremely glad that I didn't have to voice, 'Come We To the Summer' with its prolonged evocation of the poet's beloved,' in case it might have been misconstrued by the old dame. As it was…. Well!

For the salon, Ash said I need not wear the penguin suit again, which was a relief, so I opted for a light summer suit and shirt, both of which fitted me properly. As for Ash himself, he swung into exotic mode with a Spanish style beige suit, the jacket of which was as long as a frock coat, set off with a brown winged-collar shirt, and Cuban heels. Over his shoulders he threw a mauve silk Indian shawl.

I considered him critically, 'Of course, I am inured to the fact that you will always upstage me, but did you have to make me look like the driver on his night off?'

'Tonight, Jack, I have to look the part and be both entertainer and mystic…' With one finger he twirled a circular display of tarot cards, with a conjuror's flourish.

'... and am I to be his performing monkey?'

He laughed, slapping me on the back, and we caught a taxi to the salon, 'While I am busy tonight, you will be doing the dangerous work. So, no, you are "covert operations". Our watchwords of the night are "distract and deceive."'

We had agreed that Ash would take responsibility for distracting everyone: 'Once the tarot cards come out, I will not get any peace until all who want a reading get one, so you will be free to go exploring. I will try and make it the music first, then you will have to use that as your cover.'

Only the thought of the clandestine nature of my purpose brought me any appetite for the evening's events. Hidden in my inside pocket, I had my pair of collapsible divining rods, so that I could check out what was going on in Bethany's room. I was honoured that Ash trusted my judgement enough to let me loose on this task, but he said, 'You have a better feel for the rods than I.'

The house was at the posh Knightsbridge end of Kensington: one of those huge five-story early Victorian edifices that are usually split up into flats now, only this one wasn't: Madame owned the whole building – surely a testament to her artistic reputation or a very well-invested private income. We rang the bell and were admitted into a tiled hallway by the butler. The salon was clearly on the first-floor front reception room, as a convivial spill of people came and went from it down the stairs, making artistic conversation.

It was a motley assortment of recondite artistic types. I recognized Marti Gee, gossip columnist of *The Tatler*, and the Huxtable brothers, in their identical twin suits, the Tweedledum and Tweedledee of modern art. Most of those assembled were has-beens or would-have-beens, well over the hill, with a good assortment of toadies and hangers-on to keep the circle well oiled. There were scarcely any young women in the throng – probably to ensure that Madame was not upstaged. Ash and I stuck out as the youngest guests at the salon, apart from Bethany and the waiting staff.

Madame herself sat in state upon a kind of armchair throne, with a footstool propping up her tiny feet, her jeweled cane laid across her lap, while guests approached to be given her greeting or *bon-mot*. This was no salon: more like a royal audience.

As we were both taller than the majority of the guests, Madame spotted us immediately, beckoning us over. 'Welcome, welcome! Newcomers to my salon are so welcome!' she proclaimed loudly, while the toadies drew back to view us with arrested distain.

At her greeting, a great change came over Ash: our quiet, modest soul doctor vanished, to be replaced by some exotic creature who strode across the floor like a dancer, casting himself down on one knee to kiss her hand, 'Madame! It is a great honour to be among you.' He mouthed flattering nonsense to her like a man selling cut-price plates in a street market to a reluctant lady.

Zakharova preened in the face of his excessive charm then, turning her head up, fixed me with her basilisk's stare, her mouth curving into a smile of pleasure, 'And you brought your big friend,' which was my cue to step forward. I cannot adequately convey what her tone and smile implied, but they made me feel unclean.

Clutching my left hand in her tiny bird fingers, she ran her other hand up my thigh, out of sight of the company under my jacket: it was like being felt up by a hook-winged pterosaur. I had a hard job not to shudder.

Holding onto my hand, she asked of Ash, 'And what wonders have you brought for us?'

His obsequious bow belied his masterful words, 'Yes, I have brought the cards, Madame, but first you shall have music!'

This was to be my cue to depart in search of the facilities and look over Bethany's bedroom and Gaston's room, but the wretched woman shifted her feet off the footstool and made me perch upon it, running her hand up my shrinking carcass as I hunched at her feet. I composed myself by thinking just what Jane would do to her, were she present. It was a pleasing prospect in my present predicament.

Ash sat flamboyantly at the piano, warming his hands and extending his long fingers, turning them over in the light. I smiled, recognizing some of the passes he made when he wanted to calm things down. Madame whispered in my ear, 'He is a good friend to you, then? I could be a better one, though…' she promised, and her fingers resumed their unwanted wanderings.

Silence fell as Ash launched into *Reflets sur L'Eau*, one of Debussy's *Images*, with its sauntering glints of light. His performance both looked and sounded impressive, as he dived up and down the keyboard, with lifted hands at the rests, bringing interested glances from those in the salon. The music fell away to the sound of scattered applause. He continued seamlessly with Fauré's *Sicilienne*, which settled everyone back into a more conversational mode.

I shifted uneasily, for I should now be about my work, and I was desperate to be out of the clutches of this monstrous old woman. Gaston seemed to be in deep conversation with a petit Asian woman attired in Thai costume, so I was clear to start work. Taking a leaf from his book, I said to Zakharova, 'Madame, forgive me. The journey here was long, and I need the little boy's room.'

She reluctantly ceased her fingering of my back, giving me a little push with a sigh. I rose, leaving Ash to advance his programme. Bethany hovered in the door of the salon, anxiously awaiting me. She showed me - ostensibly to find the way to the facilities - but really to show me her room and the layout of the house. We ran upstairs while the company was spellbound by the playing. 'In here,' said Bethany, leaving me to it, keeping her eyes averted from me, as if I were a shameful thing, now that I had been scavenged by her employer. I had a much keener sense now of quite how La Zakharova had battened upon her youth, even as she had laid caressing fingers upon me, a stranger. I now wondered whether there was some sexual charge or undercurrent in Bethany's situation.

I speedily scoured Gaston's vast room. His bedroom drawer resembled a bank-teller's till, yielding a stash of bank notes in high denominations. There were several credit cards in a variety of names casually clipped to the back of his passport – whether stolen or just fraudulent identities, I couldn't say. Setting the credit cards aside, I flipped through his French passport. Born Gaston-Pierre Lucas in Caracas in 1955, he was a lot older than he looked. The stamps revealed him going in and out of Venezuela frequently between international destinations all over Europe. In the bottom drawer he had about a 3 ounce stash of cocaine in a plastic bag. Going through his clothes, I came across bills for a Savile Row tailors, and some roulette tokens from Crockfords. He had clearly been living the good life since his return to London. The only thing in his room that looked out of place was a brightly-painted turtle made of papier-mâché that sat on the table. As I picked it up, I discovered it was actually a box. The contents were similar to what had been discovered in Bethany's room: chimó again, but without the added ingredient. It confirmed what we already knew.

I moved quickly into Bethany's medium sized bedroom on the second floor, with its own en-suite bathroom. Several touches spoke of her: a pile of French poetry by her bed; a pin-board of friends' photos with a much younger and carefree looking Bethany smiling out; a greetings card with an image of Hokusai's wave signed by her parents; a tub of hat-pins, and a small framed print by Zakharova of doves in flight. But I had work to do. I went over the room speedily to ensure that there were no more presents of tobacco. Bethany had been keeping her door locked, she said, but it would be easy enough for Gaston to steal the key from the housekeeper's board and plant something else. If he was really trying to get rid of her, then we would catch him.

Diviners have to check their body's reaction as well as observe the motion of the rods, keeping a sense of what is held, what is moving, what is stuck.

I quietened myself to feel the room with all my senses: the smell of Bethany's perfume, the faint sound of the piano drifting up from below, a cat's whisker of anxiety, a sense of curtains revealing and concealing something, but little else.

Over the years, I had learned to dowse from Ash: we had wandered over the Downs finding springs, and ancient monuments whose remains were beneath the surface of the land. I have to report that it remains the only esoteric skill in which I ever surpassed Ash: he declared me a natural.

I deployed the rods, ranging up and across the area. The rods crossed together over her bed, where a line transected her room. I mentally inquired of the rods, 'Is this water?' Getting a sense of 'no,' I asked, 'Is this electrical cabling?' Again a 'no.' I went through the list, discovering that the line running through her bed was a natural energy line, so I diverted its route, pushing it away with my body-field, to run along the outside wall instead. These kinds of lines accentuate poor sleeping or difficult dreams: it is like trying to sleep on the Queen's highway amid the passing traffic. The bed itself had the kind of anomalies that arise from anxiety: these were just burgeoning thought-forms wrought of worry, but not anything more malign. I went into the bathroom and brought water, adding into it the salt from the screw of paper I had brought in my pocket, to help reconsecrate the area. I gave the bed a good going over, finishing with a blessing.

I was still in the bathroom tipping out the unused water when the bedroom door opened. From the smell of the waft of aftershave, it was clearly not Bethany. Improvising hastily, I stepped out of the bathroom, toweling my hands vigorously. There stood Gaston on the threshold. In a hectoring tone, he demanded, 'And what are you doing in here?' His accent was a curious mix of Spanish overlaying his original French.

'The other facilities were in use, so Bethany directed me use her bathroom.'

Gaston looked ready to square up to me, so I threw the towel down across the rods, which he had not yet noticed, and came over to look down on him. I was both taller and more strongly-built than he, but I guessed he was a coward and would back down. Rather more aggressively than I needed to, I inquired, 'And what are *you* doing barging into Bethany's room?' bringing my face down in closer proximity to his. His breath had the odour of poor dental hygiene which his Italian cologne did little to cover.

As I hoped, he drew back, but he reposted on the defensive, 'I live here.'

Mildly, and with the smallest edge of irony, I replied, 'That must be very nice for you.'

He puffed himself up like a bullfrog, 'Madame will have views about you coming into her companion's room.'

The penny dropped. I realized that his reaction was fueled by jealousy of

Madame's come-on to me! I had to do something, if only to prevent Bethany getting into even more hot water.

In for a penny, in for a pound: if Madame thought of me as Ash's 'bit of rough,' then I could readily oblige. Speaking from low in my chest, I deepened my voice, uttering, 'Who said I was interested in the women?' laying a careless hand upon the bare skin of his wrist.

That raised his heterosexual Latin blood! He was instantly, massively offended, raising his fist to me, swearing in Spanish. I easily parried the blow, and used him to pivot myself out of the room. I ran downstairs and helped myself to a large whiskey, knocking it back in one swallow.

Back in the salon, Madame was in fine fettle, with Ash leaning over an Indian tray table where the tarot cards were spread out, like an old fakir charming the memsahib, one arm intimately curved about the back of her chair. She was hanging on his every word, her hooded eyes glittering black diamonds as he interpreted the cards for her.

Ash noted my return, without drawing breath and turned another card to lay alongside the others on the Indian tray. That card obviously had a bitter flavour, for she drew back her twisted hands to her breast with shock. Then, scattering the spread of cards upon the floor, in a fit of pique, she pronounced loudly, 'Enough of the occult, let us return to art.'

She commanded the conversation to come to order once more, leaving Ash to ignominiously pick up the spilled tarot cards from the floor, all favouritism suspended. His bow to her was ignored. Casting his white hair out of his face, he sauntered up to me and drained a glass of champagne, asking casually in a low tone, 'How did you do?'

'OK. Nothing major. - I think we both know that the problem is sitting there...'

'Not here,' Ash whispered, turning into me, as Gaston hoved into view, going to whisper frantically into Madame's ear. Her eyes flicked accusingly towards us.

For their benefit, I threw one arm across Ash's back and pulled him closer, as if to kiss him, 'Sorry, but this is for Gaston's benefit!' I explained, at close range.

Not missing a beat, Ash reciprocated readily, smoothing my cheek afterwards with a lovesome finger. Gaston had registered us, with grim satisfaction, while Madame looked on with pitiable disappointment.

'Well, that's certainly put the cat among the pigeons,' Ash said, flirtatiously.

Trying hard not to giggle, out of the corner of my mouth, I asked Ash, 'Are you reading any more cards tonight?'

'I very much doubt it. Madame will probably not want any more doom and gloom poured upon her soirée...' Dropping his voice an octave, Ash gestured with his eyes, 'Shark alert at 4 o'clock!'

Whatever miserable effect we had had upon Madame, the Huxtable brothers had decided to take a shine to us. We both smiled non-committally as the gay, bland-faced twins cruised past, trailing their interest in the new talent; I hoped they quickly got the message that Ash and I were an item, as we clung together.

Unfortunately, we then had to deal with the rather more serious attentions of Marti Gee after that. He came over, all glasses and blond quiff, to pump us for our origins, but neither of us wished to appear in his catty gossip column, where many a reputation had been insinuatingly shot down by his verbal sniping, so Ash kept up a speedy banter that revealed nothing at all. I left him to it, as I didn't want my big mouth to ruin the effect.

At Gee's elbow sipping on his sherry, was a short, velvet-coated man with a balding pate who looked like a clockmaker. He introduced himself as Stephen Venables, an art dealer. 'Such a pity that Madame is doing so little new work,' he said to me, conversationally.

I readily agreed, asking whether it was because of her arthritis, 'I noticed it was severe.'

Laying a hand on my arm, and nodding at Gee, he warned me in a whisper, 'Better not say more, dear chap!' And in a louder voice, 'Gaston tells me that Madame has plans for a new set of pictures. We are all agog to see them.'

Bethany caught my frantic signaling and fortunately intervened at that point, steering us away and keeping up a steady stream of conversation about music until Gee latched onto some other unfortunate.

At that point, Madame demanded loudly that the Hungarian violinist should play to her gypsy soul. As he raised his instrument, and under cover of the music, I told Bethany that my divining rods were still on her bed, and to bring them back the next time she came.

I asked her, 'So, have we blown it? Or do we have to stay?'

'Circulate a bit longer and then wish her goodnight,' she advised quietly. 'Thank you so much for coming,' she said in a louder voice, shaking our hands.

As the last frenetic notes of the *czardas* fell away, we were ready to bow over Madame's hand and thank her, before running out into the night, making good our escape. I only wished we might have taken Bethany away with us from that vile household.

As we left, Ash stooped, ostensibly to re-fasten his boot, but I saw him draw with his fingers on the threshold, 'Just a little insurance for Bethany,' he said, enigmatically.

In the privacy of the taxi I began to vent, 'What a terrible evening! Being felt up by that unspeakable old hag, and then having to make love to you for the benefit of her tame eunuch....!'

Ash shook his head with mock melancholy, 'Ah, the sad life of a psychologist: from toy boy to bear, and all in one evening, too! But we did establish the picture well enough and can offer Bethany much better help now.'

Back at the flat, Ash turned to me in the hall, saying, '"Lend thy hand
And pluck my magic garment from me."'

'OK, Prospero!' I obliged, flinging his jacket and shawl onto the settee.
'Are we done now?'

Addressing his garments, Ash said, '"Lie there, my art!" - Yes, indeed, off with the play-acting and on with some real work!'

Ash duly penned a thank you letter, but La Zakharova had evidently found us both an intriguing disappointment, as no response came. Jane was coming home from Manchester for good, finally, and I looked forward to resuming our married life together where we had left off at the beginning of her degree course three years ago. While she had spent most of her holidays at the Beacon over those three years, I still hadn't seen her since Easter and it was now late May. Her absences were finally going to translate into a life together, and a magnificent expansiveness was beginning to flood my being at the prospect. Ash had promised that he would take Will Walton up to London with him and leave me at the Beacon to oversee things for a while, so that Jane and I could settle in together. But I also wanted to see Bethany safe before that.

Ash and I agreed that the ambivalences within that Kensington household were such that Bethany's quality of life could only depreciate. What may have begun as an honourable post and an artistic leg up for this young woman, had now become a cat and mouse game in which she could only be toyed with and made more miserable. We pondered how she might be released from her employer's clutches. The first movement had to come from her, as Ash remarked, 'When she is ready to depart, we will be ready for her.'

The weather had grown very much warmer and I wondered how Bethany would be dressed when we next saw her. Everywhere on London streets, women were already showing bare arms and wearing sandals.

Her third appointment dawned and Bethany was late arriving. We saw her decant from the taxi. She had gone into summer creams and whites, though still affecting her Thirties style, with a close-fitting straw hat and white crochet cotton gloves.

Breathlessly, she tottered into the room on heeled shoes, 'I'm so sorry to be late. Madame made it very difficult for me to leave today.'

'But it's your day off,' I pointed out, noting that she had a little more colour today.

'Indeed, but she was difficult to settle today. She demanded that I stay, but I said I had to run some errands and caught the first taxi I could. – I think she suspects something…'

'What has been happening?' Ash asked.

'She was very fussy after the salon. She kept asking about how I knew you and was very… rude about you both. Once she takes against someone, she can be very unpleasant.'

'Has she been unpleasant to you?'

'Just very demanding. I hardly have a minute's peace: she goes on and on at me.' Even now, she spoke without blame, and I wondered how long it would be before Bethany decided she had had enough. 'But tell me, what did you find? I've been longing to know,' she pleaded. She reached into her bag to return my divining rods.

'Thank you. Gaston's room yielded what we might expect: someone with a drug habit and some possibly illegal doings. Your room had a couple of small anomalies but I dealt with those,' I assured her. 'I reconsecrated it - and no, I found no more gifts of tobacco. Ash had the stuff analyzed.'

'Yes, the substance was basically chimó - the kind of tobacco that many people use daily in Venezuela, but the Tonkin Bean flavouring was masking a herb used by native Afro-Columbian witches to induce states of fear.'

Looking at Ash for support, I said, as neutrally as possible, 'There was more of the stuff in Gaston's room. Frankly, it is not the house that is the problem so much as those living in it.'

Ash said, 'I agree with Jack. Gaston, for whatever reason, has clearly wanted to scare you away by supernatural means, while Madame seems to be even more determined to keep you closer. You have a decision before you… do you stay and continue to be pulled between these two people, or do you leave?'

Faced with the truth about her fearful dreams, Bethany was about to open her mouth when another taxi drew up outside with a screech. Out of it tumbled Gaston, who belted down into the area and rang the bell over and over, until Maggie went to open to him. Her loud protestations were of no avail, as Gaston fell into the consulting room, tearing for a fight. He was pouring with sweat in a striped blazer, marching towards us in a ridiculously melodramatic way, 'So, this is what you get up to on your day off!' he accused Bethany, who shrank fearfully back. Sneeringly, he said, 'Consulting with the magician and his big fairy. Wait till Madame hears of this!'

Ash rose, 'Mr Lucas, you are interrupting a private consultation, and I must kindly ask you to leave.'

Gouts of sweat were running down Gaston's face and neck, he was so worked up. While I doubted he could do much physical damage, other than to himself, the effect upon Bethany was unmistakable as he reached towards her, 'You will come home with me this instant and leave these charlatans!'

Ash was saying, 'Miss Miller is an adult, here at her own behest, and not under your charge,' when Bethany began screaming loudly in utter horror as Gaston laid his sweaty, hairy hand upon her shoulder, as her fearful dreams became a reality with his touch.

Maggie ran into the room, asking if she should call the police.

Reaching under Gaston's right forearm, I jerked it upwards behind him, so that Bethany fell forward into Ash's arms, while I pulled the intruder wriggling and swearing backwards towards the door. He threshed about a good deal, unable to do anything much while I exerted force, using the kind of armlock I've occasionally had to use on violent mental patients: it does no harm, but is effective for all that. But his flailing left arm struck the standing mirror on the far desk, sending it crashing to the ground in a thousand splinters.

Gaston was conducted off the premises, shouting and carrying on all the way up the steps, to be deposited ignominiously on the pavement. Maggie came up behind me, 'I am going to call the police! I never saw the like,' she said, marching down the basement steps in high dudgeon.

I called after her, 'Leave it for a moment, Maggie! Ash may not want the police involved, for the young woman's sake.'

I stayed on the steps to ensure that Gaston departed, watching him stagger down the street, turning into New Cavendish Street where he hailed a taxi.

While Maggie went to fetch the dustpan and brush to sweep up the shards of mirror, Ash attended to Bethany, dosing a water glass with rescue remedy which she meekly sipped between hiccupping sobs. He also drew the white cashmere shawl from the couch around her shoulders, since she had begun to shiver in shock, and asked me to fetch her some hot tea, 'It's alright, Bethany, he's gone.'

With her face in her hands, she was saying over and over, with great determination, 'I cannot stay in that house!'

My gaze met Ash's over her head: Gaston had forced the issue for us, and now we could pick up the pieces, for he had broken her dream. I heartily prayed that the spell was broken along with the mirror and that, like a latter-day Lady of Shalott, she might be free at last.

Bethany drank the tea biddably and then looked up, fearfully, 'I don't really have to go back, do I?'

Ash knelt in front of her, looking into her eyes, assuring her, 'You never have to go back there again. Whatever you want to do now, Jack and I will help you. I'm going to ask Maggie to cancel our afternoon appointments, and we will sort it out, unless you have anyone else who can help you?'

'No. But all m-my things are in that house!' she wailed.

'We will get them back, but for the moment, you are under our care. Would you like to speak to your parents?'

She nodded, but her lip trembled again, 'But I don't know where they are!... Somewhere in Germany, I think.' She reached for her handbag and drew out a picture postcard of Cologne, 'It doesn't say where they are going next.'

'Well, that decides it! You are going to come with us to my house in the country and rest up. We will track down your parents and get your things back. In the meantime, you can relax. Maggie will stay here with you in the flat upstairs where you can rest, and Jack and I will go to your house to fetch your things.'

She gave us her keys, enumerating what she needed, 'My suitcases are under the bed, and my laptop in the second drawer of the chest.'

She also wrote a letter to Madame for us to take, giving notice and asking for the wages due to her. 'She will hate me forever,' she said, miserably. 'I've been there for her every day for over three years.'

'"Better a dish of herbs than a stalled ox within,"' I quoted quietly. 'Whatever love has been lost, remember that Madame ceased to respect you a long while ago.'

Maggie took Bethany up the flat and settled her down, while Ash and I planned our campaign.

'Look, Ash, I've no doubt we will get in, thanks to these keys, but we will not go unnoticed, what with the butler and Lucas. What kind of case do we have if they call the police?'

'We have Bethany's authority to obtain her things and, as her medical advisors, we are acting *in loco parentis*. Besides which, if they create, I have something up my sleeve that will draw the flack away from Bethany and ourselves.'

'What?'

'Wait and see,' he grinned. 'You will enjoy it.'

I wasn't so sure.

In the end, we knocked on Madame's door, announcing ourselves to the butler, who had clearly been primed to expect us, showing us straight into the dark ground floor front room where Madame sat, with Gaston at her side. She glowered in the gloom as Gaston said, in French, 'I told you that they would come!' We were not offered a seat.

Drawing herself up, La Zakharova set both hands upon the knob of her jeweled cane, regarding us with hostility, 'I am surprised that you have the gall to darken my door again, after your deceit at the salon. Gaston tells me that you have been beating him up.' Looking me up and down, she continued, 'I hope your bully boy does not intend to wreak more violence in my house?'

Ash laid a restraining hand on my arm, as I leapt to refute this, saying to her, 'Merely removing him from our premises, Madame, where he had burst into a private consultation. I believe your friend is not injured.'

'His pride is perhaps more bruised than his body,' she said, smilingly. In a more glacial tone, 'But I want to know what you have done with my companion. Where is she?'

Ash presented her with Bethany's letter of resignation. Gaston slit it for her with a knife he took from his pocket, taking care to make sure I noted the sharpness of his blade with his wolfish smile.

Madame raised a magnifying glass to the letter, scanning down the page, then looking up at Ash, 'And how do I know she has not written this under your dictation?'

'Bethany wrote that letter herself, I assure you, Madame. We have merely come to fetch away her things on her behalf. Her outstanding wages can be sent to her via my Harley Street address, unless you want to write her a cheque now for us to take. If they are not received, then I daresay that her parents will take the matter further.'

She cast her eyes, 'Her parents?' She cackled ironically, 'Don't expect much help from that quarter! I took that ungrateful wretch off their hands. She deserves nothing. I am minded to keep her things here in lieu of her services, running out on me like that!'

Ash appeared to expect this response. Removing a slim piece of paper from his inside pocket, he held it teasingly before her, saying, 'In that case, you may like to know what has been going on under your very nose. Bethany has given you excellent and dedicated service, as you know, which is more than can be said for Mr Lucas whom you have let into the heart of your home. He has gone behind your back in a manner that proves him to be both a thief and a deceiver.'

Ah! so it was gloves off, at last!

Madame turned her saurian neck towards Gaston, 'What is this?' She narrowed her eyes at him, then back to Ash, 'Of what are you accusing him?'

Ash unfolded the paper, reading aloud, 'Sold to D'Arcy Fine Art, Pimlico Rd on the 9th May: 15 prints from the *Paris Printemps* series, 7 preparatory sketches for *Sous Les Saules de Marie-le-Courbière*, and 2 canvases in oils of *December Woman* and *Undine Verte*. – The receipt is addressed to Gaston Lucas, and the sum given to him for these purchases by the gallery is £403,685.'

Ash handed her the receipt, but her hands would not or could not grasp it. The paper fell to her lap and thence to the floor. Lifting her jeweled cane, she brought it down, spiking the receipt with the ferrule. Turning on Gaston with a voice that would have made strong men blench, she shrieked, 'You sold my *Undine Vert*?'

Rising to her feet, she lifted the cane and began to belabor Gaston's shoulders. He brayed in alarm, like a recalcitrant donkey, trying to ward off the blows. Ash indicated that I should start on the packing upstairs.

I burst out of the room, having to skirt round the butler and the two maids who had been pressed to the door listening in horrid fascination, and ran upstairs, throwing things into Bethany's cases as quickly as might be. I tipped the spill of her jewelry into a corner of the case and looked around again. I had everything stashed as best I could, except for the photos on the cork-board. In the end I wrenched the whole pin-board bodily off the wall, tucking it under my arm, and ran back downstairs where Ash was administering first aid to the unfortunate Gaston, now prone on the floor.

Madame had already called the police, so we cut short our farewells and fled, chucking the keys back through the open front door into the house once we were clear. Throwing ourselves into a taxi, I breathed, 'Whoever would have thought the old dame had that much strength! Was he much injured?'

'Just a few bruises, and a cut to the chin where she landed one on his face, but he will live. She will prosecute him for theft and he will undoubtedly bring a cross-prosecution of GBH, but I would not like to be the jury that had to decide on that verdict, I have to say. She is over 80, after all!'

'What about us?'

'Oh, I don't think we will figure very high in the scale of things.'

'How did you know about the stolen prints?'

'Well, we both heard Bethany's suspicions. I thought I would enquire whether any substantial amount of Zhakarova's art had recently come onto the market. The auction houses revealed that *D'Arcy Fine Art* had recently moved on some recent acquisitions, and that *Undine Verte* was up for auction. Since it was one of her signature paintings, I thought it unlikely that she would have parted with it so readily, so I told them my suspicions. It was Stephen Venables who got me the photocopy of the receipt – in return for a small donation towards his retirement fund. I think he was already suspicious of Gaston and had his own axe to grind with Madame...'

It wasn't until after we had driven Bethany down to the Beacon, that I thought to ask Ash about the night of the salon, 'What did you write on the threshold of Madame's house that night?'

'Just a piece of medieval folk magic, no more. I drew a sigil that helps expel evil from a house.'

'Well, that certainly worked!'

Bethany stayed with us for a week while we helped her recover from the effects of her servitude. Her parents were finally located in Florence where they had gone for a second honeymoon, coming on to collect their daughter on the way back to Maine. We did not find them particularly responsible, for they seemed to have had towards their daughter the attitude of turtles to their eggs, but even they could see that she needed time to leech out the unhealthy influences of Madame and her thieving relative.

For myself, there was nothing left but to help Jane clear out of her flat in Manchester, and bring her triumphantly home to the Beacon where she could begin to help us in our work. We brought out the last of her boxes, having to put them on the back seat, as the boot was full. That was when I noticed, 'All that sitting down and studying has done you no good at all. We'll soon get the extra weight off with a few forays up Hartsworth Beacon.'

'Well, Jack, it's going to take a few months longer than that, I'm afraid...' She had the most peculiar look on her face. Densely, I could not read it, so she obligingly turned sideways.

'Oh my God! Jane, you're pregnant!'

'Well spotted, doctor! Yep, those were some very productive Easter holidays, Jack! Looks like we're going to have a little Capricorn or an Aquarius!'

I wrapped her in my arms, 'I don't care what our baby is, as long you are both ok.'

I wondered how the news would be welcomed at the Beacon, but there was nothing to worry about. Wendy and Gillespie were delighted: they didn't see their own grandchildren as often as they'd like, since their son and daughter in law had emigrated to Canada. Ash just beamed and was not at all put out that our future plans for staffing the Beacon needed to be adjusted.

Six weeks later, we were all at breakfast when the postman brought a letter for Wendy from her sister in Kent. As she opened the envelope a cutting fell out. Unfolding it, she read down with growing incredulity, exclaiming, 'I don't believe it!' Holding it out to us, with eyebrows raised, 'And *what* is the meaning of this?'

The cutting was headed *The Tatler*, and already several weeks out of date. It was the Marti Gee column, describing our eventful evening at Zakharova's salon, and in the middle, a photo – taken by what means I know not – were Ash and myself, caught in a tight clinch, with the heading 'Mysterious Companions at Elizaveta Zakharova's Salon.'

I groaned, 'Tagged for eternity!'

Ash glanced at it, 'It's quite a good likeness of you, Jack!'

Jane snatched it from his hands and read the article aloud in an increasingly gleeful voice, 'Who *are* these mysterious companions who graced Madame's salon *ce soir*? We were entertained to a sparkling rendition of early 20th century French piano repertoire, played by the white haired, enigmatic man in the stylish suit, while La Zakharova evidently warmed to his more macho companion...'

I splurted out my coffee, 'Macho! I'll give that spectacled worm macho!'

Turning to me, Jane said sweetly, 'So this is what you get up to in my absence! I had no idea you also batted for the other team, Jack, you never said!'

Ash keeping a dead pan face assured her, 'It's alright, Jane, he was very gentle with me!'

I swiped him over the head with a rolled-up copy of the *South Downs Gazette* while Jane read on, 'A certain pair of artistic twins found the pair as delectably mysterious as myself, and we await the birth of their next new creation. What wonders might they spawn together? Unfortunately, the gorgeous twosome ran away early, like a pair of naughty Cinderellas, leaving not even a slipper behind.'

'Thank God for that!' I proclaimed. 'At least he didn't get our names!'

Ash peered at the article again, 'I'm afraid we will not be too difficult to identify. It's a good likeness.'

I responded, 'Well, the next person to call me Ash's companion is going to be thumped good and proper, I give notice.'

As for the real companion of this story: a lovely photograph of Bethany helping to sail a windjammer off the coast of Maine arrived with a letter of thanks from her in due course. It was the first time I'd ever seen her in trousers. At last, she looked like herself, and not some pallid imitation of Virginia Woolf: a happy windblown young woman with the whole world before her. As for Gaston, he was finally sent down for theft of Madame's pictures, for illicit international art dealing, other fraudulent dealings. I believe he was finally extradited to France, as Britain didn't wish to have the keeping of him. As for Madame, I imagined her growing into increasingly embittered and malevolent old age, without the youthful energies of her companion to revitalize her.

Caitlín Matthews

Case 7: THE MASK OF ANTIMONY

I will not jump with common spirits, And rank me with the barbarous multitudes.
William Shakespeare – *The Merchant of Venice* 2.9

Shakespeare once observed that all the world was a stage and all its men and women merely players, and so it sometimes appears, but when the play begins to take over your very life …? I have noticed that, in the world of the theatre, there are actors who become obsessively attached to one particular rôle. Whenever this part comes up for audition, actors will swarm out of the woodwork, sometimes even out of retirement, to read for it in the hope that they will have another crack of the whip at playing Richard II, or whoever it is, despite being well over the hill.

Of course, some parts can only be played in the prime of life: so it is a lucky actor who gets offered King Lear when he's in his forties or fifties, and an unlucky one who gets to play it when he's in his seventies, since Lear is one of those parts that requires the endurance and stamina of a man in his prime. I once saw the great Angus McPhee play Lear back in 1993 at the age of 72: it was brilliantly and poignantly portrayed, but utterly exhausting, as I observed when I passed the stage door just as McPhee left the theatre on that dark night. A companion had to hold him up as they proceeded down the half-timbered streets of Stratford-on-Avon to his rooms. It was humbling to see the cost of playing so massive a role upon so great an actor.

The actor who came to the Harley St consulting room that morning looked in somewhat worse shape than had McPhee. Martin Napier, favourite of many a romantic and historical tv series, and renowned for his classical stage work, was a man of about 45 years. But something had gone badly wrong. His powerful voice sounded strained, 'I've had the damnedest run of bad luck. My old dresser knew about you from when you helped Daphne Weir* with her troubles a while back, so I thought I'd give you a try.'

'Tell us about it,' Ash asked.

We both already knew something of Martin's fortunes because his face had been recently plastered all over the media. In an attempt to keep up his finances, he had agreed to play Djon Djago, one of the major characters in *Marscape*, a space-epic that had bombed spectacularly at the box-office due to poor direction and a shaky script. Pleased to have acquired a stable of classical British actors, the US creators of the film had over-estimated their projects's

*See *The Trouble with Daphne Weir* in *Diary of a Soul Doctor*.

success in a publicity campaign that saw billboards on the approach to all major cities, posters on the sides of buses, and phone boxes, and a general sense of overkill that made you want to avoid the whole thing. The film company were now in disarray, and overproduction of the model spaceships and characters from the film had resulted in most of these figures being reduced in supermarket aisles across the world.

A very jaded Martin remarked, 'Yes. There's nothing worse than seeing figures of yourself in a cut-price box on the reject shelf. There're enough Djon Djagos to melt down into plastic buckets for every person in China, I imagine. They'd be more useful, frankly! - No, while that humiliation ranks alongside the farcical tomato sauce adverts I did straight out of drama school, that's not the reason I've come to see you.'

He accepted another cup of tea from the pot, 'All this has come about because of a part that I've been trying to get for some years. I don't know why, but this play has haunted me since I was a schoolboy when I first studied it.'

The part was that of Nevio, the hero of the Jacobean Revenger tragedy, *The Masque of Antimony*, by a little-known playwright, Ralph de Lacy. Bastard son of Gilbert de Lacy, lesser scion of the Earls of Ulster, Ralph had grubbed a living as a minor poet and playwright in the early days of James I's Stuart court in Whitehall. Sent down from Oxford for philandering, de Lacy was a troubled man whose single claim to fame was this one play, which had been seldom reprised since. The play dealt with the attempts of Nevio to alchemically create a goddess from the body of an enchanted serving girl, Belinda, and install her as his mistress, in a kind of ghastly parody of Pygmalion, foreshadowing Mary Shelley's *Frankenstein* by a good few centuries, while echoing elements of Marlow's conjuration of Helen of Troy from *Dr Faustus*. It must have pandered precisely to King James' twin terrors of women and the supernatural, though it did not carry the charge of Shakespeare's *Macbeth*, nor yet the incantatory verse of Marlow's work. It was a rare curiosity, but one desired by Martin above all things.

Martin told us, 'I finally auditioned for the part of Nevio and got it, without contest, despite *Marscapes* bombing so badly. We are part-way through rehearsals now, and the director, Anthony Bournville, thinks it will be the best Nevio ever seen. *The Masque of Antimony* is due to play for 7 weeks as part of the National's Restoration Season but, though it's not opened yet, my life has gone down the tubes big time!'

'What's happened?' I asked

'Flavia, my wife of fourteen years, has left me. We've been pals since drama school and no-one who saw us together would ever believe we could part. I was just starting rehearsals at the National when she walked out on me – and it was not for someone else either!' he said, defensively.

'What reason did she give?' Ash asked softly.

'That she couldn't bear to be in the same bed as me.' He wept in bewilderment, 'My lovely girl gone! It's been hell, I tell you.'

After a silent interval of tea-pot filling and furtive mopping of tears, Ash asked, 'Why do you think the play is the cause of this break-up?'

Martin's eyes seemed to glaze over and a different character began to look out from them, haughty and self-satisfied. Ash and I exchanged glances. This strange overlay soon melted away, and his sad eyes refocused upon us, 'I suppose it's an unlucky part, like the Thane in the Scottish play.'

Superstitious actors are two a penny, but this seemed a highly unlikely reason to me.

Ash started with the obvious, 'Tell us, what is it about the part and the play that draws you?'

Martin gazed into the middle distance, head on one side, unconsciously modelling that handsome countenance to us in profile, or perhaps, as an actor, he couldn't help himself? Tossing back his famous drooping quiff of brown hair, he finally said, 'I was drawn to the sheer audacity of Nevio – I mean, trying to conjure a goddess out of a serving girl! Making a silk purse out of a sow's ear, so to speak....' He ran on, eulogising the detestable character of Nevio.

I was glad that neither Jane nor Wendy were in the room to hear such casual male superiority, but Ash was onto it, 'Could it be that the character's attitudes have begun to overlay your own, within your relationship?'

Martin blanked, then bit his lip, 'Oh! You know, I hadn't even thought about that... Yes, I suppose it does happen sometimes with parts ... but Flavia is an actor herself, she knows what it is to carry a part – it does kind of butt into your life sometimes. She would surely have known to make allowances for that,' he ended, doubtfully.

Living with a cross between Dr Faustus and Dr Frankenstein might have proved the last straw for his wife, I privately thought.

'How do you feel in yourself when you are in that part – I mean your day-to-day sense of who you are?'

Martin gave Ash an old-fashioned look, 'Are you implying that Nevio is taking me over?'

'Well, is he?' Ash kept his voice in neutral.

Again, the change overcame Martin, 'As it happens, I have never felt so good. It's as if I could go anywhere, do anything. I feel right up there, on form, just the ticket.' This buoyant arrogance opened a sudden window onto Nevio at his most triumphantly overbearing: like Shakespeare's Richard III on speed. This sat incongruously beside Martin's protestations of bad luck.

There seemed nowhere else to go after this, as the interview kept being cross-tracked by Nevio, which made it difficult to clarify what Martin himself felt about things, but we did due diligence in making a list of the kinds of bad luck Martin felt he had inherited as a result of his role. We managed to get a basic client history out of him, and made a fresh appointment to see him in a few days, after we had done some more research.

'What kind of man gets a kick out of playing a character who is a first-class rogue, without a shred of humanity?' I asked, unable to understand his compulsion.

Ash looked up from his note-taking, 'Oh, quite a few actors love parts like this! Think about it, Jack! The ability to do what you like, how you like, and with whom you like? I would guess that Mr Napier has led a rather more circumscribed life than Nevio, wouldn't you? Law-abiding, honest, responsible, in the main.'

'I don't know,' I scowled, 'But when it comes to throwing off restraint, you can get much the same effect after dementia sets in, and that's not a pretty sight, either.' I mentally tidied away past visions of elderly people roaming naked through the ward, after all normal self-restraint had been cast off. 'I feel sorry for his wife, personally.'

'It might be useful to have a word with her, if we are able. To get some sense of what she experienced.'

'We're not opening a side-line in marriage guidance now, are we?'

He grinned, 'No, but I imagine that much *superbia* and self-dereliction in a spouse would be cause enough for separation. I just have the feeling that he will be needing her support if he is to come back after this run.'

'I wonder how the rest of the cast is managing?'

Ash nodded, 'I was wondering that too. His Belinda needs to be a thick-skinned actor, for sure!'

'If he is being taken over by this character, is he really safe to be loose on the streets?'

'Worrying about the Jekyll and Hyde effect? I would like to attend some rehearsals to judge better what is going on at closer hand. Let's do the research first! If I see the next client alone, will you go to the London Library and look up the *Masque of Antimony*, and we'll see? It's not a play I know at all well. Whatever clues lie in the text itself it would be good to be fore-armed before the next session.'

So, with Ash's London Library ticket in my pocket, I took the bus to

Piccadilly, penetrating its august walls to gain more information for our quest. The librarian finally came back with the volume that I needed, *Minor Jacobean Playwrights* by Kendrick Allen. I riffled through and found *the Masque of Antimony*, where I got the gist of the story. I was interested to see that the play had been created from the remains of an earlier masque, one designed by Inigo Jones, and was much admired by James I's queen, Anne of Denmark, who had played the part of Juno in it. De Lacy's play still retained many elements of his original masque, making it a kind of musical play, with a chorus acting as the narrator, and a *deus ex machina* of gods who occasionally look in upon the scene. The surviving plans of the masque looked impressive, with grandiloquent sets and costumes. In his analysis, Allen commented that the gods took a more backseat role in the play than they had in the masque. I noticed that in the costume designs for the masque, Nevio was played in a sequence of half-masks that changed as the action went on, warping his once-handsome face into the sneer of pride, then lechery, finally ending in a rictus of fantastic ruin.

I riffled through the pages of the tightly bound green volume that had landed at my reading station. The key scene was soon found. Having first inveigled the serving girl, Belinda, into his bed, Nevio then goes on to attempt his enchantment; rendering her compliant to become the embodiment of Venus.

> 'BELINDA: What place is this? So baleful and so dark?
> O Master, leave me yet one candle's spark!
>
> NEVIO: (*kindling a light and holding it aloft*)
> My cell 'tis, lady; where, instead of masks,
> Music, tilts, tourneys, and such court-like shows,
> The hollow murmur of the checkless winds
> Shall groan again, whilst the unquiet sea
> Shakes the whole rock with foamy battery.
> There, usherless, the airs come in and out;
> The rheumy vault will force your eyes to weep,
> Whilst you behold true desolation.
> A rocky barrenness shall pierce your eyes;
> Where all at once one reaches, where he stands,
> With brows the roof, both walls with both his hands,
> A giant, fathomless as Saturn, come to break the bands.
>
> BELINDA: What vastness reaches for my very soul?
> I sink down. I am emptied out.... Ah, Jesu save!.....

BELINDA *sleeps. The curtain is drawn upon her.*

NEVIO. Sit now, Delight, my spaniel; rouse not up,
Lest that the lady take offence at your alarm,
While I call forth the substance of my charm.
Come, wand of art! Now waken necromancers!
Scotus who knew, yet did not know, the dark;
Antick Virgil, he who brast the bounds of death,
Bringing Anchises to his sorrowing son;
And all ye panoply of hell who lurk below,
Arise, arise! Upon the form of this ignoble flesh,
I paint. O spirit of Antimony,
Make here your best device: mask well,
And hold in darkness this *grogram* girl. (*a cheap scratchy fabric*)
Just as the wolfsbane purifies the gold,
Slake back my minion; here fix upon
Her frame the *sarcenet* of Venus. (*a fine silk fabric*)
Make her a beauty, terrible to behold!

Music sounds. NEVIO pulls back the curtain, disclosing Belinda attir'd as Venus.

BELINDA: What mortal orisons disclose
The daylight to my waking eyes? Ah, magister,
How are you shaped for sports venereal?
Every pleasure now to you be op'd.

NEVIO: O mistress *anadyomene*, (*risen from the sea*)
From Saturn's loss, our age's gain arise!
Sweet alchemy! Time, place and blood,
How fit you close together! Heaven's tones
Strike not such music to immortal souls
As your accordance sweets my heart withal.'

There followed what can only be described as a chorus of satyrs inciting Nevio to serve Venus in the most physical way. After engaging in an orgy, portrayed as a dance, Nevio delves into much darker magic; fuelled by his alchemical experiments, which also give him untold wealth, he meddles in the lives of his dependents, to their ruin, murders his nephew for a slight that his brother put upon him, and attempts to overthrow the Venetian state by making alliance with Ottoman forces, as he drifts from being human into a fantasy figure of his former self. His belief in his own powers, boosted by Venus, finally cause him to overstep all discretion where, to prove his abilities, he causes the goods for sale on the Rialto to rise up, as if inspirited too, so that bolts of cloth fill with wind and walk about as invisible forms, embodying his spirits. Thus, he is unmasked as a necromancer in public.

Nevio's moralistic brother, Juliano, whose son was murdered by Nevio, then calls upon the Doge of Venice to restrain him from any further magic or treachery, and Nevio is finally run to earth in his alchemical cell, while Belinda, who is brought into sanctuary of a near-by church, for her own protection, breaks down into madness and jumps into the canal. Nevio dies from being struck by a bolt of lightning, after having being confined in the ruins of a pagan temple where he is awaiting execution. It was all desperate stuff, hardly anything to uplift or entertain in any way, unless you like your drama over the top while a chorus sings you to ruination. It was simply the story of man far-gone in hubris who, without restraint or humanity, makes hay with whatever falls in his path.

His death speech was by far the most anthologized of the whole play:

NEVIO: This now my cell, hard by the reverent ruins
Of a once glorious temple, rear'd to Jove,
Whose very rubbish (like the pitied fall
Of virtue most unfortunate) yet bears
A deathless majesty, though now quite ras'd,
Hurl'd down by wrath and lust of impious kings,
So that, where holy Flamens wont to sing
Sweet hymns to heaven, there the daw and crow,
The ill-voic'd raven, and still chattering pye,
Send forth ungrateful sounds and loathsome filth;
Where statues and Jove's act were skilfully limn'd,
Boys with black coals draw the veil'd parts of nature
And lecherous actions of imagined lust;
Where tombs and beauteous urns of well-dead men
Stood in assured rest, the shepherd now
Unloads his belly, corruption most abhorr'd,
Mingling itself with their renowned ashes:
There once a charnel house, now a vast cave,
Over whose brow a pale and untrod grove

Throws out her heavy shade, the mouth thick arm
Of darkness yew, sunproof, for ever choak'd;
Within, rest barren darkness, fruitless drought,
Pines in eternal night; the steam of hell
Yields not so lazy air; here, now, my cell,
And ever through the ruin'd casement fly
Jove's outrag'd lightnings down. Strike me, immortal gods!
From hence my shivering soul give up to thee,
Who has the sun enslav'd and every virtue
Bent to tawdry trinkets.

And so, Nevio dies, stricken by lightning - not even half repentant - to be discovered by his erstwhile pet spaniel, Delight, who licks his face while everyone else onstage derides his master as an apostate villain, and the chorus sing him off to Hades. I made a detailed outline of the plot, and then asked the librarian for some photocopies of a few pages, taking them back to Ash who pursued them with some alarm.

'A deeply-dyed villain indeed!' was his response, as he laid aside the last page.

'The only character who has anything pleasant to say about Nevio is Silvio, his erstwhile drinking companion.' I read, '"His appetite is as insatiable as the grave: as far from any content as from heaven. His highest delight is to procure others' vexation, and therein he thinks he truly serves heaven; for 'tis his position, whosoever in this earth can be contented is a slave and damned; therefore, does he afflict all in that to which they are most affected. The elements struggle within him; his own soul is at variance within herself; his speech is halter-worthy at all hours. I like him..."'

'A loveable rogue fit only for the stage?'

I made a face. 'Undoubtedly! ... Oh, I know what I was going to ask you, what exactly is antimony in the context of this play?'

Ash took down an encyclopaedia of alchemy from his shelves, opening to the page. I could see that the symbol of antimony written like so:

'But isn't that the sign for Venus?' I protested.

'When at this angle, it becomes the emblem for antimony, the very antithesis of Venus.'

The entry read: *'Lupus metallorum*: The grey wolf or stibnite, used to purify gold. As the sulphur in the antimony sulphide bonds to the metals alloyed with the gold, these form a slag which can be removed. The gold remains dissolved in the metallic antimony, which can be boiled off to leave the purified gold.'

He continued, 'The Egyptians used a compound of antimony, stibium, for eye-make up, or *kohl*, and alchemists used or made different compounds of it in their experiments. The implication is that's how Belinda is changed in the play, I imagine, by the application of magical make-up. Antimony has a lot of different forms. The ore of antimony is bright and silvery; but it was often depicted as a wolf devouring a king, a symbol of its voracious attack on other metals in the alchemical emblems.' He opened out one of the folded illustrations from the alchemy book, to show me.

'It's the first of the *Twelve Keys of Basil Valentinus* by Michael Maier from 1618, so it's pretty much contemporary with the Masque. You can see how the king is devoured by the wolf in the foreground – it was supposed to show how antimony devours, or rather, unites with all metals except gold. In the background, the King, having been purified, walks away hale and hearty, while the wolf is consumed by fire. When applied to gold, antimony makes it look like silver, and is said to be purified by it, which is why the gold is symbolised by the king in this image. Of course, any actual ingestion of antimony would make you very sick indeed, and cause death, if you had enough of it.'

'Umm! I remember my chemistry well enough. Am I right in thinking that physicians used to actually prescribe antimony? I have a half-memory of something…a pill made of antimony that you swallowed, and reused, after judicious cleansing…?' I thought I'd seen one in the Welcome Collection of medical oddities.

Ash nodded, 'Yes, also some households kept a cup made of metallic antimony in which you were supposed to put Moselle wine overnight, to drink in the morning, to help you purge, or recover from any over-eating.' He made a face, 'I would prefer my Moselle in a clear glass, please, if you are offering me any!'

I peered down at the king being devoured by a wolf in the engraving, 'So, what are we to do about our friend? Are we going to need a magic pill to cure him of Nevio?'

'I think we can say that Nevio is under the influence of antimony in that play, his humanity eaten away, but whether Martin will be able to walk off as blithely as the king in this picture, I am not so sure. We need to learn more.'

The next appointment for Martin Napier came around, but he phoned the night before to say he could not make it, and could we instead come to a rehearsal, when he could talk to us in the break? It took a lot of moving of appointments, but we did so. The rehearsal room was right the over in Canning Town in the East End. It turned out to be a converted factory, where the brick walls were unplastered, and the ceiling resembled an aircraft hangar.

In the underheated hall, a thin, harassed woman was trying to choreograph a scene where the full panoply of the masque had to be employed. A line of eight characters muffled in their outdoor clothes, was sitting on high bar-stools as Martin mingled with a group of dancing masquers, all doing a complex dance. The pianist had to keep playing over the same phrase of music, to the thin woman's exasperation, 'From the top again. Starting positions!' she cried, as everyone slumped their shoulders and scurried to regroup.

Antony Bournville spotted us at the door, striding over to us in high boots, and overcoat, 'Are you Martin's guests? Please take seats over here.' His breath hung in the cold air.

He sat down himself, 'God know why I decided to do this thing! I must have been mad. – I hope you will be discreet, you know we don't usually have previews of rehearsals?'

'We shall be as silent as the grave,' Ash assured him. 'Which scene are you doing today?'

Bournville flapped a script at us, 'See for yourselves. Whether we'll ever be able to equal the elegance of Inigo Jones' drawings, I've no idea, but props and costume say it's possible.' Looking over at the actors learning their moves, he raised his extensive eyebrows, 'When everyone has worked out their right from their left foot, that is…'

It certainly helped to read what was not quite yet represented before us:

'The cornets are winded, and the travers that is drawn before the masquers sinkes downe. The whole shewe presently appereereth: the syde of a steepely assending wood, on the top of which in a fayre oak, sits a goulden eagle, under whose wings sitt in eight several thrones, the eight masquers with wisards like stares, their helmes like Mercyrye's, with fayre plumes of carnation and white, in antique doublets imbrodered with stares. They sing:

Audiacious night makes bold the lip,
Now all court chaster pleasure,
Whilst to Apollo's harp you trip,
And tread the gracing measure.
Now meets, now break, then fain a warlike sally,
So Venus' sports, and so the gods may dally.'

The set-dressing of a magic curtain behind which sit a chorus of demi-gods in starry costumes might clearly raise the ante a little, in terms of audience beguilement, but it was presently far removed from the chilly, fidgeting star-beings on their bar-stools swinging their idle legs before us, as the company tried and kept failing to dance the 'gracing measure.'

We particularly observed Martin, while the choreographer did her best on a chill morning with actors unused to the conventions of Jacobean dance. He seemed to be unremarkably himself while he was learning this dance routine, sharing the frustrations of the others. Since Martin's own interaction with the dance was but brief, Bournville called him and a boy actor away into a side room, inviting us to observe. For our benefit, he set the scene, 'So this scene is set in a churchyard at night, where Nevio has set up a meeting with his nephew.

You have to imagine dim blue lighting, and an open trap for a newly-dug grave, stage front'. He threw down his overcoat to mark the grave. Raising his voice, Bournville called, 'And in comes Julio…'

Martin, with a stage dagger thrust in his belt started pacing up and down as Damien Price stepped in. He was a child actor with a long acting career behind him, having played the cheeky son in a long-running family comedy on tv since he was six. He was now twelve. With round innocent face turned up to greet his uncle, his clear unbroken voice rang out,

'Uncle Nevio, are you here, I'faith?
Why do you frown? Indeed, my mother said
I should call you uncle, that she did!
Buss me, good uncle. It is the truth,
I love you better than my father, indeed.'

Martin stepped up to kiss him, with an aside,

'Thy father? Gracious, O bounteous heaven,
I do adore thy justice! He comes into my hands,
So that my quittance might be vindicate!

In winsome tones, young Julio tried his uncle again:

'Truth, since my mother died, I loved you best.
Something hath anger'd you: pray you, look merrily.'

To the audience, Nevio spoke sarcastically,

'I will laugh, and dimple my thin cheek
With capering joy!'

Then turning to the child with enforced cheer said,

'Chuck, my heart doth leap
To grasp thy bosom.'

Yet, while embracing his nephew, he spoke to himself,

'Time, place, and blood, how fit you close together!'

Then raising his voice, holding the child away from him, said with sickly sweetness,

'Heaven's tones
Strike not such music to immortal souls,
As your accordance sweets my breast withal!'

Then, drawing the boy back again to his chest, Nevio went on, speaking to himself, while running his hands across the boy's back. Something was definitively changing, for a creepy metallic cadence shivered Martin's voice, as if he were talking with a raised soft palate,

'O that I knew which joint, which side, which limb
Were father all, and had no mother in it;
That I might rip it vein by vein, and carve revenge
In bleeding traces.'

Julio, who had tried to wriggle away from his uncle embrace, then cried out, in authentic fear,

'O God, you'll hurt me! For my mother's sake,
Pray you don't hurt me! An you kill me,
I will tell my father...'

At this point, even Bournville was beginning to be alarmed, as Martin's Nevio seemed possessed of a darker spirit than even the script belied,

'Come pretty tender child,
It is not thee I hate, or thee I kill.'

Damien took several steps backwards, with real terror in his eyes, and we rose to our feet, for what was happening before us was beyond acting now. Martin did not stop. Rather the icy distain of Nevio poured venomously out of him. He closed on Damien with,

'Thy father's blood that flowers within thy veins,
Is it I loath; but, being his, thus, thus,
And thus, I'll punch it out.'

In this speech, Nevio was supposed to strike Julio with his stage poignard several times, but Martin was using his fist against the boy, and we all made a rush at him. Bournville and I restrained him, while Ash drew Damien, bawling his head off, out from under him.

'What's got into you? Are you alright, Damien? God almighty!'

'Lie still, while I look you over.'

'Martin, come back to us.'

But Martin staggered forward to the front of the rehearsal area, with both of us still holding onto his arms, to where the grave was marked by the thrown-down overcoat, uttering the end of the scene. With a precision of diction that out-Richarded even Olivier's Richard III, he spat triumphantly into the auditorium,

> 'Now barks the wolf against the full-cheeked moon;
> Now lions' half-clammed entrails roar for food;
> Now croaks the toad, and night-crows screech aloud,
> Fluttering 'bout casements of departing soul!
> Now gape the graves, and through their yarns let loose
> Imprison'd spirits to revisit earth:
> And now, swart Night, to swell thy hour out,
> Behold I spurt warm blood in thy black eyes...'

He raised his forearms, as if they still held the corpse of Julio, over the open trap, as might a man lift up the World Cup, inviting us to congratulate him.

Bournville could take no more, and slapped Martin smartly round the face, 'Stop that now!' Martin fell back upon me as I took his weight, then dropped to the floor. 'Ow! Why did you do that?' By his affronted voice, we knew he was back, and that Nevio had departed.

Bournville stood uncompromisingly over him, 'If you've injured that boy, I'll make sure Equity take your union card off you, by God!'

Damien sat folded up over his stomach in a chair, eyeing Martin's apologetic outstretched hand with suspicion. Ash said, 'I don't think there is any internal injury, but best that he is checked over!' An ambulance was called, and the boy went with one of the cast to hospital for a check-up. Damien's parents were called, while rehearsals fell in disarray.

Knots of actors stood around, casting alarmed or knowing glances at Martin. I heard an older man say to a sad-faced actor, 'Didn't I say that he'd be found out? If it weren't for the mortgage, I wouldn't have played in this thing, not for all the tea in China.'

I asked the older man which actor was playing Belinda, and he nodded sideways, 'Valerie Masters, the one with the top-knot. She is fed up to the back-teeth with him, too!' But there was no time to talk her or the rest of the cast as Bournville, dragging Martin by one arm, thrust him at us, 'Take him away with you. I don't want to see his face again until I hear that Damien is alright.'

A contrite Martin was walked back to the Tube with us, still bewildered by the events of the morning. 'Why did I hit him? I can't remember now. Should I hand myself into the police?' he asked, miserably.

'No, but I think you need to go home,' said Ash. 'One of us will stay with you for a while, and we'll find out how Damien is doing.'

'Should I pick up some medication for him?' I whispered to Ash as we stepped into the carriage, feeling that some anti-psychotics could do good work to slow up whatever was happening.

He shook his head, 'I don't think Nevio is going to raise his head again today.'

'You said that before,' I reminded him, grimly, horrified at the speed of Nevio's escalation.

We accompanied Martin back to his bleak lodgings where he had been since his break up with Flavia. They turned out to be two small adjoining rooms in a rather indifferent third-rate hotel with a broken lift, most unhomely. It was soon clear that Martin was still trying to pass off the latest incident as yet another proof of his bad luck. Neither of us were being convinced.

Over a cup of tea, Ash asked him, 'Have you ever had any experience of a part taking you over before?'

Martin stopped sipping his tea, 'Not really. I mean, every actor has some idea of the character he plays as really existent, or no-one in the audience could experience any suspension of disbelief. Do you really think Nevio is taking me over, then?'

Ash left a long pause, 'What do you think? Given that Damien had some very real bruising to his torso!'

Martin put his head between his hands moaning in despair, 'I'll have to give up the part, won't I?'

'Do you have any sense of when Nevio is slipping in?' Ash asked him.

'None. I just feel I am invincible, and by that time, he is in and that's it.'

Ash and I exchanged glances.

I went off to phone Bournville, to get an update on Damien, and discover the status of Martin in the production. At my return, he shrank back onto the bed, 'It's bad news, isn't it? I've killed him!'

I allayed his fears, 'No, Damien is quite alright, though Bournville doubts that his parents will let him continue in the part, so Julio will have to be recast. As for you, he says that if we give you a clean bill of health, you can return, but we only have a few days, or the rehearsals will become too advanced. – Your understudy is going to step in till the end of the week.'

'Is that all the time we have?'

'I'm afraid so. It's over to you, Ash!'

After the ill-fated rehearsal, we urgently discussed the case. I was still all for giving Martin anti-psychotics as an immediate solution, as it seemed irresponsible that he should continue in the part without them, even if the cast would agree to act with him.

'Given that we have just a few days, I want to investigate as much as we can before we go down that route. Martin is well aware how near the edge he was, and now he needs some good support.'

'Should he go down to the Beacon for a few days? I could take him.'

'I would like to ask his wife a few questions, and see if she will look in on him.'

Martin had given us Flavia's number, as there was no-one else in London who he might call upon to deal with his immediate care; since she was down as his next of kin, Ash phoned her, outlining the situation.

'She didn't sound very surprised,' Ash said, afterwards. 'According to her, Nevio has been coming on since rehearsals started, which is why she threw him out of the house. His obsession with the part goes back a long way, apparently. She will only come over to be with him if someone accompanies her.'

'Well, I don't blame her. So, should he step out of the part now?'

Ash said, 'Possibly. There is nothing in his history to suggest that he is susceptible to any kind of overlay like this. It is entirely out of his own character. His reputation as an actor has been built up from romantic and historic parts where he is the hero. I feel increasingly certain that we should be asking "Who has played this part before, and what happened to them?"' It was a question that Ash asked his friend, the theatre historian, Cressida Friedrichsen. That same night, we caught up with her in the balcony bar at the National Theatre, after she had given a talk as part of the South Bank's *Theatre Through Time* series. They knew each other from a time when they had taught together on a psycho-drama seminar years back, about which they warmly reminisced. Carefully not giving a context to his question, Ash introduced it into the conversation by saying, 'I was surprised to see that they are putting on the *Masque of Anitimony*?'

'It's not often revived,' Cressida said. 'Unless you go down the full masque end of things, à la Inigo Jones with dance and music, when it becomes like an opera, or else translate it into a modern setting where it just becomes a miserable story of degradation, there's not a lot of point to my mind. It hasn't caught the imagination of many companies in the last century. Although, they are saying that Martin Napier's performance will be the event of the century in some quarters.' Then she lowered her voice, aware of where we were seated, 'But others are more doubtful.'

'Really?' Ash didn't let on where we had been most of the day.

'Our Martin seems to be taking on the part rather ... more robustly than he should?' Clearly the theatrical bush-telegraph had been working overtime that day! She went on, 'He's a good actor, but Nevio is a rather one-note character in his satiric determination to plumb the lower depths. I just wonder whether our good-time BBC box-set hero is quite equal to Nevio's malevolence? I mean, especially after the Djon Djago fiasco – what a terrible piece of miscasting was there....'

Incuriously, Ash asked her, 'So, is there some theatrical tradition about this play in general? I can't recall anyone playing it before....'

Cressida sipped her Campari, raising her beautifully pencilled eyebrows, 'You mean, is it like the Scottish play? Well, as a matter of fact, there is! It's pretty much forgotten now, but one of the early actor-managers, Ambrose Phillips, went off his head in the part and the play had to be taken off back in 1829. Phillips had played it as a burlesque melodrama, which was very popular then, but it's had a bad name since then. Several actors tried to do revivals of it, in the 1920s and once during the war, then it was attempted by Gina Maddox' touring company in the 70s, but that was a wash-out, due to the strikes. Antony Bournville is trying to buck the play's reputation by going back into the whole masque tradition, from all I hear.' She directed us to some sources at the Theatre Museum, which is where we repaired to the next day.

Armed with this information, we did some further research in the confines of a little backroom. The twentieth century productions were easier to look up. Reading between the archived notices, it was clear to see that previous actors in the role had not fared well. Occam Bentley in 1927 lost his voice on the second night, while Gina Maddox's protégé, Timothy Sweetman, had famously gone off the rails afterwards, sinking into a spiral of drug-abuse and degradation.

The archivist, Christina, brought us a large folder containing a play-bill for Phillips' *The Masque of Antimony*, from the Theatre Royal in Norwich, where it had been played alongside an Elephant Dance, some Turkish Musicians, and Benedict Franks, the child prodigy, as well as a comedy of the *Shepherd's Hay*: a very full evening's entertainment back in 1829! In a separate archive box, was a group of pictures associated with the play, showing the melodramatic cast with Nevio foreground in a doublet, striking an attitude that passed for good acting in those days. We were about to put them back when another item fell out of the box: it showed a posthumously-engraved image of Ambrose Phillips, dead in a straightjacket. 'What on earth is this? I don't remember this scene!' Ash said, looking at me curiously.

Ever since Cressida had told us about Ambrose Phillips, something had been tugging at my remembrance. I exclaimed, 'The Lincoln Straightjacket case!'

Ash looked at me quizzically, while I explained, 'It's a famous case that changed the way they restrained the mentally ill! It was this case that motivated the general reform of mental health care, from that moment onwards. But I had no idea it was Ambrose Phillips who died!' I turned over the image to find out, 'It says here, Phillips was committed to Lincoln Asylum – it must have been shortly after his final performance as Nevio - he was found dead of strangulation, having been left over night in a straitjacket without any supervision, a case that went down in infamy.' But while Phillips may have not died in vain, that still left us with our current problem.

Ash was thoughtful, 'So we have a very clear lineage of things going wrong for the players of Nevio!'

'I never made much of theatrical superstition till now! What was Bournville thinking of? With a track record like this….!' I exclaimed.

But Ash was ahead of me with, 'I wonder who first played Nevio?'

We appealed once more to Christina, the archivist, who rolled her eyes at our naïve expectation: 'Strangely, we have very few records of the early 17th century: a small matter of the English Civil War and the Interregnum…?' Of course, very few records of the early Jacobean theatre survived the forcible closure of the theatres in 1642 by the puritanical Cromwell and his Parliamentary henchmen.

But she nevertheless went off, returning triumphantly with a small, fragile book bound in leather. Her air of triumph was well warranted, and it was clear that she was pleased as Punch, 'I shouldn't be showing you this, as it's about to go off, but since it is relevant… This is a partial register of performances from the 17th century for the Red Bull Theatre in Clerkenwell, and I hope you realize how rare this is! Please put on those white gloves, now! It was part of the Christopher Beeston bequest that was found at Cockley Hall in St Albans late last year.' She regarded it longingly, 'You are lucky to see it, as it is going off to the conservators at the British Museum, and then onto Stratford's Shakespeare Centre where it will be kept. You know that Beeston was one of the share-holders of the Red Bull Theatre in Clerkenwell, and one of the company of Queen Anna of Denmark's men? We don't know more than the name of the person who held this book and managed the Red Bull back in the early part of James I's reign. He's only mentioned a couple of times: Clement Shadwell. I'll hold it for you and we'll look together.'

With Christina laying the book on a stand and sitting between us, we peered over the pages, taken aback to be examing a real Jacobean manager's theatre register, written in brown ink with a quill pen. She turned the pages. It took a while to understand Shadwell's writing. Between the box office takings, were many accountings, whereby its owner had listed moneys paid out for properties, costumes, building work, and contracts with his players. In the records for May 1607 was:

'§ pd vnto Rafe de Lacy the some of xx s. w' was dve vnto him for Masq of Antimonie'

'20 shillings? What? For a whole play!' I exclaimed.

The archivist smiled, 'The entrance price to a play was a penny, or more if you wanted to sit down. It is likely that de Lacy may have been given an advance by Shadwell, and this was just what was owing. – Just think, this was the same year that Shakespeare's *Antony and Cleopatra* was played at court!' she cooed.

The next relevant entry was rather surprising,

'§ M/dom that the 27 of Jeuley 1607 Rafe de Lacy for to serve me ij years in the qualetie of playenge for five shellynges a weacke for a year. He hath covenanted hime seallfe to searue me & not to departe from my company till this ij years be eanded. Restraynte be granted then to go for the tyme into the contrey and after to retorne agayne to London yf he breacke this then to forget (illegible) for the same a hundreth markes. Wittness to this John Brackan.'

'It looks as if de Lacy served as a player himself then?' Ash breathed.

Christina told us, 'We aren't sure that he served his term of two years, as agreed. The clause about going to the country was pretty much standard at this time, in case a player had to be loaned to another company which was playing up country, as they often did in times of plague. A hundred marks is a lot of money, but we don't have the details about whether de Lacy reneged on the deal.'

'Does that mean that he might have played Nevio himself, then?'

The archivist frowned, 'It's very doubtful. Only the top billing actors would play title parts. It looks to me as if de Lacy was down on his luck, if he was treading the boards – acting was not the work of a gentleman!'

Further down we found,

'§ *the some of xi s. for one embjadered cloake of ashcolered velluet & a payir of longe silke stockins in crymsone colour for Nevio.*'

'Well, whoever played him had a handsome costume!'

The ledger was frustratingly taciturn on the matter of the play, except for the returns:

'§ *2 August 1607: Rcd. At masq of antimonie xxxj s.*'

'Receipts of 31 shillings - that's probably the takings for a couple of days, I imagine. 350 people in the audience was not a particularly good house,' said the archivist. But there was no more information to be had, as the register came to an abrupt end. Christina said that the Red Bull probably had a change of management, and that Shadwell's book was set aside, but she promised to keep looking for more clues for us.

Out on the streets of Covent Garden, I said, 'For all this research, we are no nearer to solving what's up with Martin. What are we going to do?'

Ash asked me, 'I have an idea, if you agree with it. I want to set up a walk-through of the past players of Nevio, and you are cast as my time-travelling spy.'

'Do I have to audition for this part?'

'No, you are quite perfect for it! Let's go and fetch Martin, as this is something he can witness and perhaps benefit from.'

We swung round to check in on Martin, finding him listless and unhappy. Like a statue of guilt, he gnawed upon his knuckles, appealing to us for some hope. 'I've been sitting here wondering how I'd survive prison,' he admitted.

'Has anything changed? Did Damien's parents press charges?'

'No, but I feel it hanging over me.'

We told him what we had discovered from our researches and he calmed down considerably, 'I had no idea that other actors have shared my fate. What lies behind it all, do you think?'

Ash said, 'We're going to find out now, if you are agreeable. If we are not successful, then I think you need to come and stay at our house in the country until we have got to the bottom of it.' And he explained what he had in mind.

Back at the Harley Street practice, Ash, myself and Martin, pushed the desk and the chairs back so that we had the full length of the room, then Ash laid out various lengths of ribbon, filched from Maggie's desk drawer, stretching them across the floor in a line at intervals of three feet.

I asked, 'What's this?'

'Think of each of the ribbons as the separate rungs on a ladder through time. This end by the window is now, the other end by the wall is the first performance. Martin, I'd like you to sit sideways onto the ladder, so that you have a front row seat on this performance. Jack is going to explore the time-ladder on your behalf.' Martin nodded uncertainly.

Turning to me, Ash said, 'Jack, I want you to step forward up to each line and, as you do so, step into the shoes of actors playing Nevio, with me guiding you back through time. You have an excellent somatic grasp of things, I know. Your job is to report what you find as you step forward onto the next rung: no need for you to give up yourself into any kind of psycho-drama or become the actor in question. Just be yourself, looking through the eyes of each of the performers, and reporting back as you go – what kinds of feelings or sensations they have.'

'Is this some kind of Family Constellation thing?' I asked.

'Very like it, but I would prefer us to think of it a time-travelling experiment.'

I took off my shoes and stood, as instructed, my shadow falling forward over the lines of ribbons stretching before me with the strong afternoon light behind me. With this sort of thing, you need to have a good grip on who you are first, if you are to come out in good order, so I took time to establish my own presence before stepping into the arena of this puzzling story. I'd had some exposure to this kind of thing before, though it hadn't always been led by such discerning people as Ash.

'When you are ready, step forward to the first line: stand just before the ribbon and feel what it is to be Martin.'

I dutifully toed the line, allowing my body and senses to experience standing in Martin's shoes. 'I feel if as my head and my feet are not quite held together by anything in the middle. My stomach is churning like a washing machine.'

From the sidelines, Martin nodded vigorously at Ash in confirmation, 'That is astonishing! Ash indicated that he should remain silent.

'Now Jack, will you step onto the ribbon as Martin in the part of Nevio?'

Not without considerable trepidation, I inched my toes onto the first ribbon and stood, swaying a little, as the part took its effect. 'I'm feeling very similar, but now my head and feet are even further apart, and they have no relation to each other.' Carefully, I attended to my sensations and feelings, my beliefs and understandings, as Martin playing Nevio. 'I feel as if I could do anything, that no-one else matters except me. I feel supremely powerful. There's more than a touch of *schadenfreude*: or perhaps it's more like the kind of destructive impulse that small boys have to push things over and make a mess, just to see what will happen...' Then I hit something nastier and took a sharp step backwards.

'What's happening?' Ash asked.

'I had to step back from something very nasty. It felt as if I stayed there, I would be propelled into something from which there is no return.'

Ash looked quizzically at Martin whose face was white as a sheet, 'He speaks the truth, utterly!'

Ash continued, 'So, leave the period of Martin's performance behind you, and shake yourself to let it go. Now you are now going back into the 1970s, with Gina Maddox's production. Feel what it is to be Timothy Sweetman first, before you step onto the ribbon itself which will represent the part of Nevio.'

I stood in Sweetman's shoes, feeling his raw, mercurial optimism, then I stepped onto the ribbon as his Nevio in the *Masque*, being more careful to keep my neutral distance from things, 'I'm feeling chaotic and unstrung, as if I were a bit drunk, out of control in charge of a vehicle...'

Martin breathed, 'Oh, that is remarkable!'

'Ok, so shake off that performance and leave that era behind, stepping forward into the 1920s. Be aware of Occam Bentley, what is happening there?'

Standing in Bentley's shoes, I said, 'I'm aware of his weariness. He is feeling washed up and out of touch.' Stepping into Bentley as Nevio, 'I get an immediate blast of energy, as if I had been given a tonic or pick-me-up.' I toyed with feeling the lure of Nevio for myself, for just a second. Suddenly I started to cough uncontrollably. Ash brought me water, instructing me to move off that ribbon. 'Are you alright to go on?'

'Yes, that was like his system was suddenly getting a whole spoonful of Indian spices – it was too much for him!'

I then moved onto the 1829 rung where Ambrose Phillips stood. 'I get Phillips' sense of himself as competent and in charge. I feel his humanity.' I moved unto the rung of his Nevio. 'Everything here becomes highly charged and coloured. He feels able to do anything, especially when the music is playing.' I tapped my foot to the rhythm that I could feel, then something darker, 'Now it's like I've been tempted to walk out onto a tight-rope. The angle of the rope is impossible, though, and the lights are very bright... It makes me feel dizzy.' I stepped smartly off that ribbon; to right myself, I had to clutch the side of the desk.

Ash was at my side, concerned, 'Is it alright to continue? We can stop here, if you'd rather?'

I shook my head, 'No, let's continue. What's this next rung?'

'I've put in an 18th century rung on the ladder: we don't have any information about performances of the *Masque*, but just in case there was one. Try it out and see.'

I stood before the next ribbon, trying to sense the 'someone unknown' who might have been a player in that era. I shook my head, 'This is like an inoperative phone box. If someone attempted Nevio here, they left no trace I can pick up.'

'Very well, then step up to the 1607's original performance line. See what was the experience of the first one who played Nevio at the Red Bull.'

I stood in front of the ribbon waiting, trying to feel and sense. 'Things are accelerating very fast. I have a sense of shame - no, more like I am being judged or held to account for something. It's not like the other actors at all. They all felt like actors – people who take on a part with skill – this feels uneasy, queasy even.' Then, stepping onto the last ribbon I reeled, as Nevio's first performance moved through me, 'Good God! It's like being on some drugged-up high!' A Jacobean psychedelia of perspectives enwrapped me. I breathed deeply, trying to report back, 'I've been hit with a stream of stuff – can only do shorthand - women finding me attractive and how! Men envying me my beauty and skill....' A kaleidoscope of impressions and sensations unreeled through me. In a voice I hardly recognized as my own, I flung out my arms, saying, 'I want to shag the whole audience... it's wonderful.' Abruptly the image of Martin holding out the corpse of Julio broke through this whirl of self-admiration, and I was feeling sick to my stomach. I took a step back, saying, 'I just got how Martin feels – it is resonating here, still.'

Ash stepped in beside me, closing his eyes. 'Yes, I see,' he said.

Looking back down the line, to the eras I walked down, I suddenly had the sense of grandmother's footsteps, and that something lay back before the first performance, 'I think there is something one more rung back.'

Ash looked deeply into my eyes, nodded, and together we stood on an invisible rung further back in time. An unmistakable sense of envy, frustration, and retaliatory vengeance lurked here. 'This is whence the play emanates,' Ash said. 'The author is eaten up with it. He has projected onto Nevio everything he wished he could do, but was powerless to affect. He was constrained by his frustration, eaten up with envy and fury, and that powerful retaliation is still resounding.'

He turned to Martin, 'If you are any kind of praying man, will you please do so now? We have something to clear: pray for all those actors who played Nevio and received the curse of its author instead of fame. Pray for love of them.'

Martin nodded, clutching his hands together, unable to speak.

Ash stepped out of the constellation to pick up a bronze bowl from the top of the filing cabinet; he poured water into it, muttering a blessing over it, 'Let's clear the way!' he said thrusting the bowl at me. I held it as, at each rung of the time-ladder, he sprinkled water over the ribbons, saying, 'Whatever pain, envy or fear held you in thrall, be free of it now. Time passes now into eternity, and into peace. You who have held the pain all this time, let it loose now into the peace and mercy of eternity! Be free to pass where you need to be, as love returns to fill the void.'

Solemnly, we proceeded back up the time-ladder until we were standing near the window before the first ribbon, where Ash asked Martin to stand in his own place, saying, 'Look back down the ladder of time, Martin, and see all who have played Nevio before you. It is your privilege to bless them all now and let the players pass to their rest.'

'May I?' Martin took the bowl of water from Ash.

Without any prompting, Martin walked to each ribbon, reciting the words of blessing from the immortal words of Prospero, sprinkling each as he went, his wonderful voice achieving full release as he went down the line:

> 'Our revels now are ended. These our actors,
> As I foretold you, were all spirits and
> Are melted into air, into thin air:
> And, like the baseless fabric of this vision,
> The cloud-capp'd towers, the gorgeous palaces,
> The solemn temples, the great globe itself,
> Yea, all which it inherit, shall dissolve
> And, like this insubstantial pageant faded,
> Leave not a rack behind. We are such stuff
> As dreams are made on, and our little life
> Is rounded with a sleep.

Ash walked beside him, out of the field of the story we had uncovered. Martin came at last to the end and hovered, uncertainly, looking to Ash for guidance.

'Just leave the bowl beyond the last ribbon, for poor de Lacy: he needs his own merciful quietus.'

It felt right that Martin himself should be witness to and actor in this. He regarded with compassion all the different actors who had played Nevio, and on behalf of them had spoken their release. He walked back to the top of the line and turned to face the window and the future of his own particular time-ladder. Behind him, I could sense the piecing out of an old pattern that was flying free of its retaliatory constraints.

Martin said quietly, 'For all who come afterwards, may the way be clear!'

We were all silent while those words took their effect. Then Ash went to his desk and struck the Tibetan singing bowl, whose long echoing round closed the circle of the story we had uncovered.

Martin turned and looked at us both, 'Is that it? Has it passed?'

Ash smiled, 'How do you feel?'

'As if I had been at the best performance in the world, ever!' He burst into applause, then hugged me, 'Thank you! If they were passing out the awards now, I would make sure you had one!'

Overwhelmed by his sincerity, I observed, 'I don't think they give awards for understudies.'

'I've never seen such a wonderful thing in my life – it's like magic!'

Still shaking his head in disbelief, Martin asked, looking to me for confirmation, 'So, it was Ralph de Lacy, the author, who played Nevio the first time?'

'It felt like it when I was standing it – I know it's not hard evidence...' I said.

Martin was bewildered, 'But the reason he wrote it was almost like a curse upon actors! Why? What caused him to be like that?'

'I don't know much about de Lacy, but he did once dedicate a volume of his poetry to 'his most esteemed and best beloved self!'

'Was the poor chap some deeply-dyed narcissist then?'

Ash said, 'No, he was just a deeply disturbed and gifted man whose fate was to live in a time of genius playwrights, I suspect. From the internal evidence of that time-ladder, I would say that de Lacy suffered from some kind of mental illness, possibly he was a schizophrenic.'

'But if he was some kind of minor nobility, what was he doing going on stage in the first place?' Martin couldn't understand.

'Maybe de Lacy was just stage-struck?' Ash suggested.

'Or like Christina said, just down on his luck?' I added.

'Can we find out something more about him?' Martin pleaded.

Ash pulled down the volume of the *Dictionary of National Biography*, which yielded the following information: 'Ralph de Lacy was born in 1572 and died in 1631. The illegitimate son of Sir Gilbert de Lacy, a lesser scion of the Earls of Ulster, and Catherine Donnelly, his seduced ward, he wrote a number of masques, and two collections of satiric poetry. He married Mary, daughter of royal chaplain, William Runyon. De Lacy's career was a pugnacious and contentious one. Ben Jonson had a personal feud with him and is said to have beaten de Lacy up and taken his pistol from him. Jonson's word on de Lacy's plays was that 'in his tragedies he wrote his father in law's preaching, while all his comedies were written *by* his father in law.' Not content with physically beating him up, Johnson satirised him in his play, *Poetaster*, as the wretched poet Crispinus who, as a punishment for his temerity in plagiarizing the poetry of Horace, is taken to trial and given an emetic to spew up the difficult words with which he had overloaded his vocabulary. After these superfluous words have been thrown up, Crispinus's sentence is to be locked in a dark place in solitude. Shortly after this, de Lacy foreswore the theatre, to retire as the rector of Syddenham St David, in Dorset. Apart from *The Masque of Antimony*, none of his other plays survived him.'

There were no more details to be had, because De Lacy's archive had long since gone up in smoke during the English Civil War.

'What now?' Martin asked.

'What do you feel about playing Nevio now?'

Martin considered. I thought he would say he was giving the part up, after our afternoon's efforts, but I was wrong. Like the good creative actor he was, he simply said, 'I – I will play Nevio as the author, not the character he wrote: I will play him as a man who is trying to balance mental illness, but who increasingly gives into it. It will give Nevio grounds for compassion. I don't think anyone has played him like that!'

Ash inclined his head, 'Play him like that and Nevio will go to the pitying hearts of your whole audience.'

After Martin had gone, I said to Ash, 'You know, you have taken the mask off Martin and restored the face of Nevio?'

'It is astonishing what antimony will do to a chap!' was all he said.

We gave Martin a clean bill of health and rehearsals resumed. Martin got back with Flavia, as a result of our intervention and reassurance, and both of them went to visit Damien and his parents, and to apologize in person. Since Damien had rather enjoyed the nine days wonder of being 'the actor that Martin Napier beat up', ('though it was like being beaten up by a teddy bear' was what Damien was reported to have said about it!) Martin came back to the part, with the reassurance that there would be no repeat performance of Nevio's attack.

A couple of weeks later we received a call. It was Christina, the archivist from the Theatre Museum, 'After you went, I started to check through our archive for any more clues and drew a blank, but I spent an afternoon last week with a colleague who has been researching the Royal Chaplains of the Stuarts, and he came up with something that I think you'll want to see. As long as you promise not to publish it anywhere, he is happy for you to read it. When I put the phone down, I will send you a fax with his notes.'

She was as good as her word. Out of the fax machine came chuntering the following, headed by a handwritten note: 'This extract is from the diaries of William Runyon, one of James I's chaplains.' Then in modernized spelling the following typescript read, "At the urging of my daughter, I have this day redeemed her miserable husband RdL from his Babylonian captivity, paying that monstrous tyrant Red Bull Shadwell the bond, that RdL be utterly quit of the boards, so long as he live a retired life, for the good of his soul." This quitclaim is confirmed in Runyon's book of accounts, "Item: 45 marks to C. Shadwell, that RdL be released from his bond." We cannot prove that RdL is Ralph to Lacy definitely, but it seems to me likely.'

'I see de Lacy's father in law managed to beat down Shadwell by more than half the hundred marks due if Ralph reneged on his contract!' I said.

'Nothing like the influence of royal thumbscrews when you want erring relatives to toe the line,' Ash remarked. 'I suspect that de Lacy would have been taken off the boards before long, if my suspicions are correct.'

There remained one last thing to do. After learning about the latest research, Martin was adamant that we should respectfully visit the grave of Ralph de Lacy at Syddenham St David, to ensure the rest of his eternal soul. As well as giving a generous donation to the church's upkeep, Martin read aloud de Lacy's poem to *Everlasting Oblivion* at the monument, the poignancy of its words now utterly clear to us all, especially his clear sense of oblivion while other playwrights would be remembered:

> Thou mighty gulf, insatiate cormorant!
> Deride me not, though I seem petulant
> To fall into thy chops. Let others pray
> For ever their fair poems flourish may,
> But as for me, hungry Oblivion
> Devour me quick. Accept my orison
> My earnest prayers, which do importune thee
> With gloomy shade of thy still empery
> To veil both me and my rude poesy.
> Far worthier lines, in silence of thy state,

Do sleep securely, free from love or hate
From which this living ne'er can be exempt,
But whilst it breathes, will hate and fury tempt.
Then close his eyes with the all-dimming hand,
Which not right-glorious actions can withstand;
Peace, hateful tongues; I now in silence pace,
Unless some hound do wake me from my place.
I with this sharp, yet well-meant poesy
Will sleep secure, right free from injury
Of cankered hate, or rankest villany.

He had to swallow a couple of times, to keep emotion in check. After a pause, Flavia laid a small garland of daffodils and irises under the modest plaque of the erstwhile playwright, saying in a voice of infinite pity, 'Rest well, poor soul! Heaven knows, I could not give up the stage.'

'At least he went from the stage to the pulpit, which as Olivier used to say, was a different kind of platform!' Martin took her hand, kissing it in imitation of a bejewelled Jacobean nobleman with a carnation behind his ear.

The rest, as they say, was history. *The Masque of Antimony* finally came off at the National Theatre and we were there on the first night, to ensure that everything went well. But Martin's Nevio was a well-tempered, intelligent performance, of a man sliding from lechery and hubris into obsessional revenge, the more effectively because it was played by one used to sympathetic and romantic characters, and who knew the backstory of de Lacy. It was the show of the season, going into history as the first performance not to be dogged by a player's breakdown or madness. Of all the actors in all the worlds who ever wanted to play a part so badly, Martin Napier proved he was the king of them, taking Nevio out of the realms of revenger-tragedy into the very real tragedy of schizophrenia. And not one of his reviews mentioned *Marscapes*, for the unlamented Djon Djago was quite forgotten.

Case 8: THE STALKER BEHIND BARS

Time itself shall shortly cease, the sun look dim with age, and nature sink in years, but thy soul shall still remain unhurt amidst the war of elements, the wreck of matter, and the crush of worlds.
From an early 19th century Jewish sampler

Of all the cases that have come my way over the years, the ones that I find the most personally trying concern those where clients have been abused as children, whether verbally, violently or sexually. A righteous, protective anger rises in me, and I have to work hard to hold it in check. Now that I am a father myself, that anger has transmuted somewhat: I am older and I hope wiser, though the urge to protect and defend the innocent, and to prevent their abuse has never left me. I've sat on family mediation boards and held my ground when a morass of inter-generational abuse has been laid bare, but it has never been easy. Only latterly have I been able to find any compassion for the abuser or the molester: Ash showed me the way of it a few years after I first came to the Beacon.

From the time when I started working with Ash, I noticed a particular phenomenon that often attended the inception of some of his cases. The referral call for a Marc de Kayser came from the Jungian analyst, Rabbi Ariel Klein, asking Ash to see his client. An appointment was duly made at the London practice room, notes of the case were made, but de Kayser never showed.

'Why do so many clients do that? ... make an appointment and never show?'

'Fear, sometimes, but usually because things are not yet at their worst,' said Ash. 'We could not help them until they were ready. That's why the initial enquiry is sometimes merely a feeler of hope.'

Angry on his behalf, I spoke my mind, 'Damn it, Ash! It's your time he's wasted. You could be seeing another client.'

'Perhaps,' he said, mildly, 'but no one else requires our services today. He will come.'

'When?' I asked.

For answer, he took up a compliments slip from his desk and wrote upon it while I raged on about the thoughtlessness of clients. Then, regarding me with his black-rimmed grey eyes, and with great solemnity, he consigned the slip into an envelope, licked it shut, wrote that day's date upon it and asked me take it, 'When Marc de Kayser next steps through the door, you may open this and read what it says.'

'What's this? A game of mind reading?'

'No, he said quietly, but with a twinkle, 'Just a little reminder for us.'

I consigned the envelope behind the clock on the mantlepiece, and stalked off to buy a couple of panini from the Italian deli on the corner.

Rabbi Ariel professed himself baffled about his client's non-appearance, but reported that de Kayser seemed to have taken off somewhere, and had not been back to him either. Weeks passed, becoming months, and I forgot all about the referral, until the day when Maggie put through a call from de Kayser who'd phoned in some urgency to see Ash. Five months later than his initial referral, Marc de Kayser finally came through our door: a well-groomed and personable young man in his early thirties, who worked at his uncle's recording business, specialising in educational conferencing and spoken books. He wore a wary, put-upon look, his eyes continually sliding to the side as if there were something just out of his view that was creeping up upon him. His manner of speech was educated and his diction polished, but his voice itself sounded as if someone had tied a knot in it. I've often noted that if someone is harbouring unresolved matters that they usually roost upon the vocal chords, resulting in a strained voice that sounds full of burdens.

De Kayser was ashamed, it would appear, 'When Rabbi Klein first recommended you to me, I am very sorry I failed to show up....it was...well, things were difficult.'

Ash encouraged him with, 'Do not concern yourself, please! Just tell us what you've been experiencing.' De Kayser flicked a glance at me, taking notes, 'I hardly know where to begin....'

Ash said, 'My colleague, Dr Rivers, and I have heard many unusual things over the years, and will not be shocked. We are here to help you, not judge you.'

De Kayser swallowed hard, 'Seven months ago I helped bring a high court action against Leslie Sandars, the old master of my prep school.... He had abused myself and several other boys at my school - over many years, it turns out. About three years ago, I realised that I couldn't let what he had done go unpunished any longer, as it was overshadowing my whole life. I've been unable to make or keep any relationship due to him, and so, with help of Rabbi Klein, I finally felt strong enough to bring a case against Sandars as a man, which I could not have done as a boy. I consulted a barrister who said that there was good likelihood of prosecution, so I contacted several past pupils of the school, and a small group of us decided to go forward.'

'Was the case successful?' Ash asked.

'Indeed it was. Sandars was sentenced to life imprisonment for serial and aggravated offences against the seven of us who had brought the action – many, many others were involved but didn't come forward, of course. The compounded sentences handed down to him ensure that he is unlikely to get out or to trouble anyone else again. He will most certainly die in prison.'

'So, what then is your trouble?' Ash enquired.

De Kayser shook his head, 'It sounds pitiful, I know, but I need to admit to you that, despite all this - despite the fact that I *know* he is incarcerated for the rest of his days - I still feel as if he is just behind me. He follows me everywhere....' He thrust his head into his hands, 'Oh my God, it is so awful! It is a living nightmare.'

Ash asked him, 'What do you experience?'

De Kayser licked his lips and shifted in his chair, 'I can feel it here, now. It's him - I call it "the spectre" as it's always looking me over. It feels as if I was being stroked by a long set of fingers, only they don't touch my skin but rather they reach into my very core. It is a filthy, horrible thing....' He struggled to compose himself, 'Am I going mad?'

I would certainly have said so and would have prescribed some medication, back in those unenlightened days before I had learned better, but Ash passed his gaze over de Kayser's head, then refocused his eyes to reply, 'I would say not.... How long has this been going on?'

'In a milder way, since my youth. But it has got a lot more serious since the court case. I have been aware of a shadow that seems well out of my reach but which catches at the edge of peripheral vision.'

'What manner of shadow do you experience?'

De Kayser swallowed hard, casting down his eyes with shame, 'It is in the very shape of the master who abused me...' Looking up, he protested, 'But of course, it cannot be he, because he is incarcerated for the duration and will never be let out – not even remission for good behaviour would release him, my barrister assured me! So, what is it?'

'And is the sense of being stalked present all the time, or are there respites from it? When is it at its worst?'

De Kayser said, 'It is worse at night. I feel him looking into me, as if he were perusing my body like a book. There is no end to it, save in the hours before dawn. I've been fending the spectre off for hours every night... This was why I didn't come to the appointment. I'd tried to avoid its attentions by going abroad, but I was little better for it... The stalking continued. I have been at my wits end with lack of sleep.'

Then Ash asked one of his wonderful, rule-breaking questions, 'What do *you* feel is going on?'

Unlike a majority of practitioners, Ash was of the opinion that the client, as the body's owner, knew more about his condition from the inside than we ever did, and that we should respect this knowledge. He also judged that the metaphors that the subject used were a great pointer to the causation, nature and experience of the disturbance. I sharpened my attention to see our client's somatic response, and was not disappointed.

De Kayser looked around the room as if following an invisible presence. His body seemed to be sensing what was wrong. I watched for his initial response to Ash's questioning. His shoulder blades arched and shivered, as he shielded his body, and a look of utter weariness and fear passed over his features, 'I feel as if I were a child again, waiting for that man to come in and abuse me, only this time, he comes to torment and punish me for what I have done to him.'

Ash nodded, 'Thank you, that is most helpful. I suggest, if your uncle is agreeable to your absence, that you come and stay with us down at the Beacon, near the south coast, where I can assure you the rest that you need, and a solution to your trouble.'

De Kayser's face flashed open, and we both saw what a handsome man he might be without the shielded wariness, 'Do you really mean that? - Can you really help me when so many have failed?'

It was evident from the sudden sucking in of his under-lip that he had indeed been to see many other practitioners before us, and had now inadvertently blurted this out. As Ash has often observed, 'An unfortunate feature of mysterious cases is that the sufferer will often first consult a set of fools who have no idea how to proceed. These raise and dash hope in equal proportion, while feathering their own nests with the hard-won cash of their clients. By the time we get to see them, the condition is often exacerbated, and their will to live considerably diminished.'

We had seen many such: clients who had consulted crystal therapists, reiki practitioners, Indian head masseurs, as well as witches and psychics of dubious ilk, rather than come under our roof. It seems to me that the graver the problem, the loonier the treatments the client is likely to seek out. As Ash observed, there were plenty of people along the boundaries of the unknown with the known, ready to peddle their stop-gap line of help - both practitioners who had some genuine familiarity with the unseen world - as well as many more who just thought they did.

However, I was surprised that to de Kayser's face, Ash said, 'These difficulties can be resolved by straightforward means.'

De Kayser responded with a rueful grin, 'You mean I won't have to wear garlic round my neck, or recite spells, or sit facing east for five days while fasting?' Poor chap! What a rotten régime that must have been!

'No, indeed! We only ask that you come down to the Beacon, where you will have your own room, and where you may question any of our methods. Once you've had a few nights sleep, then we will have some sessions and get to the bottom of this speedily, I feel. Can you take a few days off work?'

De Kayser seemed to centre and settle himself at this prospect. With upturned face, he said, 'I've lived with the spectre all these years. I think I can spare a few days to be rid of it.'

As we watched de Kayser hail a taxi, I turned to Ash, 'What is wrong with him?'

Ash turned from the window, 'He has a vampiric stalker, Jack. It was very clear to the view - did you not feel it yourself? You normally have a good somatic sense?'

I pronounced myself proof against the horrors that cannot be seen, and satisfied that the abuser had had his just deserts. 'What's bothering de Kayser is surely some deeply engrained guilt-trip that has been triggered by this court case?'

Ash shook his head, 'Oh, I don't doubt that he has been experiencing a living hell that even his courageous reopening of historic abuse and its airing in public cannot allay. We will have work to do, but first, that hunted man needs a few nights secure and deep sleep, so that he's in better shape for what I intend.'

'How can you be so sure that he is not merely delusional as a residue of the abuse he's suffered?'

Ash took me into his view of it, 'Did you not notice how he spoke of his spectre as both "it" and "he?" This is sure proof that what stalks him has indeed the shape of his abuser, but I am sure that the impression is masking an entity that has emanated and grown from the abuse, and now has a life of its own.'

'What on earth is an entity?'

'It is not a word that either of us should use in the presence of clients, as it makes them deeply fearful. An entity is a thought-form that arises from prolonged and intensive brooding or meditation. Despair, sorrow, passion, hate - they can all build up to create an entity – which is just a created thought form, a being with low intelligence - that literally possesses and controls someone's life. In this case, it is likely to have germinated from the sexual desires of Sandars, fed by pornographic thoughts and images that he has entertained, and fuelled by the fear and hatred of his victims... It is likely that Sandars was himself once abused in a similar way, so the entity is likely to be growing in strength and fearfulness from generation to generation, infecting and preying upon each new child.'

Still doubtful, I rolled the idea around my mind, finally admitted, 'It sounds like a truly horrible thing... but I suppose it does explain how abusers and their victims are linked, and why abuse seems to cascade from generation to generation within certain families.... I will have to think about it some more... So how will you proceed?'

Ash rubbed his hands together with some force and expelled a long breath, 'We have a soul to steal back, Jack.'

'"Straightforward means" you promised him!' I accused him.

With wide, innocent eyes, he said, 'And that is what he will get. Jack, don't you think that he needs clear and scientific answers to his questions after so much mystification? He doesn't want anything else sneaking up on him ever again.'

Marc De Kayser drove down the next evening, arriving as the first stars were becoming visible. The barbastrelle bats were flitting and foraging at fall of dusk: little darts of darkness that you felt more than saw. As he locked the car door and looked towards the house, you could see the wariness of a man who has known fear while boarding at an institutional building.

Something rather strange happened at the threshold, I remember. I came out to greet him, inviting him to follow me in. I was still talking to him, when I realized he had stuck at the door, and was several steps behind me, still on the far side of the threshold.

Ash arrived in the hall at that moment, saw the difficulty, and stretched his hand over the threshold to shake hands with De Kayser, pulling him gently over the threshold with, a very formal statement, 'Mr de Kayser, you are very welcome to the Beacon. Come in!'

Our guest stood in the hall looking first surprised, and then very relieved, 'That is extraordinary! - I feel utterly normal. The spectre has let me alone.' He felt all over his arms and head as if feeling for invisible cobwebs. 'Yes, utterly gone!'

Ash nodded, 'Indeed! This is a protected place and your shadow knows it is not welcome here.'

Wendy installed Marc in the Blue Room that looks eastward towards the curve of the Downs, and then came to find Ash, saying, 'I'm so glad that young man is here - he needed it so much...You know, he just threw himself down on the bed and fell deeply asleep. Just like that! I don't think he took in one word I said about breakfast times at all!'

Ash commanded that he should not be woken in the morning, but left to sleep round naturally.

Marc came down for a very late breakfast with great apologies, just as Wendy was clearing away, 'I'd no idea I'd overslept so long.'

Wendy put him at his ease, 'Help yourself to what you want, now, it's no trouble.' She swiftly brought him some toast and black coffee, while I joined him for another cup of tea, 'A good sleep?'

Marc had that well-rested plumped-out look of a long sleep, 'Beyond good! I've not slept like that since I was a young child.' He moved his head cautiously slowly from side to side, checking, saying in a lower voice, 'It's not there anymore! – I can't believe it! You said you would make things better, but we've not even started yet?'

'Well, I think you will find that you are feeling the effect of the Beacon, and that things will not have changed much should you step outside of it.'

His face fell.

'After you've finished breakfast, I think Ash has a few things up his sleeve, so don't despair. We will not leave you alone with it!'

After a short interview, in which Marc continually announced his astonishment at the absence of his spectre, Ash judged that our guest should be allowed to roam the Beacon and grounds, and have a few days holiday to just be himself without the overshadowing influence to perturb him. He spent most of the time, when fine, out in the grounds, but Marc did love our piano. When it rained, he just played tune after tune, until several of our guests asked if he would give a concert for them. It was clear he had joined his uncle's recording business not simply because he liked the work, but because he had both a good ear and considerable musical talent.

On the Wednesday, Ash came to see me to arrange a time for the expulsion of the spectre, 'and what about stealing the soul back?' I asked, in ironic tones.

'Oh, we'll do that at the same time!' was his response, and he outlined his intended approach.

Marc had asked me anxiously at lunch, 'Are you going to do anything soon?' A profound restlessness was upon him, I saw; his two hands were clamped across his body, holding either arm, as if he were barely keeping in check some wild beast, 'I'm not trying to force your hand, but I have the feeling that the spectre is just waiting to rush me, the minute I step out into my car.' I reported this to Ash, who pronounced, 'It is always the right time when the guest is ready.'

Accordingly, we met in Ash's consulting room that afternoon. The day was calm, and beginning to be cold, as the autumn deepened. A bright blue sky with a few high clouds sent its lovely light into the room. The last leaves were still upon the trees but any worsening of weather would soon strip them bare.

Marc could not settle, but paced up and down, and only reluctantly sat down. 'I'm sorry, I just feel a growing tension in me, like I should run away.'

Ash said squarely to him, 'That is the spectre knowing that it has a shortened lease. It is not you who wants to run away, but the spectre itself.'

Marc swallowed, considering these words, 'Yes, I understand, I think. What do you want me to do?'

'Are you, Marc de Kayzer, willing for this overshadowing spectre to depart and not return?' Ash was keeping the protocols very formal, I perceived, so that Marc was not going to feel jumped upon.

'Of course I am! Are you mad?!'

'Then, let us proceed.' Unfazed by his exasperation, Ash invited Marc to lie down upon the couch, with myself at his feet and himself at the side. Ash explained in full, 'I am going to see what has been going on behind the scenes and restore what has been warped by your experiences. For your part, please lie here. You can close your eyes or open them, as you please. Jack will be present all the time. You have nothing to fear. When I have finished my work, I will be bringing back something that belongs to you that has been displaced for a long while. I will convey that back to you by blowing it into your chest, is that alright by you?'

Marc nodded, 'Yes. I don't know what you'll be doing, but yes! Whatever will banish this awful thing.' And he covered his eyes to hide the desperate tears that filled them.

'Have you any questions for me?' Ash asked.

Marc mastered himself again, 'Will it come back?'

'No, it will be banished, and you will have your own life back again.'

Marc was unable to speak at this answer, but just made shooing gestures to Ash to get on with it. Between fear and dread, and the willingness to be done with this wretched persecution, Marc was ready.

Ash had already lit some incense and a shrine light before we began, and he directed Marc to breathe in the scent of the frankincense. Then emitting a series of high-pitched overtones, Ash ran his hands four inches above Marc's body, as if to feel where the displacement was situated in his body-field, searching and stopping, then finally spreading his hands along the body field as if he were smoothing laundry.

Ash then modified his own breathing, closing his eyes, going deeper. My job was to watch both guest and practitioner, to take notes if necessary.

I have seen Ash 'go out' many times, but that occasion I remember well. Normally he would sit or lie still, but this time, his hands and body seemed very busy, as if we were scurrying about behind the scenes of Marc's sad story. After about fifteen minutes, he laughed shortly, then learnt forward to scoop something out of Marc's body. Like a man screwing up a paper bag, his hands manipulated what he had taken up into some other shape and threw it towards the window, which he had left open a crack at the top. Whether by co-incidence or not, a crow flew past at the exact same time, turning wing towards Hartworth Beacon and beyond. I could swear that it took away whatever Ash had thrown, but maybe I was being fanciful.

Ash went back into quietness for a moment, as if gathering himself. Marc had by this time closed his eyes and his restlessness had ceased. Occasionally, he moaned a little, as if with the memory, like a man in a light dream, but his own breathing evened out and his features relaxed. A few minutes later, Ash was arising and blowing into his chest, making passes over the body-field again to check the results. Then he brought the incense and wafted it over Marc who opened his eyes in wonder, patting his body with both hands. 'What have you done? It feels different.' He sat up. 'Tell me, what happened?'

'What you call the spectre has been taken away.'

'Will it come back?' was Marc's very reasonable question.

'No, because I have also brought back the part of your soul that was taken from you in that assault. While that soul part was absent, the spectre had a nice comfortable place to be, hiding in the place that the soul-part had vacated. Now that that soul part is returned, the spectre has been evicted for good.'

It was very unlike Ash to go into this kind of detail, but he had promised transparency. Someone as intelligent as Marc was would not be content with less: heaven knows, he had suffered the bamboozlement of numerous charlatans and wafflaly New Age practitioners to deserve an adult explanation.

Still, Marc had a bundle of questions: 'Soul-part? Where has it been? Who had it? How did you do that?'

Ash composed himself to convey the story, 'I will tell you, if you would like. Problems often cannot be healed this side of the worlds, because we need to go beyond time and place into eternity and space to find the solutions. That is what I have done: gone to the other side of the worlds that we don't see, but which are just as real as this one.

As for the soul: the soul is not a single thing, but a flexible composite, made up of multiple understandings and functions, governing different modalities. Together, these work like the instruments in an orchestra. When one of the first violins drops out of the music, the music still continues, as your life did, but should the single harp be removed, the music cannot sound like it did.'

Ash was using the metaphor that Marc well understood in his telling, 'What you experienced at school robbed you of a part of your soul. The shock of this loss caused you to suffer a void into which what you called the spectre could lodge – made up of disgust, pornographic fantasy, and sexual obsession. It has been taken away, be assured, and it had its origins elsewhere. Sandars no doubt knows it well.'

'But where did it go? I don't want it to hurt others!'

Ash nodded reassuringly, 'What made up your spectre has been gathered up and sent away, held within a field of amethyst where it can be purged and dismantled. Think of it, if you will, as a kind of wrecking yard where the pieces that made it up are slowly leached out and neutralized. It will not get out and hurt others.'

Marc breathed more easily, but he asked, 'But where was that part of my soul that was stolen?'

Patiently, Ash began, 'If I tell you that in my vision while I worked, I was aware of a conservatory with a statue of Adonis upon a plinth....'

Marc went white, his eyes wide with amazement, 'But Sandars had such a statue in his rooms! How could you kn....?'

Ash nodded, 'I was shown it, and how Sandars was obsessed with this beautiful form. For him it was his inspiration. But in my hand, I found myself holding a conker – the same kind of horsechestnut seed which schoolboys play conkers with. I was shown to smash the statue open, and there within the centre of it was your soul-part, looking like a boy sheltering from a storm. I took you out and left the conker behind on the plinth.'

So that was why Ash had laughed: a wonderful school-boyish swap of soul-part for a conker!

Marc opened his mouth, but nothing came out. Finally, he said, 'I believe you. You couldn't have known about that statue, but you are right. He doted on it, and stroked it over and over while he was preparing to abuse us.' He suddenly stopped, as understanding stuck home, 'Sandars has been brooding over my soul in the same way, hasn't he?' He began to cough, which soon turned into a retching, so I hastily fetched a tray, which was all I had to hand, and after Marc had heaved over it for a bit, bringing up bile, I brought him some water and handful of tissues.

'I feel rid of it, and of him, truly,' he said. I noticed that his voice had achieved a full release. It no longer sounded as if he was talking through a sore throat.

'I am glad to have been of service,' Ash said.

Marc sat up, 'Thank you! – You have done what so many cannot.'

'Go and rest now, and perhaps tomorrow, when you have slept on it, we will talk again.'

We had a less formal debriefing the next morning, after breakfast over some coffee. Marc looked like a different man: it seemed to me as if he could almost have had some kind of special skin treatment, his face looked so radiant.

Ash said, 'I can see you do not need to stay here any longer.'

Marc smiled, 'No indeed. Your work has done the trick. What instructions do I have for after-care?'

I could see how much that question pleased Ash, 'Now you will have to find a new way to live - now that you are no longer the victim, that is. I think you will find it much more empowering to take up the threads and themes of that returned soul-part as your main concern. It will be a different discourse now.'

Marc nodded, 'I dreamt of Sandars last night but it didn't make me anxious anymore. He was looking old and sad, like a man that has lost something precious to him. I almost felt pity, were that possible.'

'Well, Sandars still has a lot more to clear, but that is his task, not yours. Perhaps now you will consider him in a different light, now that you are rid of the spectre, and have some pity upon him who still suffers?'

Marc put his coffee cup, as if in protest, then he said, 'Do you mean that my spectre is something he also knows?... That he has not caused it?'

Ash nodded, 'Indeed so. He is a fellow sufferer like yourself, caught in a web of horrific gratification that holds him captive.'

Marc thought swiftly, a variety of expressions modifing his features, 'You are the very first person I know who ever spoke of Sandars as if he were a human being and not a paedophile.' There was wonder and self-doubt in his voice. He stared out of the window at Hartsworth Beacon and the squally wind that was shaking leaves from the oak trees. Turning to Ash, he said, 'I think I understand you. You make me realise that I have allowed myself to become superior to men like him. Being a victim has given me the superiority of innocence, and cast my predator as the only guilty one. But that is not true, is it?'

I was very moved and somewhat bewildered by these words coming out of the mouth of this intelligent young man, but even more so by what Ash replied to him, 'You have liberated your soul from an old story, by this very means. You can now make your own life, without looking over your shoulder, if you live by that principle and keep it before you always.'

After Marc had set off for Surrey, for he would not stay longer, I challenged Ash about this mysterious exchange, 'What did you mean?'

'A lot of lives are lived with a sense that we are individually superior or better than others. The sense of being innocent because we have suffered, the certainty that those who made us suffer are guilty and inferior – these are things that can cause great imbalance in the world.'

I disagreed, 'But many awful things are done, like the evils that Marc and his fellow schoolboys suffered...'

'Indeed so! But *all* human beings come with the propensity to do terrible things. Change but one circumstance, and you or I could do worse than Sandars.'

I felt my own superiority rise in the face of his words, but bit back my protestations. The last leaves on the sycamore tree whirled wildly in the wind, spirally down onto the window ledge. I tried hard to understand, 'Are you saying we need humility in every place and circumstance?'

'Neutrality is how you and I approach our guests and their cases, trusting that healing will find its way into their souls. If we believed for a moment that we were superior to our clients, we would violate that trust, and our treatments would be hollow and worthless.'

I nodded, 'I think I understand. But where does that leave Sandars? Where does he fit in all this?'

Ash nodded vigorously, 'Precisely! Today's work will stir him up too.'

'You mean he will also feel it – how?'

Ash considered the best metaphor to explain it to me, 'Let's say you and I were yoked by chains of desire and attraction on one side, and by the chains of disgust and repulsion on the other, and someone suddenly severed them, how would you feel? We have seen Marc's end of the story and what has resulted – for him it has brought freedom from a vampiric stalker. But what do you think today's work has wrought for Sandars?'

'You mean that he... oh, you mean how he appeared in Marc's dream this morning... as if he had lost something...?'

Ash waited patiently on my understanding, head on one side.

The penny finally dropped. 'Ah! Of course, you smashed his statue of Adonis.'

What Ash had done seemed to be a very satisfactory end to the case but, in actuality, it was just the first half of it. A month or so later, we were contacted by Christine Machen, the niece whom Sandars had appointed as his next of kin. She had been an appalled witness at her uncle's court case and had subsequently developed a sense of obligation towards Marc and the other men who had been abused by her uncle as boys. She had gathered from Marc that Ash and

I had therapeutically supported him, and now wanted to ask our advice. She phoned to tell us, 'My uncle is very unwell and is unlikely to live long, but the governor reports that he is suffering very badly. Although he's not a very religiously-observant man now, he needs some kind of help: he doesn't want to die with all that he's done… he's terrified of the judgement to come, I think. He was brought up very strictly, I believe. I've spoken to Mr de Kayzer who's told me a little of what you do, and I really feel that my uncle could also benefit from your help. I know it is tremendously presumptuous of me to even ask but… there is no-one else'

She told us that Sandars had been imprisoned at HMP Wallerton in Devon, a predominantly sexual offenders' facility. Had he been younger, he would have been undoubtedly classified as a category A prisoner, likely to reoffend and to be of danger to the public but, due to his age, he had been downgraded to a category B prisoner, as one who was unlikely to need maximum containment. Considering the length of his sentence - currently standing at 19 years – he was unlikely to see release since he was now 83 and in poor health.

With growing horror, I listened in on the conversation which Ash put on speaker, exclaiming when he ended the call, 'You're not seriously going to go to see that paedophile?'

'You saw the nature of the entity that was tailing Marc. Do you think that Sandars doesn't experience it also, as well as feeling the full weight of what he has brought about?'

Folding my arms over my chest, I forthrightly proclaimed, 'I don't know and I don't frankly care!'

'So, for you, like everyone else who has written him off, Sandars is just a non-human without rights, then?' he challenged me. 'Would you leave him with the burden of remorse, shame and pollution still in place, without attempting to deal with it?'

My eyes caught the plaque on the desk, given to us by Rabbi Klein: 'May I never see in the patient anything but a fellow creature in pain,' and tried to feel my way back to the conversation we had had on the morning that Marc left the Beacon, but I had lost the sense of it in my instinctive response to abuse. Maimonides' words reproached me. I acknowledged to Ash, 'I'm sorry. I suffer from faulty understanding and the usual prejudices, as most of us do. Of course, I will come with you.'

Her Majesty's Prison at Wallerton was a relatively modern facility, with a purpose-built wing for sex-offenders, so our visit was not as harrowing as I had thought it might be. It was as far away from the old forbidding stone Victorian prison house as could be imagined. We might have been visiting some ordinary light industrial plant or offices, except that the prison was situated by itself in the deep countryside behind high fencing.

At the entrance, we were searched, signed in, and shown to the Governor's office, for we were expected.

'When we received the visiting order for you, I did wonder if Sandars was going to turn a corner finally.' The Prison Governor wore a quizzical expression. He was David Anderson, the Quaker, famous for his writings on prison reform and his championship of political prisoners for Amnesty. It was under his watch that HMP Wallerton had been converted into a model prison with separate chapel, work regimes, and exercise yards for the different categories of prisoners housed there. He shook hands warmly with us both, and it was soon clear that he knew the scope of Ash's work. He told us that though Sandars had been amenable to rehabilitation therapy, it was clear that his paedophilic compulsion remained largely unchanged. Most of the prisoners in the forty-bed wing that housed similar paedophiles and sexual offenders, lived in what was called 'a therapeutic community' – mostly for their own protection. They were encouraged by a series of incentives to earn enhanced levels and privileges in that community, through their participation in the sexual offenders' treatment programme, but Sandars had remained somewhat withdrawn, mostly due to his advanced age and educational background.

The Governor called in the young Anglican chaplain, to give us an update on Sandars' progress. He confirmed, 'While Sandars has attended the sexual offenders programme regularly, he remains consumed by a sense of shame. I've been unable to provide the kind of help he needs. Conventional religious approaches are doing nothing, and the psychiatrist is at a loss. Sandar's desire to see anyone other than his niece is a good step forward, I feel.'

The Governor rang a bell on his desk, 'Then I think I will permit you both to see what can be done to alleviate his state of mind. He is a very sick man, I fear.' A few minutes later a short man in a very tight warder's uniform knocked at the door.

'Come in! Mr Wilson, will you please conduct these gentlemen to Mr Sandars? I have given them permission to see him in the side room of the ward. You may remain outside until they knock.'

The warder strode ahead of us down the well-lit corridors to unlock the various pass doors, his self-important propriety almost a cliché. As we came to the prison sick-bay, he muttered, 'Scum they are, bloody chomos!' I pulled Ash's sleeve, querying this remark with raised eyebrows.

'Prison lingo for "child molesters," he whispered back. I felt properly chastened about my own over-reaction in the presence of such judgement, wondering if the Governor knew he had so censorious man as this attending sex-offenders.

Although this was a modern prison facility, the process of passing through that many locked doors had a salutary effect on me. Though I could see prisoners working in a relaxed way in the vegetable beds through the reinforced glass giving onto the grounds, or being taught how to lay bricks in one of the many rehabilitation classes that encouraged offenders to take up an apprenticeship, I have never felt so enclosed, and I speak as someone who has worked in secure mental units. Most incarcerated mentally ill patients did not usually spend unending amounts of time locked up these days, but the sheer drag of time within a prison pressed heavily upon me as we followed.

In the prison sick-bay, just three occupants, one of whom had a cast on his leg, were leafing through magazines. They looked up with curiosity at our entrance, and away as quickly when they saw we had not come for them. Two orderlies were pushing Sandar's bed into the side room where we were to see him, one holding up the drip. The ward and side room were without ornament save for a discreet geometric frieze around the wall. It was the only splash of colour in that clinically spare setting.

Wilson marched in ahead of us, 'Look sharp, Mr Sandars, you have two doctors to see you!' He made no move to leave until Ash looked pointedly at the door with, 'Let's give the patient a little privacy, shall we, Mr Wilson?' At which point, the warder sniffed and strode out, hovering outside at the door.

The man lying in the hospital bed was both frail and elderly, wizened with care and heavy with years of predation. I had been expecting some monster, I suppose, but here was a man I might have passed any day in the street. Sandars was preternaturally thin, the planes of his skull sharp, his frame diminished from poor absorption of nourishment, which accounted for the drip. But the area around his arm where the canula had been applied was almost black with bruising. He did not have the look of a man with many weeks left.

Ash spoke warmly, modifying his voice to that narrow room, to reach its captive patient. 'Good afternoon, Mr Sandars, I am Dr. Richard Ashington, and this is my colleague, Dr. Jack Rivers.' Ash extended his hand, and Sandars' wrist twitched, but he was too weak to raise it, so he nodded his head in acknowledgement of us both instead.

The voice that responded was dredged up from antique depths, 'I thank you for coming to see an old derelict like me.' His accent was cultured, charmingly old fashioned, with a diction rarely heard today, but the arrested fear in his eyes spoke more to me. And I, who had expected to be disgusted, was filled with pity at the wreck this old Classics scholar had become.

'My niece tells me that you are skilled in cases like mine?'

'Indeed so. Tell us how we can help you? How would you diagnose your condition, sir?'

Sandars blinked at this unwonted appellation of respect, smiling ironically, *'Aurius teneo lupum,* that's what I've been doing all these years, and I know it.'

'No man should have to hold the wolf by the ears that long,' Ash said softly. 'It's time enough for the compulsion you have been under to depart, I believe?' Ash looked around, aware of our being overlooked through the window adjoining the sick-bay with this side room. I stood up and drew the curtains in the very face of Wilson's sneering countenance, saying, 'I think we can do without an audience.'

'Tell us, when did the compulsion start?' So it was that Ash began the slow uncovering of Sandars' story, beginning with his own experience of sexual assault as a young boy at prep-school, the utter betrayal of his parent's stubborn disbelief about it, and the slow, long slide into paedophiliac addiction that had marred his whole life. I stood by the door, distancing myself from what appeared to be an essential and intimate confession of a burdened soul. It was a story of overshadowing, I recognised now, one which, despite a harsh religious upbringing, had asserted itself, becoming impervious to either righteous action or integrity of mind, laden with overriding imperatives of gratification and justification

Sandars' voice pattered on, like dry leaves swept up in the whirling wind into which he too had been caught up. To my ears, it was clear he was penitent, ashamed, and at the same time captive, overcome by the same entity that Ash had removed from Marc. 'I was held prisoner long before I was convicted,' Sandars admitted to Ash.

'And do you now want to be released from it?'

Sudden hope flared in his eyes, and was as quickly dashed, 'Ah, you ask the question that our Saviour posed to the halt and the blind! Indeed, I do! With all my heart, were it only possible!'

Ash closed his eyes, as if praying. Like a singer reaching for an impossibly high note, his whole body seemed to take on bulk as he reached down into himself, drawing something up into him.

Then, without any more preparation, Ash did something I have never before seen, and never saw ever again. He laid his hand gently upon the prisoner's chest, as if drawing out the poison that had accumulated there. Then he leant swiftly over and kissed Sandars on the mouth, like one drawing evil out of him by benediction. Then he rose, swilled his mouth with water from the bottle in his pocket, and spat it down the sluice.

'Begone! And trouble him not again!' his voice shivered in the air of that sad place.

Sandars lay calm and empty, one tear held upon his cheek. He felt his chest, much as Marc had done, astounded to find himself free. His wondering eyes sought out Ash, like one in whom a miracle had been wrought. He uttered, 'you have removed it! Thank God!'

'Is there anything more we can do for you?' Ash asked.

Sandars shifted his shoulders. Without any thought, he replied, '*Carthago delenda est*. We both know that!'

Even an indifferent scholar like me, could understand that one: 'Carthage must be destroyed.' It was clear and right, for death could not be long behind, since Sandars had nothing left to sustain him, and had surrendered to his fate. The collapsing veins, the milky eyes, all told their tale.

He continued firmly, with conviction, 'You have released me, I thank you from the bottom of my heart. I want no more… I shall eat and drink nothing for the next few days, and I think that will do it. Please tell them here that I do not want to be forcibly fed nor resuscitated. I will go without fuss. Christine has my wishes in hand.' He could speak no more, but turned his head to one side, relaxing like a boy passing into a trusting sleep.

'Let him sleep,' Ash said to the orderlies who cared for him, before we were conducted back to the Governor's office, where we conveyed Sandars' wishes in more professional terminology, and walked back to the car. I hoped that they would honour his wishes.

Sitting beside Ash as we sped eastwards along the motorway, I asked, 'What on earth did you do back there?'

'Just some traditional sin-eating, Jack. Sandars couldn't live any more with the weight of it, not without passing it on first.'

I was astounded, for I had always understood sin-eating to be some benighted Welsh custom that survived after the Reformation had forbidden confession: in those days, so that the freight of sin should not remain with the dead, a poor or indigent person was brought in to literally eat the sin of the deceased by taking bread and salt from the top of the dead person's coffin. I had not thought it to be such a physical process as Ash had demonstrated. I was in awe of his courage and compassion, for there was no way I would have laid my mouth over that old reprobate's, 'And is a glass of water all you are going to take for that?' For it did not seem enough to me.

Ash agreed with me, 'I will take the burden of it to place where it can go free finally, if you will be so good as to take the road coming up to the left.'

We drew off the motorway, taking many turnings until even the little villages and settlements ran out, and we were on a narrowing B road, leading I knew not where. The region was unknown to me, but finally Ash directed us down a single track, dead-end road to the verge of a steep hill. We left the car half parked on a bank, and walked up the steep slopes, Ash striding ahead with me following behind, just in case. It was only when we reached the summit, with the wind tugging at our clothes, that Ash began to sing into the wind, letting loose the longest lamentation I have ever heard, filled with the grief and despair of children, together with the shame and guilt that Sandars himself had carried. And the winds lifted it far into the air, fragmenting and diminishing it as the sound fell away.

We drove home in silence, Ash sleeping some of the way, until we reached the welcome of the Beacon. After such a visitation, neither of us could face London. We both yearned for the homely house that had sheltered the lost and the desperate so many times. In need of its restoration ourselves, we turned the lane to see its welcome lights twinkling between the wind-wracked trees, with a need to not think, to not know, but to lie down, like over-worked animals in their own stall, and wait for the hope of tomorrow's dawn.

In the aftermath of this case, Christine Machen reported her uncle's death a few days after our visit. She and ourselves were the only people at the funeral at the crematorium. I was struck by the enormity of it: that no-one else came to witness Sandars' departure, that there was no-one who was glad that he had lived. As for Marc, he has sent us many other guests over the years with a kind of proselytizing zeal, that other broken lives might be mended, as his had been. Since his marriage, he has been a regular benefactor to the Beacon, bringing his wife and children to visit us once a year.

It was some months after this case that our cleaner, Edna, at the London practice rooms asked about the rather dusty letter she had found behind the clock. Did Ash still want it? How long had it been forgotten? Did we want it posted?

Ash placed the slim envelope into my hands, demonstrating, 'It is still sealed.'

Puzzled, I took it: the front of the envelope was blank except for a date back in the previous April. I opened it and read, 'Marc de Kayser, 23rd October. And his fellow sufferer, 9th December.'

Finding last year's desk diary in the bottom drawer, I thumbed back through it, until I found the entries. They matched the associated cases: the first being the time Marc kept his first appointment, and the other, the death day of Sandars who had gone to meet his Maker shortly after our visit to the prison.

'Now how did you do that?' I demanded.

Ash just smiled enigmatically.

Caitlín Matthews

Case 9: CLOSING THE CIRCLE

One deceit needs many others, and so the whole house is built in the air and must soon come to the ground.
Baltasar Gracián – Oráculo Manual

The middle-aged couple on the pavement outside looked tired and dejected, crushed by the impact of London. The fact that they had walked up and down outside for some time was not lost on me, for I had seen many individuals haver like this outside Ash's consulting room, afraid to come in. But I couldn't stand seeing their legs go up and down past our basement window anymore.

'Shall I welcome them in?' I asked Ash, as I drew aside the curtain to observe them more clearly.

'No, let them decide for themselves. No-one can coerce them into asking for our help,' Ash said, sitting at the little upright piano which he'd installed in the Harley St consulting room since his return. It was his favourite kind of relaxation between clients. To me, he seemed massively unconcerned, although only yesterday he had had a long phone call from the haunted-looking woman now wandering up and down outside with her husband. Their daughter was in trouble, it appeared. It sounded like a police matter to me, as I had forthrightly told him.

Finally, Maggie buzzed through that Mr and Mrs Wharton had arrived. They looked ill at ease in these surroundings, not being the kind of people who would normally frequent a consulting room. Doug Wharton was a builder who exuded a downright scepticism. He sat with folded arms, defiantly and militantly armoured against any kind of nonsense, as though to cover the hangdog shame at being where he was. Laura, his wife, was clearly the driving impulse of their visit. Her anxiety muted a buoyant personality that normally made light of life's inequities, I guessed, taking the edge off her husband's brusqueness, though now there seemed little of that energy left in her tired eyes.

Ash was very patient with them both, despite Mr Wharton's frequent and rebarbative comments: he clearly regarded us both as barely a cut above the abductor of his daughter. I reckoned that he had decided to play along with his wife, on the understanding that you might need to set a thief to catch a thief. As they both sat silent on the edge of their chairs, Ash asked, 'How can we help you today?'

'As I said on the phone, our daughter, Evelyn, has gone off and joined something called the Order of the Golden Serpent. It's run by a person called Kyros Kyriakou... he seems a frightful man.'

Ash's eyes narrowed in recognition.

Mr Wharton said, 'And we know where she is: we tracked her down to the old canal wharehouse building in Icenfield, you know - the one with the boarded-up frontage. God knows what she's up to in there!'

'We do know she's somewhere inside! We've even seen her, but she won't speak to us,' Mrs Wharton declared. 'We've tried several times.'

Ash patiently let them rehearse their vain efforts again, then asked, 'The question is, does Evelyn want to come out? Or is she being coerced to stay?'

'That's what the police asked us. We can't say, but we want her back.'

They were in that awful position when relatives become cult members, when neither police nor social workers have an entrée without it being an overt matter of crime or public safety. But, as responsible practitioners, we had to have the consent of the party in question. I wondered whether Ash would refuse to take the case at this point, but he continued questioning them.

'Is Evelyn in touch with anyone else?'

'She used to be close to her brother, Michael, but he has also tried to speak to her, and she never even comes to the door. He was shown the dogs the last time he tried. Her colleagues at work have no idea.'

'Is there no boyfriend?'

Mrs Wharton shook her head, 'Evelyn had just split up with Adrian – they'd been together for three years and we thought they would be married.'

'It's a waste of effort, I tell you,' Mr Wharton advized his wife, with rough kindness, impatiently fiddling with his cap.

'How did she seem to you, when you saw her?' Ash asked.

Mr Wharton replied, impatiently, 'She was pale and wan, and didn't want to spend any time with us.'

'She seemed distracted, as if she were trying to remember something important and couldn't,' Mrs Wharton observed sadly.

I had not been privy to the preliminary phone conversation with Ash, so I asked, 'How old is Evelyn?'

'She's 28....'

Mr Wharton interrupted his wife, 'If I could get my hands on that bast.....'

His wife nudged him.

'And how long has she been with this group?' Ash asked.

She went on, 'For over two months, but we only found this out in the last fortnight. Her friend Mary and she went to a public talk, and they both signed up for a course of further talks with this Kyriakou. Mary said they fell out about it: that she ended up walking out of the first talk because she thought that the man was unethical. Unfortunately, they didn't talk for a few days, and so she had no idea that Evelyn had been taken in by him. It was only when Evelyn sent her a message to ask her to look after her cat that Mary realized that she had joined the order.'

'We did the research, now what are you going to do?' Mr Wharton demanded, pugnaciously.

'Kyros Kyriakou is a child of Greek Cypriot parents who came here in the 60s,' said Ash. 'He has a very bad reputation of taking advantage of his devotees. He....'

'Well, you would say that, wouldn't you?' said Mr Wharton, muttering, 'The bloody pot calling the kettle black....'

His wife laid her hand on his arm, 'Doug, dear, don't make things worse! These gentlemen are trying to help us!'

Ash replied for us both, 'Whatever help we can provide, we will. We will need to infiltrate his outfit, but there is no guarantee that Evelyn will want to come away. We can only see how the land lies, and what kind of hold he has over her.'

Wharton flung up his eyes, 'I told you we should have gone to a private detective, woman.'

'With the greatest respect, sir, I doubt that a private detective would have the right profile for this job. Kyriakou is a slippery and unscrupulous character. Only someone who has some idea of how he could jump would be equipped to deal with this person.'

We took as many details as could, with Mrs Wharton being very helpful and her husband shaking his head at the wastefulness of it all. They left us with a photo of Evelyn in her graduation robes, black with a teal hood, when she had taken her veterinary degree from the University of Nottingham. Her long blond hair spilled from under her mortar board, and she looked well and happy, with her life before her.

After they had gone, I asked Ash, 'Surely, we can't take this case. Evelyn's made her choice, which is unfortunate, but we are not a rescue service!'

'In normal circumstances, I would refuse to be involved, but if Evelyn is in with Kyros Kyriakou, then she is in danger of her life.'

'Who is he? How could he harm her?'

'I didn't want to speak about Kyriakou's activities in front of the Whartons, but he is what the world considers a black magician: someone who uses others to advance himself. He preys on the weak and gullible, as well as holding them in fear. – We have crossed swords before. – Though she may not know it, Evelyn is in the equivalent of a burning building: the longer she is under his charge, the riskier it will become. Kyriakou doesn't hold onto people for long: they burn out or he disposes of them.'

'But you heard the Whartons, no-one gets through the door, and whoever's within isn't interested in coming out.'

'If Evelyn cannot get out, then someone will have to go in, with a legitimate purpose,' Ash concluded.

'Who?'

Ash considered me, head on the side, 'I think you are going to have a burning desire to learn more about the work of this order.'

I protested, 'But I know so little about anything magical!'

'That's why you will be perfect for the job. Brains and brawn in the service of magic. It will be irresistible to him.'

'But won't Kyriakou know I work for you?'

'Oh yes, but only because I'm going to "sack" you. You can then go over to him for employment to get back at me: so, you will become doubly useful to him.'

I frowned, 'Why would he find me so very desirable?'

'Because you are a doctor and that is a very useful person if you are doing the kinds of things and taking the kinds of risks I imagine he is taking. To his mind, you would be able to sign death certificates for any unfortunate accidents, prescribe drugs to render the unwilling malleable, and all manner of useful skills would be at his command.'

I shuddered, 'I'm not going to do anything that would cause the GMC to strike me off, am I?'

'We should be able to crack you out before that.'

'*Should* be able to....?' I cried, throwing up my hands.

'At least do the research with me, and make up your own mind.'

Icenfield was a minor town in the south that had fallen upon hard times, since the canal trade had passed it by. It was used to transport goods from Christminster down to the coast at Toot Barton, near Frisdon, back in the 19th century, but as it no longer joined onto the more northerly canal networks that connected the coast to Andover and the north, it had fallen into neglect, and today the canal, though largely navigable, was mostly for recreational and holiday use, apart from a few ageing hippies and other enthusiasts who lived along its decaying moorings.

We drove over to look about. The old canal wharehouse was pretty easy to find. Ash and I did our own recce, passing the Kyriakou's HQ in the car twice, quite slowly. Set back from the road and bordering the canal bank, the building had the look of a minor municipal office fallen on hard times: once it would have held all manner of goods, ready to lade, and the canal offices would have been full of clerks. Victorian civic pride had now fallen into urban decay, complete with graffiti. Not the most prepossessing premises for a magical outfit, I thought.

Behind the graffiti and the boarded-up windows, it told a different story, as I discovered later, but it was not for the fainthearted. Anyone bold enough to knock on the front door had to pass the dogs lose in the yard and, beyond them, the villainous, moustachioed factotum who sat at on a broken chair at the half-door, picking his nails with a commando knife, as I discovered to my cost. What I did not realise beforehand was that these preventatives were far less effective than the ones that were already in place: the willingness of the members to stay, and their fear of offending against their Magister, as they called him.

For the moment, we gave the premises a wide berth and explored the little town, which did not appear to be prospering. Many of the local shops were closed or about to close down, though the sub-post office in the newsagent seemed to be doing a roaring trade, until I remembered that it was the last day of the month and pension morning. Ash and I agreed to separate and pump anyone we met for information about Kyriakou's HQ. He took the north, and I the south side of the street, before meeting back in the carpark.

Wandering into the greengrocers, I bought a bag of granny smiths and enquired what was the boarded-up big building along the way? I was told that it was some Greek millionaire's development of the canal offices, but in the bakery, they thought it was some kind of commune. In the funeral directors, where I made noises about looking for a good firm to do my own funeral, come the time, the man on the desk let slip that someone had died from Kyriakou's place recently, and that the undertaker's rival - a funeral director from Withybrook, the town on the next lock along the canal - had been given the work. The undertaker keenly felt the loss of this opportunity, apparently. I ditched the funeral leaflets he'd given me in the nearest bin, not wishing my corpse to be attended to by such as he.

Then I struck up a conversation with a lady walking her poodle; she told me that people from the commune came into town seldom, but that they looked like zombies, 'On drugs, I don't doubt! she said darkly before her dog pulled her to the next lamppost. It was clear that Kyriakou's outfit was not much liked, and several people told me that they'd wish he would go somewhere else.

Back at the carpark, Ash and I compared notes. He had learned that, while people did not emerge often from Kyriakou's place, that even arcane beings like his devotees had to eat sometimes. Ash said, 'The butcher told me that they were always asking for any spare off-cuts of meat for the dogs, which he was happy about at first, but now he thinks that the meat goes to the devotees.'

'Sounds grim!'

He showed me a flyer, 'I found this stuffed into the leaflet rack in the New Age shop. The proprietor seemed to know nothing about Kyriakou's real activities, or I doubt she would be so willing to display them. I removed all of them.'

The leaflet was printed with an indigo banner at the top proclaiming, 'The Secrets of the Unseen World' with the gold sigil of the erect serpent embossed upon it. It gave the times of his lectures. It looked as if there was a monthly public lecture series, which was probably the method by which he gained new recruits. These were followed by a series of three lectures to which only those attending the public lecture might come. After that, one might apply to join the Order of the Golden Serpent.

It was very short on detail, though there was fulsome information on how one might donate to the Order - it filled the back page, along with a series of endorsements, of which the following will give you a good idea:

'I have been in perfect health since following the meditations of the Magister.' - Anita, of Worcester.

'Since I discovered the secrets of the universe, I have achieved a happy and successful business life. By scientific persuasion, I have gained control over my fate' – Pratesh, of London.

'My twin soul has been found at last, thanks to Magister Kyros.' Carey, of Edmonton.

This nonsense was followed by an inset picture of the Magister himself: a balding man of about 50 who had trained his dark hair, and eyebrows to best effect, like the archetypal magician. Attired in a purple robe with the gold lamen of a serpent about his neck, Kyriakou smouldered out of the frame with the dark eyed iconic intensity of a film star. The short biography accompanying it was a mélange of unprovable statements about his supposed guru-dom:

Drawing upon the mysteries of ancient Greece, Magister Kyros Kyriakou has discovered the secrets of the unseen world through the inspiration of the Ascended Masters. He is regarded internationally as a true initiate who can open the way to telepathic vision and the deep wisdom of the Olympian Gods, revealing how you may achieve health, wealth and happiness. His mission is to spread this knowledge for the genuine good of mankind.

'And make himself a cartload of cash!...What a farrago of nonsense!' I said, casting it down. 'Do I really have to do this?'

'Of course not. It is for you to choose.'

I told him, 'The undertaker said that there'd been a recent death from the premises... he didn't say who it was, but do you think it could be one of the devotees of the Order?'

Ash went still, 'It is quite likely. I'll have a word with Sergeant Hobbs and see if can find out anything. – If you decide to do this, Jack, I will ensure that you go in prepared and that there is support ready when you need it. This man is too dangerous altogether.'

I was duly booked to attend Kyriakou's public lecture which was the following week.

Ash advised, 'It's unlikely that you will have any personal contact with him tonight but, just in case, pick out a couple of phrases from Kyriakou's talk that might demonstrate what you are looking for in life. Feed them back into anything you say. And keep your eyes and ears open. If he or anyone asks you, you are "a seeker after truth."'

'Well, no-one can argue with that!'

The lecture was held in the old Masonic Hall at the other end of Icenfield. I duly paid my money at the door to a dull eyed woman of indeterminate age; she wore a kind of indigo wrap over her clothes. Inside, a young man with a similar wrap, only his was shorter and without sleeves, led me to my seat; he was a lot keener than the woman on the door, but neither of them struck me as shining examples of great success or health. The sleeveless robes looked a lot like university commoner's gowns – a menial kind of garment indicating that you were still in training, with the front strips hanging down to the thigh. The event wasn't exactly sold out, and the audience rattled a little loosely in the auditorium, even though we had all been seated together in the same section near the front.

The lights dimmed, and Kyriakou made his grand entrance dressed in a sweeping indigo robe with bat-wing sleeves, to the sound of hyped-up, canned symphonic music. He was much smaller in person, but just as intense as in the photograph. As the music fell away, he bowed his head over the microphone, as if in holy prayer, then raised his bald forehead so that the spotlight chanced upon it, making his appearance to a Greek icon complete. Mystagogue or maniac – he could have been both.

He was a good speaker, I'll give him that, with a deep penetrating voice that would have made an Orthodox deacon proud. He rummaged about in the Greek Mystery tradition, larding it with lots of Atlantean and Egyptian references, with bits of Plato thrown in for respectability, finally coming to the peroration of his talk about the wonderful work of the Order: apparently, he had the only genuine link with the past and could therefore lead us forward to the future with proper authority. Those who followed him would gain a remarkable amount of benefits, from success in business to restoration of health. He followed this with descriptions of those who had wilfully ignored his wisdom, all of whom seemed to have come to unfortunate ends - I had the feeling that this part was for the benefit of any wavering devotees. His concern was also for those who, like ourselves in the audience, wandered still in darkness.

With large glistening eyes, he asked in a dramatically pitying voice, 'And what may the multitude do who have lost their way amid error who, by the guidance of poor shepherds, have been lead into the ravine of confusion?'

Answering his own rhetorical question, with arms outstretched like a very scary Jesus, Kyriakou proclaimed, '"Seek one that may lead you by the hand and conduct you to the door of Truth and Knowledge, where the clear Light is pure from Darkness, where seekers are not drunken but sober, and who in their heart look up to him who guides them."'

Sounding genuinely moved by this quotation, he then ruined the effect by pointing to his own chest and adding - after a significant pause - 'I – I am that initiate, chosen of the Hidden Masters, blessed by the Olympian Gods, who will take your hand and lead you surely.'

Under normal circumstances, I would have guffawed aloud at such rampant narcissism, but controlled myself sufficiently to look suitably awed instead.

The Order's indigo-wrapped members all applauded loudly at this point, to mark the end of the talk. The dull-eyed woman then proclaimed that the Magister's followers would move among us and take our responses and questions. Several of the audience had already started to pick up their bags and coats, prior to departing, but more of the Magister's devotees filed out of the side doors with clip boards and pens, pinning every audience member down. The Magister himself had been whisked away.

I was caught by an earnest woman in swept-up spectacles who wanted to know my response, 'It's to help the Magister improve his lecture series. He is keen to be relevant in this modern world.'

Muttering a few inanities, I cast my eyes around in case Evelyn might be one of the clip-board brigade. Nodding and answering yes or no in a distracted way to my interviewer, I saw that Evelyn was two rows in front of me, speaking with a woman who clearly wanted to depart. Evelyn's hair was bundled into a ponytail. Her face was bare of make-up and the hollows under her eyes betrayed lack of sleep. She had a lassitude about her that spoke of illness or medication, though she was employing a ruthless, hectoring style of questioning, like an inquisitor, completely ignoring the woman's need to go. Finally, the woman rose, pushing past Evelyn in impatience.

I took this opportunity to send Evelyn a commiserating smile at her dismay, realizing that there might be penalties for devotees who did not fulfil their quotient of audience interviews. She barely registered me.

'Do you have any questions for the Magister?' my own earnest interviewer was asking.

Turning back to her, I said, 'How will the Magister answer my questions since he has left the stage?'

'Oh, he always comes back for genuine seekers,' she enthused, with pen poised, 'And what is your question?'

Wanting to get out of there myself, I pointed to her wrap which came with sleeves, 'Why do you wear these things, if you are allowed to tell me?'

'These robes with sleeves are only conferred on those who have made the unreserved dedication,' she said zealously. 'The ones without sleeves are for the neophytes,'

I didn't seek to know more and emerged into the light of day, wondering how serious this was. Whatever the unreserved dedication was, Evelyn must have already taken it, since she was already wearing one the wraps with sleeves.

Back at the Beacon, I played the lecture back to Ash, for I had taken the office dictaphone with me. He maintained a grim countenance throughout Kyriakou's recital. 'He even quotes *the Divine Pymander* to his own benefit!' he said, shaking his head.

'What's that?'

'Ironically, it is one of the texts of the *Corpus Hermeticum* - a soul's NeoPlatonic guide to living a well-regulated and spiritual life: however, it actually ends with the warning that "the whole nature and composition of those living things called Men, is very prone to maliciousness," which in this case was never truer!'

I gave him my report about Evelyn, 'What is the unreserved dedication? Because, she was wearing one the robes of those who have taken it.'

Ash went grey, 'Then it is even more urgent that we get her out, if we can. She is young and blond - just the kind he preys upon. – The Unreserved

Dedication is the commitment that an initiate takes to their highest ideals: it is only taken when someone is mature enough and ready to dedicate their life to the Great Work.'

'Then you have taken it?'

'I have. But Kyriakou's version of it is more like a Faustian pact: those who make it under his tutelage open themselves to his predations, thinking that they are dedicating themselves to a spiritual power. In actual fact, it comes down to a dedication to him personally, and all that implies.'

'Have you heard from Sergeant Hobbs?'

'He spoke off the record, but I gather that the death was of a man who had an untreated heart condition. The coroner found no suspicious circumstances, but there well might be.'

'What do we do now?'

'You know I would go myself, but Kyriakou knows who I am. Are you willing to try and get Evelyn out?'

'Yes. I think it is worth a try. From what I've seen so far, it's an unhealthy set up and we need someone to condemn it to oblivion.'

Ash then stood up, saying formally, 'Since your work has been so exceedingly unsatisfactory, I am dismissing you, Jack, from your employment at the Beacon as of this moment.'

My face fell, 'You're serious?'

'Indeed so, Jack! If Kyriakou thinks your dismissal a fraud, he will quickly sniff it out. You will pack your things and leave immediately. I will tell the staff what has happened, and you will make no contact with anyone here but me from here on.'

'Without saying goodbye to Jane?' I had not factored in that at all.

'Of course not: you may say goodbye to Jane. But she will stay here: she is an important member of staff and in her condition, she must not be put into hazard.' Jane was now in her fifth month.

'But where am I to go?'

He passed me a piece of paper, 'This address is that of Bodger, an old friend of mine in Icenfield, who has agreed to have you stay. He will see you right, and you will have to rely on him for local support. If you need to leave messages for me, he will contact me. He knows what we are trying to do. We have to prepare for the fact that you will be incommunicado for at least some of the time, till you have proven your worth.'

He passed me a small bag of paperback books, 'I would like you to look through these while you're away, to get the lie of the land.'

I looked inside: they were cheap trade paperback editions of *Secrets of the*

Western Way, The Ancient Greeks, Gods and Goddesses of Olympus, The Sevenfold Path, and *Magic for Today.*

Ash told me, on all accounts, to stick as near to the truth if possible in any dealings with Kyriakou's outfit, 'Since you want to come over as dissatisfied, think of some event when you really were, only apply your dissatisfaction to being in my employ.'

'That's easy, I shall cast my old registrar, Miles Knighton, in the role as my provocateur. I've always hated him, since he gave me many an evil time.'

Ash grinned, 'There is nothing like the genuine emotion of past wrangles!' Now, be helpful to Kyriakou, but not too helpful! And use your best offices to speak to Evelyn.'

'Any other instructions?'

'Yes.' He held out his hand, 'You had better give me back the Dictaphone. If you are caught using it, your cover is blown.'

I reluctantly handed it over and went to pack my bag.

Jane was excited about my mission, 'So, you're going to go in with guns blazing?'

'I am not exactly cut out to play James Bond, my love!'

But when she kissed me, she nonetheless urged me, 'Go carefully out there!'

Laying a hand on her bump, I kissed her for a long time, 'I'll be back soon! You take care of yourself and the little one.'

As I cast up and down the lock, I opened the piece of paper to refresh my memory of the address, 'Bodger, Wild Fennel, Decoy Drain, Icenfield Lock.' There were a bewildering variety of crafts along the moorings, from power boats to houseboats and narrowboats, but no obvious method of finding which was where. Autumn leaves were already streaming down steadily from the line of poplars and willows on the opposite bank. The little run-down backwater looked picturesque enough that September day, but I had little time to consider the view as I cast up and down.

Finally, I found the name I had been searching for on the side of a very superior narrowboat. *Wild Fennel* was painted in bottle green with yellow flashings, her name emblazoned on the side with a spray of fennel leaves. Never having been on a narrowboat before, I was uncertain how to gain attention, so I knocked on the side of the craft and called out.

A man peered out from the stern.

'Bodger?' I asked.

'Sure thing, mate. Come on along!' He beckoned me along the bank.

Bodger turned out to be a delightful, bright-eyed wiry chap with a neat beard, brown as a berry from being outside; the wrong side of 60, he would probably continue to look the same age until he died. His deft and careful movements were those of someone used to living in a small space, and he was obviously handy in many ways, as I saw from the small lathe standing on the aft deck. Bodger also came with a strong Bristolian accent, 'Oi'll put a brew on, step aboard, mate!'

When I told him I'd never been on a narrowboat before, Bodger went into full explanation. Most people moored off the canal in the backwater known as Decoy Drain were, he told me, actually living on houseboats – pontoons with a mobile home attached to them, I learned – dwellings that had his contempt, for the Bodger lived proudly in a semi-trad narrowboat.

Beckoning me onto the *Wild Fennel*, he told me, 'A semi-trad has more deck space, see - more seating and storage capacity,' He took me over his craft with all the cheerful enthusiasm of an estate agent. The semi-enclosed aft deck was open to sky between two bulkheads and was set up with his lathe, which just fitted the space. A number of well-turned bowls and dishes were stacked into a wooden tomato crate beside it, which Bodger had to move to one side for us to enter the interior. 'Got to deliver these to the craft shop, Oi must! Come on down, my friend' It was certainly snug inside, with a fold-down table dinette with hob and oven, as well as a neat bed with its own wardrobe. I could not help but be enthused with his arrangements, with wooden cupboard built ingeniously into the available spaces. The wooden shelves with their raised lip 'fiddles' to stop things from sliding about, held an array of bargee handicrafts, with brightly enamelled plates and copper-lustre jugs.

I exclaimed at their beauty, '"Roses and castles" is what we call that kind of decoration – what the toffs call "canal folk art,"' he told me, putting on an impossibly intellectual accent. 'We just loves 'en.' The roses and castles decoration extended to all parts of the narrowboat, while the swan's neck, the S shaped steel bar that connected the top of the rudder to the tiller, was painted with candy-stripes of gold and green.

The coverlet on his bed was hand-woven wool with repeating lozenges of leaves. What with the mixture of canal water, bottled gas for the cooker, diesel, and freshly baked biscuits melded together with the fragrant tobacco in Bodger's pipe, how easily I could be charmed, like Ratty and Mole, into 'messing about on boats.'

'You married, Bodger?' I couldn't help asking, as everything look so neat, speaking of a woman's hand, but I was wrong.

'Never got the hang of it, Jack! – Which isn't to say that I don't hold with the ladies: there's many a one on a Saturday night, if you know what I mean….?' He nodded to the bed. 'What about you?'

I told him about my Jane.

He poked his pipe at me, 'You're a lucky man! You keep her sweet, mark me now!' Dunking the excellent biscuits, we drank our tea down. Bodger said, 'Now, Oi got you all sorted, like Ash asked. Let me show you!'

I followed him along the canal bank to the mooring next along, where there was a houseboat that had seen better days, 'Oi know she don't look much, but she's watertight. Oi put in basic supplies for you,' he said, noting my fallen face.

The houseboat, *The Mary Anne Lee*, was nothing like as characterful at *Wild Fennel*. Inside, it had the 70s décor of a bad porno film. I put down my bag on the bed, while he showed me where things were.

'Oi rents her out seasonally, but now the Autumn's here, she's all yours. You need me anytime, just knock on the side. Ash said you might need some other kind of help, p'raps? You be sure and find me. If Oi'm not in, you'll find me at the craft shop in the High St, or you can leave a message for me: Edna will pass it along. In the evenings Oi goes down the *Waterman's Dog* up the way,' he pointed to the pub on the main canal side. 'Now, if you'm not able to get out, Oi walks along the tow-path behind that old wharehouse every night at chucking out time. You can listen for my whistle,' and Bodger whistled the theme from the old BBC series *Dixon of Dock Green*. 'You 'as any trouble, Jack, you whistle me back.' As we walked up the tow-path together, we worked out a series of suitable tunes to act as signals, so that I could keep in touch and report how things were.

Bodger showed me the back of the canal wharehouse on the other side of the canal to the tow-path we were on, 'See, you can't get access to the landward side of the wharehouse any more since the Greek bought it, but it's still possible from the canal-side.' From behind, the wharehouse looked a lot better than from the front. It still had its wooden loading lofts, to which a pulley would have lifted merchandise onto the first and second floors, and there was an arched shipping hole at water level, now closed by wooden doors: 'That's where barges could be unpacked undercover.'

I didn't answer. The windows from this side seemed as dirty as at the front and this was the place where I would be incarcerated soon, if all went well.

The next few days, I eked out a lean, bachelor existence on the houseboat, mourning the loss of my wife, my comfortable bed, and the joy of the Beacon. I tried to make good use of the time reading the books Ash had given me, like a student sitting an exam. Despite their lurid exteriors, the books were actually straight, no-nonsense reads, written by people who had their heads screwed on.

I managed to sit through the succeeding three lectures that week. Kyriakou's style was much less showy than in at the public lecture, though the hard sell was stepped up. Of the 30 or so people from the first talk, only 8 remained for the succeeding course. Ash's homework had enabled me to sort out the received facts from the less than kosher ones the Magister purveyed. I learned the name of my interviewer, Angela, and finally expressed myself interested in joining the Order. I could see from her exultant face, that she would be winning Brownie points at her success in bagging yet another neophyte. She duly passed me a form which was headed 'Magister Kyros congratulates you for seeking to redeem yourself from error and confusion!'

'You will never regret it,' she said warmly. I sincerely hoped not.

The form went on to ask my personal details and profession, and then some more ambivalently framed questions, such as, 'Do you believe in the Cosmic Laws of the Hidden Masters?' Since I had no clear idea what either of these were, I wrote, 'I hope to deepen my belief,' which I felt was a suitably ambiguous response. I nearly laughed aloud at, 'Do you believe that you are worthy to receive the Secrets of the Unseen World?' To which only an egotist would answer 'yes,' so I did, while I marked 'no' more modestly against, 'Do you have the gift of telepathy?' adding, 'but I would like to have it.'

The clincher was the last question, 'Do you promise not to divulge the secrets with which the Order of the Golden Serpent will gift you to any third party?' I wrote 'yes,' making my own mental reservation against such foolishness. This was clearly how Kyriakou kept control.

One box more awaited my attention, 'Have you ever belonged to any occult or magical group before?' In this response I was honest, writing 'no,' adding, 'but I have worked with Richard Ashington who has just sacked me.' It was made clear that service at the temple was required for the first few weeks. I signed my name with less than enthusiasm.

Three other people were also signing forms. We were asked to wait in the canteen while Kyriakou inspected them. I looked over the other applicants critically: a desiccated man in his fifties, a younger man in a thin jacket whom I judged to be a computer nerd, and a large middle-aged woman with an aggrieved air and an untreated thyroid imbalance who was laboriously filling in her form, the tip of her tongue protruding with effort.

Within minutes, Angela, my bespectacled interviewer invited me back into the hall, glowing all over her face, 'The master will see you himself.' From her tone, I gathered this wasn't usual.

Kyriakou was waiting, 'Brother Jack!' His shrewd black eyes regarded me closely. He extended his hand, giving me a masonic shake, with which I did not reciprocate. I was not invited to sit, but rather forced to do so, for he continued to hold my hand as he lowered himself back into his chair.

'I see you are a doctor?' he said, finally releasing my hand from his grip.

'Specializing in mental health at present, but yes, I have seen general practice.'

'And you are a genuine seeker?'

'I am.'

He leaned back in his chair, steepling his hands, 'Tell me, why then did you not gain the wisdom you seek with your last employer, since he is a known practitioner of the magical arts?'

Shaking my head with grievance, I ranted, 'Oh, Ashington was just impossible! He promised a lot but gave nothing.' Summoning up visions of the vile Miles Kingston and his slave-driving methods, I spoke resentfully, 'He just wanted me to run his damned nursing home for him. Hardly a day off, and no thanks for it. I told him that I wouldn't stand for it anymore, and that he had promised to initiate me, but failed to follow through. I told him he was a selfish bastard. Only now, he won't teach me his secrets. - We had a row, you see, and I ended up out on my ear.'

I showed him the dismissal letter that Ash had prepared for me.

'And so have you removed from his premises entirely?' Kyriakou sounded as if that were a pity.

'Yes, I've taken a gaff here in Icenfield, to be nearer the centre... I hope you don't want me to go back to Ashington's place?' I said in alarm.

His lips curved in a commiserating smile, 'No indeed. It all sounds most disagreeable. Let us pass over it.' I discovered later that this was his standard response to anything inconvenient.

He regarded me with those unblinking black eyes, letting the ensuing pause grow between us to see if I was unsettled, which I was not. I saw immediately how he was using the hypnotist's technique of capturing my gaze. I accordingly looked just a little to the side of his eyes, as Ash had shown me to do with persuasive people, nonchalantly letting my left arm cover my solar plexus, to keep him out.

Kyriakou registered these subtle resistances with a smile, and then continued, 'So, you want to join us, brother?'

'If you will have me. I am a hard worker.'

Looking over my build, he agreed, 'I can see that, Brother Jack. Tell me, what is it you seek?'

'I am seeking the truth,' which was my honest purpose, after all.

Nodding to the hovering Angela, he stood, commanding me, 'Come!'

I stood uncertainly, while Angela made me kneel before Kyriakou, pressing my shoulders down and putting a hand behind my knees. So, I duly knelt.

'Raise your hands to me, brother!'

I lifted my hands to have them enclosed by Kyriakou's own. A waft of cloyingly exotic oils billowed from his robes, 'Do you swear allegiance to the Order of the Golden Serpent, to serve me, your Magister?'

'I do so swear,' I responded, with what I hoped was the appropriate fervour, hoping that my crossed feet would countermand this insincere promise, since I could not cross my fingers.

As Kyriakou smeared some of the exotic oil that drenched his robes upon my head, I filled my mind with my own opposing prayer of dedication - to Ash and all that he believed in and practiced, and to the way of light that it might shine upon my family, so that I would not be tainted by this dangerous charlatan.

Lifting his voice, he cried, 'Gods of Olympus, Hidden Masters, behold I bring you a new neophyte.'

One of the meagre indigo wraps was forced onto my body, but since my dimensions were not quite those intended by the manufacturer, I could do no more than get my forearms into the thing.

'I see we will have to make you a new garment, my brother,' Kyriakou said, letting go of my hands. 'Go now and fetch your things, and follow me to your new abode. Brother Michael will go with you to help.' He nodded to the hovering acolyte.

'Yes, I will.' I said struggling to right myself without the use of either arm as they were still jammed behind me in the daft indigo wrap.

With his face very close to mine, Kyriakou said, in a tone that brooked no refusal. 'You will call me Magister, or Magister Kyros.'

'Thank you, Magister,' I muttered, bowing my head in supposed reverence, but actually chewing my bottom lip to stop myself saying something less reverent.

I was ushered out. Brother Michael had to help me out of the indigo rag. I noted how he kept his robe on, without a trace of embarrassment or awkwardness as we walked through Icenfield together, and wondered if this invigilation was a requirement to ensure the newly-made neophyte didn't bunk off.

As we entered the lock, I realised how wise Ash's choice of dwelling had been. Brother Michael would clearly be able to judge from my surroundings what my actual circumstances were. This part of the lock looked very rundown, and the houseboat appeared the very epitome of poor choice, last-ditch housing. My miserable possessions were quickly gathered up and off we went to Kyriakou's HQ.

Now, in my misspent youth as a grammar school boy, I had bought a Californian badge urging, 'Drop out and join a cult,' which I inexpertly sewed onto my backpack, along with a few other subversive inanities, like 'Make love not war', and 'Go, go, Gandalf!' But I had no idea then quite what the reality of a cultic existence involved.

Inside, the old canal building was a hidden world of toil, hunger, and peer snooping. My new fellow neophytes had been sectioned off and taken to a part of the building where leaflet production and mailing out of literature took place, to become unpaid office staff. But I was treated differently. Within a few hours of my arrival, I was given a room of my own – the others slept in male or female dormitories, I discovered later, created by the simple expedient of dividing one of the wharehouse floors with a chip-board divider. Men and women were segregated for most activities except eating and obligatory attendance in the temple which was three times a day – before breakfast, lunch and dinner.

My measurements had been taken, and by late afternoon, the women in the sewing room had run me up a sleeveless indigo robe of my own. The thing was a damn nuisance, catching in doors and generally getting in the way. When no-one was about or when gardening, I tied the front flaps behind me, for which I was frequently reprimanded.

The décor of the old wharehouse was sparse. Coir matting was laid along the corridor and some moth-eaten carpets in the main rooms. The walls had been given a rough bucket of whitewash. The only place where the decorations went over the top was in the temple, to which I was led on the first evening. The walls were hung with indigo curtains and gold trimmings, like theatrical curtains. The focal point of the shrine was a large brass snake which stood before an embroidered shimmering star. A cloud of incense hung in the air. Here, after some kind of ritual dedicated to the Evening Star, I and my companions were introduced as the new neophytes. The devotees, I saw, sat according to their grade, with the long-sleevers to the front and the no-sleevers to the back. There were clearly other insignia marks among the devotees that I had somehow missed before, for some wore lamens with different coloured ribbons round their necks. Evelyn sat near the front, with an expression of weariness. I wondered how I would get to converse with her.

After this, I returned to my room, having partaken of an indifferent supper, consisting of a bowl of unidentifiable soup with no notifiable protein with it, just a thin sliver of cheese, with a couple of bits of bread and margarine scrape on the side. An apple was intended to act as dessert to this feast. It was served with water. If this were the kind of food his followers lived on, it was unsurprising that Kyriakou's devotees looked half famished and lacking in energy. I doubted I would be able to sustain myself long on this kind of diet.

Seeing my face, Brother Michael whispered to me that it was unfortunate I had arrived on a fasting day, but they were due a feast in a few days, he promised.

It became clear to me that Kyriakou kept his devotees hungry and motivated by means of feasts: deprivation of nourishment was a despicable way of controlling people. I cursed myself that I had not thought to put any supplies into my bag when I packed up, and was now dreaming of the carton of nuts and raisins left on the table in the houseboat.

Bedtime was determined by a bell, which rang at 9.30pm. I went to my bed grindingly hungry, intending to read one of the books Ash had given me, but lights-out came at 10pm; the lights on my floor must all have been on the same circuit. I lay in the darkness, considering my fate, squinting at the luminous face of my watch, from time to time. I was beginning to drift off when I heard the *Dixon of Dock Green* whistle coming from the tow-path below. Blessing Bodger's name, I duly whistled back the theme from *Hill St Blues*, to indicate that I was alright. I would have liked to make it clear that I needed food supplies as well, but we hadn't arranged any more subtle messages than our main agreed signals.

Stealthily, I tried to learn the layout of the building, and soon learned that I did not have access to the whole house. I discovered that the front entrance gave into the front yard where several large dogs were loose. A villainous looking man in a white gilet over his naked chest sat at the half-door, playing with a commando knife, which he kept throwing at the door post. His aim looked good, if the penetration points were anything to go by. Certainly, no-one would be able to get in or out here. Brother Michael told me that his name was Stavros, that he was a fellow countryman of the Magister, and that I should on no account anger him.

The yard at the side, where I was set to develop a garden plot, was at the western side of the wharehouse, where containers and old sinks full of earth were growing the last tomatoes of the year. The walls around it were very high, making the wharehouse a prison on three sides, unless you were up for a swim in the canal.

The upper floors were out of bounds, and only those wearing the right lamen and robe might ascend to them. At the top, Kyriakou had his own quarters, to which entrance was only possible by giving the password of the day. No-one ever seemed to know the password, except certain of the young women and men, I noted. A couple of long-sleevers were positioned on the stairs as guardians during the day to deter anyone going up.

On the second morning, after the Morning Star ceremony in the Temple, one of the sisters, a woman of about 20 tried to mount the main stairs and was prevented, 'But I need to speak to my mother urgently,' she cried. She was reported by the guards on the stairs and made to stand in the temple holding the heavy candlestick until lunchtime, sniffing miserably through the service. There was no public phone, and the only private one seemed to be upstairs.

Listening to that poor woman's unheeded grief, I felt my resolve stubbornly harden. If my fellow beings were suffering in this place, then I would share their sufferings, if only to be a witness. Whether Evelyn came out of here willingly or not, this state of affairs should not continue, I swore my oath. My witness of these petty humiliations would bring Kyriakou down. But in the meantime, I also had to keep up my own spirits. During the compulsory meditations, I visualised myself back in the Sanctuary at the Beacon, invoking the angel Raphael, the healer. I needed to equalise and balance myself, to have spiritual nurture that sustained my soul in this barren place, where everything was so unbalanced, and I felt comforted, being in solidarity with Ash who sat and meditated there every day. I yearned for the Beacon, to be able to laugh and banter, to do ordinary things, and to determine my life for myself.

My own tiny room was located at the back of the building, overlooking the canal. Having it was a privilege, but I had to pay for it. On the third day, now considerably weakened by lack of nourishment, I was summoned to Kyriakou's downstairs audience chamber, 'Now that you have settled in, I would like to assign your duties. It is expected that all neophytes do some physical labour, if they are able: you will work on the vegetable plot which we are developing. I hope that suits you, brother?' I assented to this seemingly pleasant task, without any quibble.

Kyriakou then asked me to examine two or three of the devotees, because they have been a little unwell recently, 'I'm sure you can manage that?'

'Well, I don't have any supplies with me and cannot prescribe. So, if there is anything out of ordinary, they will have to be referred to the local GP,' I replied, unhelpfully.

Kyriakou had obviously not expected this. 'But you are a licenced doctor?'

'Indeed, but I may need to revalidate my licence if I am to work here,' I told him, knowing full well that he would not be savvy of the legalities.

Opening a drawer, he pushed towards me a plastic tray container of different pills, 'You may prescribe from this box, then, since it is so difficult.'

I ascertained at a glance from the unboxeded tablets within that he had a goodly array of what looked like antipsychotic and sedative drugs at his disposal. I wondered how many of these he doled out, to whom, and why, and when and where he had obtained them.

In the tiny room allotted to me, with Brother Michael as my stooge on the other side of the door, I duly examined each of the devotees in turn, finding that the man was severely under-nourished and had an infected cut on his arm, while both women showed signs of anaemia and fatigue. All of them had suspicious skin eruptions that were inclined to weep, and one woman exhibited mild ataxia, with involuntary twitching of one of her eyes. I had to search my memory to put these symptoms together, for they were not something I had ever seen, except in a text book, but I suspected potassium bromide. Still used in some veterinary medicine for seizures in dogs, it had not been given to humans for a couple of decades due to its toxicity. It was a very crude sedative, in any case, but it would certainly account for the listless nature of many of the devotees I had seen.

I did what I could for my patients, sorting out the infected cut with the help of a few things in the kitchen, where I was permitted to rummage in the inadequate first aid kit. But apart from rest and better nourishment, and the cessation of whatever was being put in the food, there was nothing more I could for them. The food preparation areas were not particularly clean and the floors had not been washed down for a while.

Now I was in a bind. My clear duty was to stop this, and report Kyriakou's outfit to both the police and the local public health inspectorate, but I needed to contact Evelyn and see if she would come out voluntarily.

There was a noise outside my impromptu clinic, so I opened the door to find that Brother Michael was pushing Evelyn away. She was asking to see the doctor.

'Please let her in,' I said.

'But you have seen all the patients that the Magister has on his list,' he bureaucratically objected. Looking at his clipboard, he pushed Evelyn away with, 'You are supposed to be on kitchen patrol today, sister.'

So, I went and knocked on Kyriakou's door, walking in without waiting. I caught him with his purple-socked feet up on his desk, leaning back in his leather chair smoking a spliff, like a very relaxed Zeus. His brows darkened, and the feet descended floor-wards, 'How dare you come into my presence without permission!'

'Magister, I am very sorry, but I thought you would want to know that one of the sisters is being kept out of my clinic.' I spoke with authority, looking to him for support, but he did not stir himself.

'Have you not seen Brother Ken and Sisters Melissa and Janet?'

'I have, but Brother Michael is keeping another one from seeing me. I don't know her name.'

He looked into the corridor and seeing Evelyn, hesitated for a moment, finally saying to Michael, 'Sister Evelyn may see Brother Jack.' To me to said, 'Let me know your findings.' Like hell I would!

Evelyn sat down, gathering her full indigo robe about her. I had rehearsed this moment for the last two nights, but had not expected to gain it within a medical context which, though it gave the best privacy I could muster in this snake-pit of snoops, it was unfortunate in that she would regard me as Kyriakou's tame spy. Her eyes looked red, and she kept touching them as if trying to wipe something away.

'Hello, my name is Jack. What can I do for you?'

She blushed, 'I am concerned that my cycle hasn't come round as usual.'

I asked her a few questions about her medical history before asking the obvious question, 'Is there any possibility that you could be pregnant?'

There was a minute shocked hesitation followed by a definite 'No!

'Is there anything you are particularly worried about at the moment?'

She was not looking at me, but addressing the wall behind, 'I am missing my usual routines, I suppose. I feel run-down and tired. And I have a strange metallic taste in my mouth that not even toothpaste will remove.' This symptom was undoubtedly caused by bromide toxicity.

'May I examine you? We can call in another sister, if you would like one.'

'No, that's alright.' She drew off her robe. While I examined her, without disturbing her clothing too much, I kept up general conversation, 'Have you been part of the order long?'

'No, just a few weeks.'

There were a series of flea bites up her legs, and her eyes were crusty with some minor infection, 'Has it been rewarding for you?' I asked, tapping her chest.

'I felt it was, but I don't know now...What about you?'

'It's all a bit strange to me,' I admitted. I thought it was safe to say, 'I'm not sure it's entirely my cup of tea.'

She looked at me closely for the first time, 'You are not like anyone else here. You sound like you know your own mind. Not like the rest of us...' there was an embittered tone in her voice, which she swiftly covered, as if realising she was saying too much.

'I would hope so,' I smiled broadly, 'I've been in practice many years now, but I remain a seeker after truth. Open your mouth, please.' As I examined her tongue, I asked, 'So, have you thought you might pursue your own search for truth outside this establishment?' This was the furthest edge my questions might approach.

Immediately, she was suspicious, 'Has the Magister been asking about me?'

'No,' I responded, 'Nor is any part of our consultation anything to do with him. I swore the Hippocratic Oath, and my care is for you. Your session remains confidential.'

'Are *you* thinking of leaving?' she ventured in a whisper.

I lowered my voice, 'As soon as I can. Would you like to get out of here?'

Before she could answer, I was aware that the door had opened a crack. I went and leaned upon it with all my weight, saying to Evelyn, in a louder voice, 'Now, I imagine that the lowered nutrition in this place and perhaps worry are mostly responsible for your amenorrhea. I can't find any other outstanding reason for it. Apart from that, you have a minor eye infection which will clear up quickly with a little cream, which I will get for you.' Realising that my pompous tones were sounding like Miles Kingston's, I asked more kindly, 'Now, tell me about the flea bites?'

She sighed, 'The second floor has old carpet and the last occupant kept a swarm of cats – it's endemic in both dormitories, I'm afraid. I've tried spraying the floor with lemon juice and vinegar, but they just seem to come back.'

'I will see what we can do about that,' I promised. 'Is there anything else?'

Fixing her eyes upon me, she leaned over and wrote on the pad, 'Did you mean that, about leaving?'

I wrote, 'Yes! – Do you want to leave?'

She said quietly, 'I'm not sure there is much to go back to, but - yes.' Then she seemed to remember something, 'But it's all hopeless, of course, since the feast is on Friday.' She seemed to vacillate between twin poles of possibility.

'What happens then?'

'You'll see,' she said, slipping away. I tore the note to shreds.

I gave it to Kyriakou on the chin, 'Magister, the main problem with those I saw this morning was malnutrition: you have to improve nutrition and standards of cleanliness, or you will see more cases like this.'

He waved my words away with his hand, 'It is the fast, no more – they will be fed more than their wildest dreams in two days when we celebrate the feast of Aphrodite – you will enjoy it, brother!'

'Nonetheless, Magister Kyros, there is a flea epidemic in the dormitories – the carpets need heat steaming. I also need to go out and get supplies: the first-aid kit is not adequate, and Sister Evelyn needs some eye lotion.'

He brushed away my concerns, enquiring with some interest, 'Is she well enough for Friday?'

'For what – Magister?' I had a horrible suspicion, which I did not want to entertain, for his interest in her was just a little too pointed.

Leaning back again, he laughed, 'Why, to celebrate the feast, of course.'

I said carefully, 'Well, the food will certainly do her good, but I don't think many of your – followers will have a great deal of energy, any more than Evelyn, especially if you keep putting potassium bromide in the supplies... Magister?'

He sat up straighter, fixing me with his eyes, knowing he had been rumbled. Then a sly smile came over his face. Congratulating me with an approving nod, he said, 'I see that you know your skill well, brother. I will have to raise you to the first level at the feast, I see.'

I realised he was attempting to bribe me with some initiation. I bowed my head, hiding my true expression from the charlatan, saying 'I'm honoured, Magister.' But I still asked, 'May I go out to get supplies, Magister?'

He pulled out the righthand drawer where he kept the petty cash box, 'How much will it be?' he asked wearily, fingers poised.

I told him and he passed me the exact money over, along with a red ticket, saying, 'Show Stavros this, and he will let you out.'

Seizing my chance, I ran to my room to scribble an explanatory note for Ash, and stuff some more cash into my pocket for food supplies, before presenting myself to the knife-wielding Stavros who was clearly no part of Kyriakou's order.

Taking the red ticket off of me, the thug beckoned with his head, 'You have a 40 minute pass. Be back here before 2.30!'

That gave me no time to get down to the canal to warn Bodger. 'What if the prescriptions take longer?' I asked.

He mouthed a bite with his bared teeth, and opened the side door.

Thinking as fast as I belted down the road towards the chemist, I saw the

Craft Shop. Crossing the road, and peering within, I found the shop frustratingly unoccupied and the closed sign still turned around. Hammering on the door, I called out.

The female proprietor looked out of an upstairs window, calling in an aggrieved voice, 'I'm closed till 3pm, can't you read?'

I called back up, 'I have an important message for Bodger.'

I heard her complaining all down the stairs. She opened with, 'What do you want?' Noting my nasty little robe with disgust, she started to draw the door to. Thrusting my note through the snecked-in door, I said, 'Please, Edna. Bodger said you would help us. That we could trust you. This message has to get to him urgently. I have to go back into that place, but everything hangs on you now. There are people there in danger.' I did my best to persuade her.

She finally took it, with some reluctance, 'Should I be calling the police then, since it's so urgent?'

'Please just give Bodger the message: he will alert my employer who will know what to do.'

At least, I sincerely hoped so. My message had been explicit. I just had to trust that Edna would do as she promised.

I speedily acquired most of the supplies I needed, with Evelyn's eye lotion, and ran back to the wharehouse, with three minutes to spare. I hammered on the door which opened: Stavros had got one of the dogs from the yard ready on a short length of leash for my benefit, its ugly snout furrowed with barking as I slipped past its jagged mouth. And so I was incarcerated for a fourth night.

I had done my best. Isolated from any communication other Bodger's whistling, I could only hope and pray that Edna would get the message through and not give on me as a waste of space.

Throughout the rest of that day, I cursed myself for not running away and for feebly creeping back, but I knew that my conscience would not allow me to leave these deluded people alone with Kyriakou; someone had to be present to fight for them. After some heavy gardening, and worrying about how I was going to get Evelyn out, I fell asleep that evening during the compulsory meditation, for which I was denied any supper. I had to stand in the Temple with the empty plate before me, like some latter-day Oliver Twist, to the great satisfaction of some of the devotees over whom I had been temporarily raised: Kyriakou's enforcers were sending the message that no-one here was exempt from the regulations.

Returning to my room, I discovered a form had been placed on my bed which I was expected to fill in. It was about making a deeper commitment to the Order, telling me that, after the unreserved dedication – should I be found worthy to do so – I needed to advize the management about how my assets and property was to be apportioned, in the event of my serious illness and death. The implication being that Kyriakou would get the lot. Those who did not take the unreserved dedication could merely tithe their assets to the Order by giving them 10%. I checked the room to see what had been disturbed, since someone had been snooping about.

I awaited Bodger's evening whistle with deep resentment and grinding hunger, this time responding to him with the *Dr Who* theme tune, which was my signal for 'things are getting bad in here.' His dulcet whistle came back with the *Ride of the Valkyries,* indicating that help was coming.

Friday dawned with early morning meditations and a complete fast, except for water. I had had so little time in town, I hadn't managed to procure any food for myself: the short commons we had been on were so severe that I was now ready to eat my bedspread, since my last meal had been lunchtime on the previous day. My only consolation was that at least I was not consuming any more bromide. I was feeling sorry for undercover spies: how did they keep up their pretence day after day? I was conscious that my own mask was near to slipping, as my own strong opinions and reactions were being squeezed to the surface.

The whole centre seemed to be both nervous and excited, with people running around on various errands; though I tried to get some guidance as to what would be happening that night, but no-one would speak about it. While the long-sleevers were all upstairs conferring, I was seconded to garden patrol, where raised beds were being constructed from old railway sleepers. It was my job to lift these into place, since there were few men strong enough among them.

Devotees were made to work in pairs, with each one spying on the other, but with Brother Jerome, a thin grey-haired man with what looked acute anaemia, as my only helper, I had to virtually Samson each of the lengths of wood personally, with Jerome dropping his end more often than he lifted. After shifting about five of the sleepers where we needed them, he looked ready to drop, so I advised him to go in and lie down for a half hour, promising to do his share. He was not reluctant to go.

I had been thinking about Bodger and what he had showed me about the wharehouse: how the narrowboats and barges used to be able to come into the water-side part of the building to unlade in the old days. Taking my chance, I dropped back to the wall of the wharehouse and inched my way along the path leading to the double doors under the arch. They seemed to be fastened by some kind of bar, from my cautious pushing on the outer door. Taking a good look round, I went back for my spade and attempted to insert it between the doors, but I could not get enough purchase unless I could stand in front of them, which was impossible. I didn't know how deep the canal was at this point, but I didn't want to have to find out, either. Somehow, I would have to get round to the interior side of the bay and undo the bar. I also realised that the canal must be at the equivalent of the lower floor level inside the wharehouse.

If I could open the doors, then Bodger would be able to draw up *Wild Fennel* inside. This idea heartened me no end, so I made up my mind that this was the only way, unless I knocked out Stavros. The bell for close of work sounded and I went in to clean off the dirt and try to remove some of the splinters that I had received from shifting the wood about. The sewing room would provide me with a needle for this operation, I was told by Brother Jerome, but there was no-one to authorize my going down to the lower floor because of the preparations above. But I knew the sewing room was where Angela held sway, so I went and sought her out in the kitchen where the no-sleevers were toiling to make our feast.

'No-one is allowed in here tonight,' she firmly blocked me entrance.

'But I need to get a needle to dig these out,' holding up my left hand which sported a long treacherous splinter.

'Oh my goodness! Go and get a needle from the sewing room right away. I can't come with you now, I have to supervise here.'

Nonchalantly I went below, so as not to alert the guardians on the stairs. I pulled out the main splinters easily by hand, and started to search the corridor for access to the canal doors. They could only be at the end of the sewing room corridor because there was a greenish stain showing on the older flagstones jutting out under the modern door. The door to the waterside was evidently locked, so I strode back to the sewing room and stole the pinking shears which looked strong enough and jemmied the door open with them, leaving a jagged scar in the paintwork.

Opening the door, I stepped into a more brackish atmosphere: canal water lapped in the darkness, but there was no light here. Fortunately, under my robe I had some supplies that I had taken from the temple the night before when I had been punished with temple isolation. While everyone had been at supper, I had taken matches and a couple of candle glasses from the storage chest, thinking to at least have some longer reading time. At the time, it felt like a small gleeful infraction that lifted my spirits: but down here in the canal bay under the wharehouse, the candles became my saviours. I swiftly lit both lamps, seeing immediately how the canal doors were fastened by a metal bar.

I finally managed to lift it by hauling on the chain that fed through a pulley mechanism. The doors had not been opened for some time, I would guess, and the chain grated and would not shift for rust. It took all my strength to release the mechanism. My muscles ached, and flakes of rust grazed my already splintered hands.

I was rewarded finally by a reluctant movement and the metal bar lifted sufficiently for both doors to fall open with a grating crash. I jumped and held my breath, expecting someone to hear, but the feast preparations meant no-one was down on this floor. Now I had to fasten the doors back somehow. I saw where the hook was and brought the near door back, tearing off the left front end of my vile robe to tie it back, in default of any rope. Lifting one candle glass, I advanced gingerly around the other side of the bay, finding that the original bolt that would have held the farther door back had long departed and that it would just have to be pushed back.

In my mind was the vision of Bodger's semi-trad, *Wild Fennel* with her white forward light, so I set one of the lamps down on the path by the near side door already fastened back, leaving the other lamp shining at the deepest part of the bay. Then I dived back through into the corridor. The door to the loading bay was too ruined to be left to the view, so I punched out the light bulb with my hand wrapped in the remains of my robe, leaving the corridor in darkness.

I put the robe back on – now very much the worse for wear - before passing back upstairs. Immediately one of the guardian sisters on the stairs saw its state, asking why I wasn't upstairs and what had I done to myself?

Mumbling about an accident, that I had caught the end of the robe in the door, I obeyed her urging to get upstairs quickly. I had not been permitted above up this staircase before, and I was clearly the last person, since she followed me up. Chanting had already began, and the rhythmic sound of a gong or cymbal was sounding over and over like a call to prayer.

The large upstairs room had once been the main wharehouse floor and remained much as it had been, without being divided into rooms. Inside, in the dimmed lighting of that huge open space, were tables laden with food and alcohol set around the room: the smells of appetizing food were making me salivate instantly. Most people in the room were probably restraining themselves from falling upon the food.

Kyriakou stood centrally on a raised podium with some of the more senior long-sleevers beside him: they had changed from their street clothes into more exotic long silver lame robes under their indigo wraps, the men as well as the women! Evelyn stood to one side, under a tented awning of heavy green brocade, like a medieval lady in an enclosed garden. Her long hair fell down about her shoulders: her robe was green and she wore a kind of copper tiara with the sign for Venus upon her brow. Draped over her head, a semi-transparent veil did not hide the fact that the green robe was considerably lower cut than any of the silver lamé ones, and that it was girdled with a wide copper coloured belt, outlining her figure very well. Her eyes were closed and she swayed slightly to the chant.

Before the podium was an altar, with incense bellowing out from the brass censer, making my head spin, with the scent of patchouli, rose and verbena, and some deeper resin or gum that made the space reek like a brothel. The chant didn't seem to be in any language I knew, which meant that was all Greek to me.

The long-sleeved guardian from the stairs came in behind me, closing the doors and ushering me to join my fellow newbies who stood wide-eyed in a little huddle near the front. She bowed to Kyriakou who regarded me curiously. I tried to keep my left side where the robe was torn away from his gaze and sidled over to join the newbies, young Eric and Virginia, who had joined that week with me.

Kyriakou concluded the chanting with a commanding gesture, like a conductor. Silence fell, except for the sound of a sibilant rattle like that of a snake about to strike. The tension ramped up a notch.

'Tonight is the feast of Aphrodite,' he proclaimed, stepping off the podium and approaching the awning where Evelyn stood. 'Let us invoke the Goddess!'

He began to make passes around Evelyn's body, as the company chanted, 'Come, O come, beautiful Aphrodite!' I had seen Ash do something similar when we did the reconsecration ritual for Caro, calling down the spirit of St Margaret upon the body of Wendy, but this was very different. This chant had an erotic charge to it, for one thing, and a deep longing that stirred the body. My own loins tightened involuntarily, and I had to think very hard of something very mundane to avoid falling into the same orgiastic state as the other half-starved devotees. Kyriakou was calling down the Goddess of Love upon Evelyn. I didn't know what to do to stop him, but it was clearly working.

Like Doctor Faustus with Helen of Troy, Kyriakou drew her out from under her awning, 'Come, all-beautiful Aphrodite, hear our prayer and bless your children.'

With swaying gait, Evelyn was led towards us newbies. Eric fell to his knees in awe as she came closer, while Virginia drew back uncertainly. I remained standing, head bowed.

'Aphrodite, chose which of these neophytes you will bless this night.'

Kyriakou was now behaving like an arch pander. Evelyn's eyes were still closed as she raised an arm to indicate. Her hand fell upon my chest.

Immediately two of the long-sleevers came, drawing off my miserable rag of a robe and attiring me in a great emerald cloak. My hand held Evelyn's as we processed around the room, with Kyriakou going ahead of us backwards, as master of ceremonies, but I am not sure that the person I was leading was Evelyn. The embodiment of Aphrodite had taken effect: as we circled, the company seemed to be working itself up in a passion of longing, stretching out their arms to us imploringly. My mind was working overtime about how we could get out of here, for I had the worst feeling about what was to follow.

Kyriakou's voice, amplified above the chanting, directed us,

'Come, O Cyprus-Born, and to my prayer incline,
whether exalted in the heavens you shine,
or pleased in this far land to dwell.
Join with Adonis pure to sing, and thee divine.
Come, all-attractive, to my prayer inclined, for thee I call, with holy, reverent mind.'

There was nothing pure or reverent in his tone or mind, as we arrived back under the awning, where he fell upon his knees before her, declaring,

'Desirous breasts and eyes of shining joy,
give to your neophyte what no man can destroy....'

He was on the point of loosening her belt, when a penetrating Bristolian accent cut the heady chant with, 'Oi'd leave that lady alone, if Oi was you!'

Never have I been so glad to see Bodger who was there at the door with Ash at his back, only Ash was wearing a set of robes so gorgeous that Kyriakou's ones dimmed to mere faded theatrical costumery. The upstanding collar of Ash's robe was a sunburst of rays, while the garment itself was a shade of rich old gold, standing stiff with embroidery.

The overhead lights were switched on full by Bodger, breaking the spell as Ash strode towards the altar. Raising his hands, he said, 'Peace be to all in this place!' His voice rang resonantly through that sleazy room, dispersing the illusions that Kyriakou had been raising.

The devotees drew together, blinking uncertainly in the harsh strip lighting, unsure what Ash's entrance portended. Kyriakou attempted to rise from his knees, protesting loudly, but I didn't let him get far. Even as he called out urgently for Stavros, I whipped off my green cloak, enveloped the Magister in it, holding him fast while he wriggled to be free. Then I tore down the curtain pull from the awning, looping it over the bundled cloak and tying it round him.

Evelyn had fortunately moved out from under it, as the heavy awning of the canopy then fell down on top of him, so at least Kyriakou was unceremoniously muffled while we straightened things out. His voice could be still be heard faintly amplified until Bodger drew aside a side curtain, revealing the sound table and tore out the leads. A few of the long-sleevers looked like they might rush us then, so Bodger and I stood stalwartly together as Ash did his work.

Pinching out the light upon the altar, and with water from a small vial hidden in his hand, Ash cast it across the altar's surface, in a wide X, 'Unclean!' He picked up the censer, casting out the burning charcoal and the incense grains into the sand-bucket that stood below. 'Unclean!' he proclaimed again. He flicked the water from the vial to the four directions, 'Unclean!'

Then coming to Evelyn, he drew the veil from off her head, and pressing down with both hands upon her shoulders, called her name, 'Evelyn! Return to us.'

She swayed and blinked, clutching out blindly as she came back into herself. I stepped forward, taking her full weight against me, holding her closely within the curve of my left arm, as her eyes flickered open.

Ash then turned to the assembly, and proclaimed, 'The Order of the Golden Serpent is no more! By the authority vested in me by the Hidden Masters, I declare it null and void. All you who have followed this false master, depart to your homes with speed, and disperse, unless you want to testify to your treatment under this roof. Kyros Kyriakou is about to be arrested by the police...'

At the sound of emergency sirens drawing nearer from down the road, chaos ensued. Many of the long-sleevers made a bolt for the door, while some of the no-sleevers fell upon the food, regardless, and began gorging, others fleeing with hams and chicken legs in hand as they scrambled to get free and eat at the same time. Kyriakou's intended orgy was swept aside, as a chaotic scramble of blasted illusions ensued. Angela's bewildered face swept past me as the groundswell of devotees made for the stairs.

I called out to Bodger in alarm, 'What about the dogs? We can't let people out if they are still loose below!'

'No worries, mate!' He called back, grinning. 'They already had a noice piece of meat with a few additives...'

Drawing off his robes, Ash told me to take Evelyn down to the canal entrance, 'And take these,' he said, draping his gorgeous robes over my shoulder. 'Bodger's narrowboat is there. Just get on board! Bodger will be there soon!'

I half lifted Evelyn with the help of Eric and Virginia who had stuck with me, as we got ourselves through the chaos of the stairs, down to the lower-ground floor. Around the front entrance there was a widening circle of panic-stricken people, fearful of dogs and Stavros, all pushing to get out. I led our little party quietly down to the lower floor along the corridor where the bright lights of *Wild Fennel* welcomed us.

As we climbed on board, we heard the sound of splintering wood answering the police swot team's battering rams as they breached the front door area above. Virginia drew off her indigo wrap, cleaned her glasses with it rather distractedly, then firmly and deliberately wiped the perfectly clean dinette table with it, before bundling the wrap into the bin. Having made her statement, she then put on the kettle to make tea as if this were a normal thing to do after a ritual gone badly wrong, while Eric havered over Evelyn, 'Is she alright?' We had lain her down upon the bed, but there was no movement from her.

'Nothing that a cup of tea won't solve,' Virginia said, sagely.

I smiled at them both, but they both lowered their eyes in shame. 'Look here,' I said, 'There's no shame in being taken in by the likes of Kyriakou. He was a charlatan who conned folk a lot more canny than any of us!' I hoped by including myself among their number that they would feel better.

Eric put his head on one side, saying eagerly, 'Whatever your friend is called, he looked like the real thing. Does he take students, do you think?' Honestly, some people are just incorrigible!

I ensured that Evelyn was alright: her pupils were enlarged and I could not be sure what Kyriakou had given her, but she was conscious and a little confused. Leaving her with my fellow neophytes, I ventured back upstairs. Police were swarming about with emergency service personal, while officers were taking care of those who had decided to stay and make statements.

Ash was coming down the stairs through the mêlée towards me when Stavros leapt out of the downstairs audience room, knife raised, intent on sticking it into me, but Bodger swiftly out-stretched foot floored him before he could attack. The knife clattered away under the feet of the escaping devotees, who by now were released into the outside world like corks from a bottle. Two of the swot team lifted the struggling thug, bundling him into the back of the police van where Kyriakou shortly joined him, casting dark eyes upon me, and even darker looks upon Ash.

'They'll want you to give a statement, Jack,' Ash said, as we met on the stairs and embraced, 'Is there anything I can get for you?'

'For the sake of heaven, something to eat before I fall over!'

While Ash helped the emergency services, Bodger duly went and fetched me fish and chips from town, which I fell upon helped by Eric and Vera. I made my statement to a wide-eyed young constable who had never seen such goings on in his whole short life.

'I only thought black magicians were in the movies,' he confided in me as I signed my statement.

After a proper medical assessment, Evelyn was given the option of staying with us at the Beacon or being conveyed home to her parents. She chose to spend a week with us first where, after rest and proper nutrition, the events leading to her joining Kyriakou were carefully unpicked: the main catalyst had been her break up with Adrian, her boyfriend, but it was an underlying unhappiness with the stark realities of veterinary practice had brought her to a critical pitch of uncertainty. As a veterinary assistant, she was finding the necessary euthanizing of sick pets almost too much to bear: 'I didn't think I could continue in my work without going mad,' she said. Kyriakou's easy assurances had arrived at the right time to offer her a life-line, she had thought.

Evelyn spoke gratefully to me, 'I knew when I heard your voice that you were in your right mind: that everything there was an utter sham. You sounded real…'

'But you still were prepared to go through with that awful ritual?'

She lowered her head, ashamed, 'I know! I'm sorry. That afternoon, I was determined not to…but, I don't know what changed things…'

Ash put in, 'Did he hypnotize you into obeying, or did he give you something?'

'I have no memory of anything else.' Her face darkened 'He didn't .... do… anything to me, did he?'

I assured her that Ash had arrived in time to stop things developing but, even had he not, 'I would have punched his lights out before he laid a finger on you.'

Her relief was palpable, 'Can my mum and dad can come now?'

'Of course!'

Mr and Mrs Wharton motored down the next day and had lunch with us. Mrs Wharton kissed me after embracing her daughter, 'That's for not giving in, and bringing back our girl to us! I knew you wouldn't let us down!' Mr Wharton had finally dropped his rebarbative air and made a goodly donation towards our work, meek as a lamb.

The fall of Kyriakou's HQ was the nine days wonder of Icenfeld, reported widely in the local and national press. I later testified in court as to the state and running of the centre, along with a handful of other ex-devotees. Remarkably few stepped forward to give statements, largely due to embarrassment, so Kyriakou did not receive the maximum sentence due to him as a result, but he had been at least been removed from the field of activity while he worked out his five years.

Ash took the verdict philosophically, 'He'll be out in 2-3 three years with good behaviour, of course, and back to his old tricks before long.'

I asked him, 'You never told me how you knew Kyriakou?'

'We trained together initially, but he was ejected from the mother lodge because of his approaches to another lodge member. He took the teachings and warped them into a series of self-promotional campaigns that led to the kind of thing that he had planned in Icenfield.'

'Well, that's cured me of wanting to have anything more to do with magic,' I stated, forthrightly.

Peering at something over my head, in a curious voice, Ash said, 'I wouldn't be so sure about that, Jack!'

Case 10: THE PATH TO THE SANCTUARY

Creating simplicity often makes the heart leap; order has been restored, the crooked made straight. But order is understanding that things cannot be made simple, that complexity reigns and must be accepted.
Marina Warner – Joan of Arc

We neither of us had slept well, which did not help matters. The argument had begun early that morning: a row to end all row: all over some tiny triviality that soon became blown out of all proportion. The more I tried to bank it down, the more inflammatory I apparently became, since Jane finally sat down on the bed and began howling. I did dimly suspected that this was not entirely about the tub of indoor roses that I had moved from where she placed it.

Feeling utterly helpless, I ran downstairs to seek out Wendy, 'I don't know what I've done, but I think she will melt down if I try to understand her any more. Can you...?

She untied her apron, 'I heard the wailing. Best you make yourself scarce for a bit and I'll try and find out what it's all about. The last few months of pregnancy are so trying. Why don't you begin laying things out for breakfast for me?'

Wendy returned ten minutes later, shaking her head to the question in my eyes, 'No, you stay here. I'll take her up something on a tray shortly. She just needs a bit of space.'

Jane's pregnancy had proceeded largely without problems but, since Christmas, and especially over the last two weeks, she had become uneasy and irritable, as well as in considerable discomfort. With two doctors in the house and a midwife just down the road, we were not unduly worried. But as the inadvertent originator of a family, I was beginning to be on increasing shaky ground myself, for I had brought her all the way from Australia to marry me, for us to live in a communal house, with only a study, bedroom, and bathroom of our own. It was little better than living in a hotel, in terms of personal space, for all that we had the run of the Beacon as our home. I had begun to look about for a place we could call our own, only to discover that anywhere this near to the coast meant an inflated price-tag that was well beyond our pocket. And now the time was drawing closer when we would need our own enclave. So, I was generally feeling inadequate and ineffective as a providing husband.

Ash came in, silently noting my hangdog expression. Kindly saying nothing, he passed me the sauce for my sausages. Then Gillespie breezed in with the post, having missed all the kerfuffle. Noting the heavy silence, he asked insouciantly, 'Has there been a fatality?' Ash received the post with a shake of the head and a significant glance in my direction. Gillespie duly withdrew himself to the scullery, humming 'There Is Nae Luck Aboot the Hoose' under his breath, which didn't help my mood.

I was mechanically shoveling baked beans into my mouth, when I realized that the silence had deepened yet further, that Ash was holding open a letter, staring fixedly at it. A sense of something badly gone wrong filled the already gloomy breakfast table.

'Bad news?'

He nodded.

'Anything I can do?'

Ash gazed into me with one his penetrating looks, 'It's just that I may have to involve you at a difficult time for you and Jane… I may have to bring you in deeper, to a place you've not chosen.'

I put down my knife and fork, 'No, you're going to have explain that to me, as I'm completely lost.'

'The Beacon is to be inspected…'

I frowned, 'Oh! But won't that just mean a bundle of papers to fill in, and lots of nosy individuals coming down on us?'

'No, this time it's personal. They are coming after me first, and then you. They want to close us down.'

I scanned the offending letter he extended to me and could see nothing of the kind written there, 'But how do you know that?'

With a dry quirk of his lips, Ash pointed, 'From the signature!'

It said 'William Faulkner' and a bunch of honorifics following his name. 'What? … You mean, impressive on paper, but deadly in person?'

'Something like that.'

'I thought you had no enemies? You could charm your way into Hades, past Cerberus and all his pups, you!'

Ash didn't avert his eyes, but just sighed, 'This time it's not so easy. We are going to have to seek sanctuary.'

To my mind, sanctuary was for medieval people, like the knights who killed Thomas à Becket, or those who filched goods out of people's pockets and then managed to run into a church and hold the altar cloth before they were arrested. I remembered the illustration in an old school book, of men wading out into the sea after their statutory 40 days of sanctuary were up, hands lifted in supplication, begging passing boats to pick them out of the sea and take them into exile, which was the next step because, if you turned back, the folk on the land you'd just waded out from might stone or execute you. It stayed in my impressionable young mind because of that dramatic picture.

My sense of something wrong was pretty well founded, by Ash's intense stillness.

'I thought you were omniscient.'

He sighed, 'I wasn't ever that, but particularly not this time. Melanie had her own difficulties when regulation became more common, but that was nothing like this is going to be.'

In such litigious days as these, when medical malpractice suits are the terror of our profession, it was a miracle that the Beacon had lasted so long without some contentious guest or professional body coming after Ash and our whole way of working. While Ash kept up his membership of several professional organizations, he was still regarded as a dangerous maverick in some quarters, by those who liked the orderliness of a well-regulated umbrella organization. The kind of work we did at the Beacon was way off-piste for the regulators, apparently, for all that we traded as a private and independent residential mental health clinic. So, it was hardly a surprise to hear that we were about to investigated by MHRC, the regulatory body of the General Medical Council.

Directly after breakfast, Ash called a house meeting of the staff. He outlined the nature of the investigation and why it was likely to be viciously thorough, 'The individual leading the inspection has crossed swords with me before, but now he occupies a more elevated position. I have reason to think that William Faulkner will give us no quarter, so we will all have to be prepared. Since Jane is now officially on leave, Deirdre will be covering her position.' Deirdre was one of our local mental health nurses who usually occasionally covered the night-shifts or any specific nursing duties. Jane did not protest, but I could feel the tension of protest in her hand which she suffered me to hold.

'What about the guests we are already seeing?' asked Will, sitting on the window-seat. He was ready primed to cover for me when Jane gave birth.

'Those who are already with us will remain, but we will not be taking on any further cases until this is all over,' Ash confirmed.

There was a stunned silence. The ethic of the Beacon was that we took those who needed us as soon as we could, turning no-one away. Healing had its own timetable that couldn't be hurried or betrayed like this.

'Oh, but what about the Hemple girl?' asked Wendy, pressing hand to face, 'I just got a phone call to say she'd be at the station at 3.40pm today?'

Anastacia Hemple had been, until recently, confined against her will by a coercive witch who purported to be training her up as a member of her all-female coven. Having separated Anastacia from her girlfriend Jodie, she had kept Anastacia locked in an upstairs bedroom for many weeks, under threat of physical harm. The police had finally brought her imprisonment to an end, but only after the body of Jodie had been discovered murdered in the garden of the flat they used to share, that the whole sordid mystery began to unravel. Anastacia's persecutor was clearly implicated in the murder, and was now on remand, awaiting trial, while Anastacia herself, traumatized by her forcible incarceration, had been freed only to encounter the devastation of her girlfriend's murder. The police enquiry had been too much for her to deal with, and she had suffered a brief period of mental breakdown. Being without good support, for her parents had shunned her since she came out as a lesbian, she had been referred on to us by one of Ash's colleagues in the Guild of Ecumenical Psychology. Our job was to offer her a place of restoration.

Ash smoothed his brow, as if trying to brush away the trial that stood before him; it was not like him to forget a new guest was coming, 'She must come, of course.' He took in our faces: Wendy leaning in disbelief against tight-lipped Gillespie. 'You all know how reluctantly I close our doors, but we must reduce the aggravation this inquisition is likely to raise.'

'On what grounds are they inspecting us,' Will asked, practically, trying to puncture the air of doom. 'Has someone complained about us, or what?'

'It is a scheduled inspection, which the MHRC can do at any time.'

'So, this Faulkner, is he the Grand Inquisitor, then?' enquired Gillespie, stroking his chin.

'Well, there will be no *auto da fé* with instruments of torture and pyres, but you may expect the full bureaucratic rack and psychological gas-lighting, yes.' We exchanged looks around the room, never having heard Ash speak so ironically before.

'When will all this happen?' Jane asked, in a small voice, as well she might, since her confinement would almost certainly fall within the duration of the inspection.

'It could be at any time: they are not bound to inform us, so if there are any areas that the inspectors would pounce upon, anything that you have left undone, now would be the time to do them: writing up or filing of casework, business accounts, reports, medical stock, replacement of supplies, bits of stair carpet that need running repairs, any broken instruments or equipment – you all know your duties. I will check that all the insurance certificates and registration documents are up to date: Jack, will you help me with locating the paperwork? Apart from Jane - and Jack, of course, when the time comes - I am suspending any leave that is due until after we are through all this. We need to be absolutely meticulous!'

'What are we to say to our guests about it?' Wendy asked, her brows furrowing with anxiety. Part of her bun had tumbled down, and she had neglected to pin it up.

'Tell them the truth, but keep it light: just say that we are expecting an inspection by the regulatory authority, but do not alarm them. None of our guests is obliged to accept the inspectors sitting in during their sessions, nor are they bound to answer any enquiries, though anything that they can add may well help us, of course.'

As everyone shuffled off in subdued fashion, Ash signed to me to stay behind. I wanted to know, 'On what grounds they are likely to try and shake us?'

'On the grounds of my fitness as a proper person to direct the Beacon. And, by association, whether you are also fit, I would imagine.' Since Ash returned from his three-year sabbatical, I had been registered as its joint director. 'I know we are both alright on paper,' he said. 'We've upkept our proper registrations, but it doesn't take much to start a witch-hunt in this field.'

Trying to put a brave face on it, I said with enforced cheeriness, 'Well, I hope my unspectacular antecedents have provided enough cover for your more unusual activities?'

'Let us hope so!' Ash said, more seriously that I intended him to take that statement.

'So, who is this Faulkner anyway?' I asked.

'An adversary who has taken personal offence at my existence. We have gone head to head on many a committee, as we have utterly divergent views on how things should be done. There was also some unpleasantness over the best medical treatment of a relative of his, for whom I was called to serve as a medical advocate: he has never forgiven me for the way the arbitration of that fell out. There was an inheritance involved, you see...'

'... and he felt hard done by? - It's very bad luck that he should be the one inspecting, then. But, listen, what is it that you need to involve me with? It sounded a bit gnomic over breakfast – was I missing something?'

Ash invited me to sit by the fire, picking up the smooth piece of serpentine that lay on the table. He passed his hands over its pink-speckled moss-green surface, peering into its depths, saying, 'There is a further difficulty that now arises, which I wanted to talk with you about privately. It concerns the nature of the trusteeship of the Beacon. When Melanie set it up, the foundation document was drawn up in such a way that at least the director or one of the trustees of the Beacon, should be an initiate of the lodge. She felt, back in the 1940s, that only one who was grounded in the Mysteries could ensure its proper working according to the guidelines she had laid down.' He paused and looked at me again, as if he were measuring me up.

Throwing up my hands, I asked, 'So, how has that changed? – You've not resigned from your lodge, have you?'

'No, but if this inspection removes me as director - which it could well do, - there would be no-one with that connection left at the Beacon. It would void our foundation agreement with Melanie.'

The loss of Ash from the Beacon for a second time was not something that bore thinking about. 'But surely ... you went away once. How is *this* eventuality any different? Did I not keep it running properly then?'

He shook his head, 'You did wonderfully well.' He sighed, 'But when I went away last time, Tryphena was still a trustee. Since her death, I have been biding my time, hoping that a solution would present itself.'

I cast about for solutions, 'Surely you could appoint someone from your lodge?'

'I have asked the members already. They all refused.' He looked deeply into me again, before continuing, 'But they did come back to me with a counter-proposal of their own: that *you* join the lodge.'

I sat back in my chair in amazement, 'But they don't know me!'

'They all know how much I rely upon you, upon your judgement and your discretion. They also know how much I have taught you over the years. The question is whether that teaching has borne fruit?'

I stood up and paced about with agitation, shaking my head, 'well, you really have chosen a very interesting point at which to make this known, my friend!'

He stood contritely, 'Jack, I know... I was hoping that something might have awoken in you, but I also acknowledge too how I hazarded your trust in me when I sent you to Kyriakou's establishment. I did wrong in exposing you to such a one as he, without the armour of a deeper training.'

That stopped me in my tracks, 'Now don't you take the blame on yourself! I may not have known much about ritual magic when I agreed to go in there after Evelyn but, being there, it showed me how much you *had* taught me, and how precious it was – no, *is*.' I looked towards the overclouded heights of Hartsworth Beacon, recalling my very first encounter with Ash in London so many years back. 'I remember how you received me when I applied for this job, when I had no expectations of any work whatever: I thought I had landed in paradise when I came here. To be treated with respect and brought into all that you do, well!... I didn't think such a post existed!'

The sudden sick feeling in the pit of my stomach, as if the whole world were a kaleidoscope, forced me to confront how things really were with me, and I told him frankly, 'You know, Ash, nothing hurt me as much as when you had to sack me from the Beacon, so that I might be seen to go over to Kyriakou's side. But I tell you, it was only once I was there, in that God-awful place, as one of his indentured cult-slaves, that I fully appreciated how much I was in the mould of all that you and Melanie have created here.'

Some of the hollowness left his face then, 'I am glad to have retained your trust.' And I realised how alone and exposed he must have felt, from the sudden hope that brightened his eyes.

In that same moment I also recalled what I had experienced when Kyriakou received me into his cult, when he made me swear the oath of allegiance to his order: I didn't simply cross my fingers to negate the words of my mouth, but had actively kept Ash in my mind, with all that we practiced here, and upon the light that shines in the Sanctuary in my intent. I had - albeit inadvertently - already taken the step towards what he now offered me. Without understanding what I had done, I had already made a promise and commitment to Ash's way of working: and now the time of its redemption had come. 'What will it mean, Ash?'

He raised his hands questioningly, 'What will *what* mean?'

'Being a part of your lodge?'

He threw back his head with suppressed laughter, 'Jack, you never disappoint! Will you really try it and see?'

'Well, I seem to remember reading in the books you gave me to study while I was on Bodger's houseboat, that no-one should enter magical work without first having put the better part of raising a family behind him. Now here are you - asking me to take this on when I am just about to start mine! But, yes, I will try it, if you all really want me?'

He embraced me, 'I have given some thought to that already, and how I might best support you... but, can we talk about that another day? Today, we have a lot of work to do.'

It was against such a background of threat and uncertainty, and in my case, bewilderment and wonder, that Gillespie went to the station that afternoon to pick up Anastacia Hemple. I had missed seeing her at the London practice, but had read her case notes closely. Everyone at the Beacon was well prepared to deal with the fall out, including any press attention, should it come. Already, the worst newspapers had blazoned the case across the country with headlines like, 'Murdered by Magic: Witch's Body Found In Compost Heap,' and 'Ritual Murder in Ealing.' It was probably the least suitable case for us to be dealing at such a time, but Ash would not turn her away, having once offered her a place at the Beacon.

Anastacia arrived in time for a late afternoon tea; a slight young woman with long brown hair bound with a green scarf who, standing beside the rangy Gillespie, looked like a different species of human being, she was so fine-boned. But I liked the way she turned her head towards the Beacon as if it were a rare fragrant flower. Ash came out to greet her, shouldering her backpack, but she did not allow him to take the longer trapezoidal case which she hugged to her chest, I noticed.

While she was being shown to her room by Wendy, I asked Ash, 'What was in that case? Some kind of instrument?'

He nodded, 'She asked if she could bring her psaltery here, of course I told her that we welcome music at the Beacon. – You do remember that she plays in an early music group?'

We eventually heard her playing it in her room, stroking sharp and plangent chords from its strings, but never once heard her voice beside it. When we asked, she would only say, 'My singing voice has gone a long way off.'

Regardless of imminent inspectors, our work had to go on. We began our assessment after Anastacia had settled in, giving her the next morning to roam the grounds and the house, though she said she found it hard to stray more than a few steps from the house, after so long an incarceration. Confronted with the wide-open space of the Downs and the crowding trees of Hartsworth Beacon, she seemed to suffer from a sense of vastation. She said, 'It's feels like the whole world were running towards me!'

Anastacia's case notes noted that she had been very closed down and somewhat reserved about the details of her unfortunate association with her captor. But, after gaging where we at the Beacon were coming from, she opened up to us, and we began to understand her former reticence.

'Thank you for having me here,' she began, shyly. 'After the last months, this place is balm to my soul.'

'You are very welcome, Anastacia. Now today, we just want to explore how best Jack and I can help you clear away the obstacles, so that you can begin to move forwards in your own story again.'

She nodded, 'I like that! I really do feel as if my life were stuck in this awful groove. But there are still so many missing bits, I can't always make sense of it. It's like trying to understand the shape of a late medieval motet, but the tenor line is missing, so it has no tune, only a welter of notes that keep going around. What do we do? What do you want?'

'Well, firstly we don't need you to pick over the details of what's happened all over again, but it would be helpful if we can ask a few questions to clarify where we need to come from.'

From the way she sat up straighter in the chair, I could tell how much Anastacia dreaded the re-traumatization that questioning might evoke. But Ash was careful, asking, 'Maybe you could start to make sense of things if you saw the connections between things? For example, how you came to know Nicola Farrell in the first place?' Farrell had been her captor.

'Jodie and I had talked for a long time about getting married, and someone introduced me to a celebrant network that custom-made marriage ceremonies for people like us, who couldn't get married in registry office.' (This was at a time when same-sex marriage or civil partnership had not yet been put on the statute.)

'We talked to a few celebrants, but none of them clicked with us. Then we met Nicola and she seemed perfect. She also taught evening classes on the Goddess and Witchcraft, we found out.' She clarified, 'You know, Wicca, - not black magic or anything like that…. And she ran a working group. Jodie and I were really only interested in joining a woman's circle, rather than a mixed coven, and she invited us to meetings. - We thought we'd done our research well, but we really hadn't.' She turned the fringes of her green silk scarf over and over distractedly.

Ash asked, 'What did you seek by joining such a group?'

'We wanted to be part of a magical, Goddess-based group, where we would be supported as lesbians, and where we could learn the deeper mysteries.'

'And did you feel that Nicola could do that?'

'At first, we both did: I suppose we were drawn so strongly to be part of such a circle that we didn't see what became obvious later: that Nicola's group was just a cover. She invited young women into her group to prey on them. Believe me, I've had long enough to realise that,' she said ruefully.

'What was it about her that drew you to Nicola,' I asked, always interested in the attraction factor that brought unlikely people together.

Anastacia became very still, 'I'm sorry, it's hard to remember how I was then, what I saw in her… I suppose it was the dazzle of her. She was a very physical woman, strong in her body like a dancer. Intensive, Scorpionic, certain of herself.'

The story began to fall into shape. Jodie and Anastasia were joined to the outer circle for a while, but then Nicola had started to drive a wedge between the girlfriends, by the simple expedient of preferring Anastacia to Jodie, whom she side-lined. The plan for a sacred marriage ceremony became pushed further and further back.

'I'm certain that Jodie had begun to work out what Nicola was about, or she had some suspicion. It was awful – we began to argue at home, because I wouldn't believe anything bad of Nicola at that point.'

Nicola had then asked Anastacia to come over, ostensibly to give her private tuition at her house, to prepare for a rite due later that month to bring her into the inner circle. Once there, Nicola had confiscated her phone, on the excuse that Anastacia needed to be in seclusion for a few days before the rite, keeping her in the house, at first by promises, and then by threats.

I myself remembered this kind of deprivation very well from my time in Icenfield but, bad as that was, or might have become, Anastacia's captivity was much worse. After an attempt to get out of the house, she had been chained to her bed by a four-foot length of chain attached to her ankle, a prisoner to Nicola's sexual predation, under the cover of it being 'service to the Goddess.'

'I just wasn't strong enough on so many levels for her. She drugged me at first. Later, if I didn't submit to her, I would be beaten. I've blotted out so much of that time: I can't remember a sequence anymore. My dreams and my waking sort of became one.' And so, she had endured, a passive recipient of the abuse that no-one could stop happening.

I could well believe it, as I had seen the photographs of Farrell in the newspapers: a well-built, tough woman who worked out regularly at the gym, she had herself been the victim of an abusive and criminal father, Anastacia said. As often happens in such cases of violent abuse, it seemed that Nicola had taken on the characteristics of a controlling bully, revisiting what she had suffered upon her victims. I knew that beneath the all-covering clothes she wore, that Anastacia still bore the scars of those beatings, as well as a recently-healed radial fracture to her forearm that had had to be reset when she was eventually freed.

Jodie had, of course, tried to track her girlfriend down, and phoned Nicola. The police report reconstructed events around the murder, working out that Nicola had gone over to Jodie's flat, where they had come to blows, and that Jodie's body had been dragged to the bottom of the garden and half-buried in the compost heap, covered with a layer of grass cuttings. It was only when the landlord finally came round to fix a broken window that another of his tenants had reported some weeks earlier, that he had come into the back garden and made the discovery. Even so, it had taken the police five more days to learn where Anastasia had gone: they had initially even suspected *her* of Jodie's murder. When Jodie's phone was discovered at the dump by an eagle-eyed council operative – for it had been discarded in the communal rubbish bins – the sequence of events was gradually pieced together. The newspapers had relished these events, working it up into 'a ritual murder,' instead of a jealous rival taking out an inconvenient partner.

Guilt was at the core of Anastacia's distress, 'If I had only held onto the love that I knew, if only I had not let Jodie down…instead of going after stranger things…'

Ash said gently, 'You are not to blame for being lured towards your earnest desire by one who was unworthy of being a guide. You came without guile into a situation that was a trap.'

'The only good thing that's come out of this is that no other women will ever be part of Nicola's circle ever again.' Anastacia concluded, taking bitter comfort. Nicola was likely to be charged with the unlawful killing of Jodie and the unwilling detention of Anastacia, as well as charge of grievous bodily harm, unlawful detention and sexual intimidation, but the law's delay meant that the trial would not take place for several months , although the CPS had advised that Nicola would be looking at a minimum of 30 years as a life sentence. Anastacia had no appetite for vengeance, however, feeling herself excerpted from the slow grind of justice.

'And for yourself, now - if your time here could give you anything - what would you most like to happen? Ash asked.

'To know that Jodie is alright, that she forgives me. To come back to a place where I could trust myself again. To cleanse my heart of sorrow.' She shook her head, 'To be able to sing again….?' She turned a tremulous mouth towards the window where rain was sweeping across the Downs. 'The only thing that kept me sane in that awful room was my psaltery, which I'd brought along; that and being able to meditate and pray to the Goddess.'

Still turned towards the window, she went on in a lower voice, 'I used the links of the chain as a rosary, you know, to say the names of the Goddess over and over:

'"Saving Mother, ever holy,
Pour upon us your abundance,
Spread your healing cloak about us,
Welcome us within your dwelling."'

She repeated the prayer in a low mutter, as if paying out a line to her drowning self, alone in a deep ocean. Turning brimming green eyes back to us, she explained, 'You see, I didn't know that I would be alive for so long… I made ready to die, because I could see no way out. If the police had not broken down the door when they did, I would have used that chain to make my escape.'

What terrible stories we heard within these four walls, I thought, and blessed that brave young woman who had held back terror and death by means of music and prayer!

Ash handed her a glass of water, saying, 'We'll leave it here for today.' He called Deirdre to come look after her.

After Anastacia had gone, we discussed the case, 'And I thought, Kyriakou was bad!'

'When spirituality becomes a cover for sexual coercion, it is ugly indeed.'

'So what action do we need to take?'

'I think, just to allow Anastacia to find her own level. She first needs stability, kindness, and a sense of regular normality. There will be work enough to clear the ground of the debris when she is ready.'

Busy though we were, I needed to speak to Jane about Ash's invitation. It might be a complication too far in the already quite complex life of the Beacon, and I needed to check. I found her in the greenhouse, repotting some of the house plants. She listened carefully to me in so extended a silence that I began to feel I was on increasingly fragile ground, 'I know it's not the best of times....'

'You're too right,' she said, pressing compost around the philodendron. Then, putting down the trowel, and resting her behind upon the stool, 'So, what do they do in the lodge? Is it an "on the square, with rolled-up trouser legs" kind of thing?'

I made a face at her, 'You know it's not that kind of lodge! More like a lot of meditation and ritual, I imagine. It's a monthly commitment, in terms of attendance, with some study in between.'

She observed me, ironically, 'What? In your copious spare time?'

'I suppose so... It's not going to stop me sharing parental duties, you know?'

'In that case, then you should do it .... if you really want to?'

'I think I do, and I'm so sorry for yesterday morning.'

She went on tiptoe to kiss me on the nose, 'I suppose it's all part of life's rich pattern in this neck of the woods?'

And I held her in my arms for a long time, but this time it felt like a shared silence.

'May I ask what the fish is about?' Anastacia said, pointing to the wall painting of Raphael the Archangel. We had taken her to see the Sanctuary. Her question pleased Ash, 'You're the first person to notice it straight away! It's a reference to the *Book of Tobit*, from the *Apocrypha*, where the archangel comes in disguise to companion Tobias on his way: the angel instructs him to catch a fish but to keep its heart, liver and gall. Tobias burns the heart and liver to scare away the demons that are serially killing off the suitors of a young woman, while he makes a healing tincture from the gall to heal his blind father, Tobit.'

Even as Ash explained the story, I felt its overt resonance with Anastacia's case, but she simply smiled, 'I see... May I come and sit in here sometimes? It would be lovely to meditate in here – it feels utterly peaceful and calm, that nothing can touch me here.'

'Of course,' Ash said.

From that moment onwards, Anastacia could often be found in the Sanctuary on a regular basis, sometimes bringing her psaltery to play when we were not seeing clients in the main office. I knew this because, amid all the preparations for inspection, I began seriously studying with Ash, who had set me to meditate daily in the Sanctuary. I began to appreciate the breadth and depth of his teaching in a different context from our work, seeing it from the standpoint of universal principles, where time transmutes into eternity.

Anastacia seemed to be settling down and, with the help of Wendy and Deirdre, had started to venture into the garden for short periods without being overcome by the wide-openness of space. In myself, a different kind of space was opening up, as I made meditation my daily practice. I still look back on that time as the formation of my life today, a space that is always available, to refresh me in times of difficulties.

Then one morning, I woke up very early and lay in bed listening gratefully to steady rain falling. I needed to hear it; just as the ground had been so dry recently, so my soul had been. The realization of this somehow made everything alright again. Jane lay breathing quietly behind me, her body spread across the bed in the trustful cradle of sleep. I tucked the quilt over her outstretched arm. No wonder I felt unhandy and stupid around her, and more than a little frightened about the responsibilities that the baby would undoubtedly bring. I had been stupidly taking the weight of the whole proceeding upon myself, and the rain now reminded me that was not necessary.

With a strangely happy heart, I dressed quickly, picking up one of the books that Ash had given me to prepare myself for penetrating Kyriakou's premises. It was *Magic for Today* by Ernest Steepleton: written back in the mid 1960s, it had proved a good support to me since I first read it on Bodger's barge. Steepleton had been an old gentleman, a revered magister of the Order of the Ancient Mystery when he wrote it, and this little book contained a life-time of good advice. It had become my habit to turn to it in times of trouble, just opening at random: sometimes a phrase or passage leapt out helpfully, as it did this morning, where he spoke about what overshadowed his world,

'Despite the disruption of two world wars, and the shadow of nuclear war that hangs over us, the light of the ageless wisdom still shines upon and within us, especially in those arcane schools who claim an ancient lineage. Yet the light burning upon the sanctuary within the lodge is the self-same light that shines upon every hearth. All those who foster its shining are themselves lantern-bearers.'

This passage moved me deeply and I went into the sanctuary quietly to meditate upon it, so that I might explore the feelings and images that it evoked in me. As I sat in the darkness before the light that shone upon the shrine there, I experienced a number of things that I cannot now recall, but chief among them was a succession of people who came and went in a long stream, passing the lantern of wisdom from hand to hand. I imagined them as figures like those engraved by William Blake, in the draperies of no specific era, but ageless and eternal as the Ancient of Days.

Generations of seers and wise people had verified that light from their own experiences and passed it on as a sacred trust to those who came after them: but the light had arisen first within them, as lone seekers, even now as it was burning more brightly within me. It was only afterwards that these seekers had found others in their searching for a wisdom that did not wander nor wilt in the heat of day's challenges, a wisdom that nourished and supported them. Now I longed with all my heart to be a recipient of that wisdom, with a patient longing, like one who is exiled and desires to see once more the shores of his homeland.

I was sunk in my musings when the door to the Sanctuary softly opened and Ash stepped in for his morning meditation. It was still dark and he did not see me where I sat huddled in the corner, so I observed how he saluted the light with a deep reverence, and the grace with which he entered so completely into its presence. To my wondering eyes, he appeared to be the latest in that long stream of wise ones who - though they were born to dissimilar and unrelated families – had been made into one lineage of light, as lantern-bearers who illuminated the world. I knew then that I longed to be one of that kindred.

I must have sighed, and Ash became aware of me, nodding his head towards me without disturbing the silence. We knew each other well enough now to be comfortable sharing a silence such as this. I tried to pick up the place where I had been, but it would not return to me. And then, I found my mind ranging back to Tryphena's funeral when Ash's lodge members came to honour her: although they were of different walks of life, male, female, younger or older, there had been something about them. They somehow shared the likeness of those in whom a magic casement had opened, so that they perceived with the same eyes those wonders that the light of wisdom had illumined. None of them had the inflated or distorted views which Kyriakou had forcibly tried to inculcate in his followers, slaves as they were to a demanding master who cared nothing for them. Ash and his fellow members of the lodge were different, being under obedience to a greater breadth and depth of spirit. Where Kyriakou's people had been shrunken and constrained, Ash's people bore the mark of free people. Accidentally, I had re-connected some vital component within my soul that morning.

It was going to be a day of trouble, I was sure, but my self-possession and quietness of heart that had been awakened by the gentle rain remained with me. I rose and left Ash to his meditations.

There are some things you can prepare for and others that just swipe you sideways. The inspection began that very morning. Faulkner and his crew had stayed overnight at a hotel in Christminster, evidently hoping to catch us on the hop early, but we were still up before them. Faulkner himself surged into the Beacon like an invading force. He was not what I expected at all, being clearly made for adventures on the high seas or in the deepest desert. Brown as a nut and with a vigour that would have been admirable in a pirate or independent explorer, he swarmed into the Beacon with his advance party. All that was missing was the swagger stick, really. His lieutenants were clearly primed to case the joint like CIA agents, though they more nearly equated to my expectations as inspectors: Edwin Maniciple was a bland-faced man with all the charm of a sinecured civil-servant, while the woman, Fiona Carey, sported the kind of up-swept glasses I'd not seen since the 1960s. She thrust her chin forward short-sightedly as if trying to smell what we were up to, making a derogatory gesture towards Melanie's shrine in the porch as she entered. I had to unball my fists before spreading a smile of welcome: I fear I was not a good dissembler!

Wendy courteously invited them all to take a breakfast with us, but Ash would not allow them to look around until such time as we had partaken of ours, so they had to sit restively with their tea and coffee while we ate what we could. Ash asked Gillespie if he would lay a fire in the waiting room which the inspection team might have as their own meeting area.

I could tell from the curl of Gillespie's expressive eyebrows that they would undoubtedly be receiving the full blast of his irony if they stepped but a finger from the path of righteousness, and that, once he started down that road, it would be next to impossible to head him off, regardless of the consequences. Fortunately, as it turned out, neither Faulkner nor his two operatives were fully attuned to Gillespie's broad accent, and so most of his sotto-voce remarks and asides fell on bewildered or tone-deaf ears.

It had been prearranged that none of us would be caught alone, and that we would remain in pairs as far as was possible, but Faulkner's team were alert to that, doing their best to divide and conquer. While Ash showed Faulkner the books, Maniciple wanted me to enumerate and outline the cases that had been through since the beginning of the year, which was no small undertaking.

'Are there any particular cases you want to look at first?' I asked the bland-faced man, presenting him with our total figures. Manciple poured over them for about three minutes, making notes on his clipboard in black, crabbed hieroglyphics. 'And where are the readmission figures?' he finally asked.

I had some difficulty in persuading him that we had nearly zero readmissions to the Beacon: the only one we had had that whole year was the premature discharge of a guest who had to return home to Shropshire for a family funeral, only to come back to us a few days later – we always marked such goings and comings when the guest was absent overnight as readmissions, for the sake of the books, in case there were ever any insurance problems.

'But there are always readmissions,' Manciple insisted, astounded at the single figure in the column. Our apparent success rate was itself a suspicious black mark in his book, it seemed.

'We work on the principle of a solution-based treatment,' Ash piped up from his desk.

Faulkner turned on him, baring his crowded teeth with ironic satisfaction, 'And how do you manage that piece of magic, may I ask?' Oh God, he was a piece of work, Ash was right!

'Not magic. We simply try to discover the epicenter of the disturbance, investigate it, and track forward from there to find the best treatment for our guests.'

'Guests? You are a mental health establishment, not a hotel,' remonstrated Carey. 'Patients or inmates, perhaps…'

'It is just our style of working… to give welcome to those who come to stay with us.'

However much we showed the Beacon style - Melanie's own kind and welcoming ways - the more their malicious satisfaction seemed to grow, and the more our answers sounded to my ears like the excuses of people caught on the back foot. By the end of the morning, I felt that any ground we had been standing upon had been seriously undercut. Leaving Will and Wendy to lead the inspectors into lunch, we hastily foregathered in the somewhat cramped seclusion of Gillespie's shed to confer with Ash, as if he were the football captain coaxing his backsliding team to victory after a miserable first-half.

Gillespie himself listened to our tales of woe, before adding his take on things: 'Weel, Picky didnae care for oor ordering system, and Miss Flicky nearly wet hirself whan she saw the crates of shrine candles in the cupboard. As for Dicky of Alamain, I've nae idea who stole *his* camel....'

So, Picky, Flicky and Dicky was what they instantly became: Manciple - the bureaucratic scrutinizer; Carey - who sat pulling peevishly repelling the dust that landed on her tights by flicking it off; and Faulkner - intent on rubbishing whatever we put forward.

Oh, but the laugh did us good, for all our hearts were aching with indignation!

After lunch, it was my job to show them over the Beacon, to show its facilities. I went through the procedurals of client intake and referral, showing the various interview rooms we used at different times. I personally think that Carey was actually quite impressed by our art room, but she managed to sound very censorious that we had no dedicated Creative Arts Therapist to oversee it, and was belittling of our combined skills. The outside facilities were not viewed in the best of weather, of course, although the garden was in its Autumn beauty still, due to Gillespie's care, with late-flowering chrysanthemums. They trooped glumly around the garden and back up to the main office where Ash waited.

We had already argued about whether the Sanctuary should be revealed to them, since it was the very heart of the Beacon. Ash insisted that it should be shown, but that he himself would do it.

'There is one more space that you have not seen. It is at the heart of the Beacon, and is here for anyone who needs to be quiet or have peace. This is the part of the house that dates from the early middle ages, when it may have been integral to religious foundation or a chapel to a manor house. Flicky's head came up, her pointy nose smelling something she found unpleasant. I'd such a bad feeling about it, wishing fervently that we might leave it out of their inspection; now they were here, it felt like the grossest provocation to violation.

Ash went in first, holding the door open for them to enter. Dicky's piratical eye roamed about the Sanctuary, falling upon Anastacia who sat crouched upon one of the little foot stools, eyes closed and hands raised, palms out slightly in front of her in the classic early posture of prayer: it was like coming across a Virgo Orans on the wall of catacomb in Rome. We had not known she was in there. I caught the moment as the happy wolfish smile spread across Dicky's countenance.

Flicky, on the other hand, had stuck by the door, like a character in a folk story, transfixed in horror by the wall paintings, and by the little shelf with its reliquary of St Margaret which had been set just under the triquetra window, with its own sanctum lamp which hung over it from a bracket. Flicky, I decided, had either had a very circumscribed, Bible-bashing upbringing, or she had been badly scandalized or abused by some Christian sect, from her fearful reaction. Picky showed his complete indifference to the sacred silence by walking straight into a chair, so that the echoing richochet of his clumsiness broke the Sanctuary's deep, gathered silence.

Anastacia snapped out of her contemplation and stood up, startled by their sudden ingress. I beamed her a calming look, but she was immediately wise to the unspoken aggression that was filling the Sanctuary. Like a startled deer, she excused herself and fled, having to push past Flicky who still clung to the door.

Into the silence that sought to gather itself again, Dicky asked, in well-spaced words that bore their own implication, 'What *else* happens in here, may I ask?'

Ash was onto it, though. He reiterated, in well-modulated tones, 'This is a quiet space where staff and guests come to refresh themselves, as they wish. There are no group activities held here.'

The way Dicky raised his chin revealed his disbelief in this statement, but at least he had the goodness to tidy away his wolfish glee. Picky continued to add more hieroglyphics to his clipboard, without demur, but I reckoned that, if we had had hymn books, he would certainly have been counting them by now.

Flicky's fearful ire then made itself felt. In a wild voice, she said, 'How ... can ... you...?' she gestured wildly at the Sanctuary. '....all this ....clap-trap...'

She didn't get any further as Dicky bore down on her and took her off for a cup of tea before she incriminated the inspection any more. Only Picky remained. Pushing his glasses up his nose he asked, incuriously, with his weights and measures hat on, 'How many people meet in here, did you say?'

The inspectors finally left us just after dinner the day following, having descended the next day with the addition of a specialist mental health inspector who interviewed us, and each of our guests. By the end of it, we felt wretched and somewhat soiled.

The round of daily work covered our anxiety. Days passed, and finally, the guests began to thin out, and go home, leaving only Anastacia. The routines of the Beacon slowed right down, giving the staff some time off. Will went home to visit his widowed mother in Dorset, promising to come speeding back if necessary. Gillespie threw himself into a round of garden reconstruction, before the major part of the growing season began again, clearing some space for raised beds. Wendy returned to the making of a huge quilt she had started some years previously but set aside through lack of time. Jane and I awaited the baby and made quick trips into Christminster to find suitable baby requisites. The Beacon itself felt as it was holding its breath.

Anastacia and Jane had become readily drawn into Wendy's quilt making, obsessively making up hexagons, strategically planning the pattern at every opportunity, when not sewing in silence. 'It's beginning to look like a Dorcas society down here,' I complained to Jane one day when I went down to read the local paper by the fire, only to find the table fully set up as a sewing station, strewn with hexagons and bolts of fabric.

'Go away, we're nesting!' Jane said, through a mouthful of pins. Wendy raised her head from her work, smiling and nodding towards Anastacia contently cutting out fabric on the floorboards, utterly absorbed, so I went back up to see Ash. 'It's become a sewing room downstairs,' I warned him, 'Though I think it's having a therapeutic effect on our remaining guest.'

Ash looked up from the ledger he was working on, 'Good! That is good news.'

That attenuated look he'd worn back in January on his return, had begun to reassert itself around the eyes. I was not the only one to notice it, because Wendy had been trying to feed him up again. The strain was bad enough for us, but Ash had borne the brunt of it, as the waiting went on.

'How is your reading and meditation going?' he asked.

I made my report for that week, asking at the end, 'I wanted to ask something… How do you get contacts? Everything you've given me to read goes on about people needing contacts, but I think I'm missing something.'

He screwed the cap on his fountain pen and pushed the ledger away. 'A contact is just the name for an influence that overshadows an individual or group. You have been working with me under the contact that Melanie and the lodge are tuned to for some years now: it is what our guests respond to when they begin to heal. You know it well. It was also what Faulkner and his crew took most exception to, what they palpably experienced when they came through our doors.'

I visualized their adverse reaction to the Sanctuary, understanding it a bit better now. 'I think I know what you are getting at … but a contact seems to be something bigger too?'

'That is because it is the appearance or likeness of something much greater. Take the archangel Raphael in the Sanctuary: an angelic presence is just the messenger of the Divine presence that we do not see, though we feel that greater goodness through the angel's mediation. We live under that influence here at the Beacon, as in the lodge, which is why Melanie's work can go forward. It is also why we cannot be simply an earthly institution: in order to be of service, we must back onto something greater for the healing to be perfect.'

'You mean, we all mediate the greater influence?'

'Yes: you, me, Wendy and Gillespie, and Jane too.' I noticed he did not mention Will who, it was true, had found the esoteric side of our work a bit beyond his ken. While he did his work perfectly well, and was a fine young doctor, he was not quite 'one of us.' I felt that exclusion keenly, knowing that it was I who had taken him on at a time of exigency, acknowledging, too, that this was not a case of our excluding him, but of him being of a totally different disposition.

'So, I have been in the spotlight of the contact all this time?'

Ash nodded, 'Yes, that's a good way of thinking about contacts. You don't have to "get" a contact: we each of us have a natural disposition – we are born into different "schools" of influence, if you like. You were drawn to be a healer so - had you been born in ancient Greece - they would have said that you were "under the influence of Asclepius."'

'You've told me very little about the work of the lodge, but am I to understand that the work is along those lines?'

'We mediate the influence of the greater wisdom, yes…. Speaking of which…' He reached into the corner and handed me a large velvet drawstring bag, which he held out to me, 'You will be needing this in a week or so.'

I drew out what was inside, and a slither of dark blue material cascaded out: it was a plain robe, long, with sleeves. 'For me?...But how did you….'

'…know your size? I asked Jane to give me your measurements.'

'Did you say in a week?' I suddenly felt nervous and uncertain.

'The date for your initiation into the Lodge is set for the eighth day of the moon,' Ash smiled.

'We don't use calendar dates, then?'

'Oh yes, because we all need our diaries, but we reckon our magical work by the moon, which gives it rhythm. So, please keep the 7th February free.'

I held up the robe to myself and examined the effect in the convex mirror, 'Are you sure you all still want me?' I asked, dubiously.

'We do, if you do.'

Folding it carefully, I said, ruefully, 'Well, at least this robe will actually fit me better than the last one I donned!'

We were both preparing for our next session with Anastacia, when she suddenly burst into the office, bubbling over with realization, 'I remembered it this morning.'

'What?'

'You know I said that I blanked out a lot of the sequence? Well, something came back to me, stronger than ever before. Something wonderful!'

Her eyes were shining with happiness. Without waiting for us to initiate the session, she launched into her account, 'I was in the Sanctuary the other day, and something sort of shifted. I can't explain it very well – as if some fogged-up filter had lifted off my perception. I felt different… No, I felt as if something was companioning me. Anyway, it was such a nice feeling, I didn't want to say anything, in case it went away again.'

'Something else happened….?' Ash prompted her, as she sucked the fringes of her shawl, reflectively.

'Yes, I had a dream. I was in an oriental market, looking for a white silk dress. There were hundreds of stalls selling silk and cotton, but I couldn't find the kind of dress I was looking for: it had to be a particular kind of white. And then, over the heads of the stallholders, I saw her - it was Jodie waving at me, just like she had come to join me in my search. I've not been able to reach her or see her in my dreams at all until this morning.'

'How did she seem?' Ash asked, careful to not stop the flow.

'She looked lovely, like she'd just got out of the shower. She was shining…

But I was so excited to see her that it woke me up. I tried so hard to go back into the dream to be with her… In the end, I just lay in the dark, savouring the precious sense of her. And then, I remembered where I had had the feeling before.'

'Where did it happen? When?' Ash asked

'It was one night when I'd been left in the dark, chained to the bed. I was really struggling, desperate, trapped. Nothing I could do for myself would set me free. It must have been in the small hours, I don't know, because there was no clock – Nicola'd taken my phone away. I couldn't see any way out.' She caught her breath with the terror of it momentarily, then remembered to inhale again. Turning her face up to us she said simply, 'I was lying in the dark when help came to me.'

We waited to hear what kind of help, but she was held in the wonder of it, staring into that timeless moment.

This time, I prompted her, gently, 'How do you mean?'

'Help came to me in the dark.' She repeated, and then refocusing on me, said, 'I know now that, by that time, Jodie must have been dead - perhaps many weeks dead - but she still came to me in the dark!' Tears ran down her face at the memory, 'But how could I have forgotten that? All this time, I've been longing for Jodie... why did I forget?' Now she was angry at herself.

Ash passed her the tissues, saying, 'The impact of trauma is sometimes so great that the mind and the soul shut down the short-term memory: sequence, detail, remembrance can all slip beneath the surface of recollection.'

'Even the good things?'

'Sometimes.'

She pursed her lips, 'Some things I would not want to remember clearly, it's true, but the memory of Jodie's presence would have kept me going.'

'I'm sure that it did! Think, Anastacia! Jodie's very last actions were spent trying to search for you: it is no surprise to me that she came to you in your darkest hour.'

The thought of these two friends who wanted the best for the other, and who would not let the other go without help moved me deeply.

With great resolve, Anastacia said, '*She* came for me, and now I want to do something for *her*.'

We discussed what she wanted to do and what was possible. Jodie's body had been released to her family already; but because Anastacia and Jodie had no recognized relationship under the law, at that time, Jodie's mother had gone ahead with the burial anyway, excluding Anastacia from the funeral. It was a needless cruelty on top of all that she had suffered.

'Jodie's mum blamed me for getting her killed, I think,' Anastacia said stoically, inured to such prejudice. 'No, what I want to do is hold a private memorial for Jodie, with just our friends, in a place that will welcome us.' Shyly, she turned in the direction of the Sanctuary door, 'If it was small, could we hold it here?'

'Of course! We would be very glad if you did.'

'Then, can you find me the book with the story of the angel and the fish in it please? I want to see if it has something I can use.'

Ash pulled down the *Apocrypha* for her and Anastacia strode purposefully away.

Next Thursday came round very quickly. Like Anastacia, that week, I returned daily to the Sanctuary to do my meditation, and to try and regain my former sense of the initiates as light-bearers through time, but, as Anastasia had found, fears often got in the way, and so I spent a largely fruitless time in mental havering.

I turned to Jane for reassurance that she was still alright with this step I was taking, because I didn't want anything to overshadow these last few days of her pregnancy, 'Look, I can put this off or pull out, if it feels at all....'

She kissed me, 'Oh, Jack! Go and do what you need to do! I'm not going to stop you if your heart is set on it... Think of it as paving the way for our child's daddy to be a better father...You know that Wendy and Gillespie will be with me, so if the baby comes tonight, I will be ok.' Having anticipated all my possible avenues of escape, my wife helped to decided me.

That night I drove with Ash to Aldhampton, to the large brick house set amid brooding rhododendrons. We entered by a porch, where the door had been left unfastened. Then I was directed to a back room to go and change, and await the coming of the Herald, the officer who would conduct me to the temple. The room had only a small high window. I had not been told how long I should wait, but it seemed about an hour – my watch was packed away in the bottom of the bag. When I became fretful, I tried to still my breath and meditate, as instructed.

Then the Herald came, a woman I recognized from Tryphena's funeral. She wore the same robe as myself, but with a yellow sash over it. In her hand was a white wand, 'The Lodge awaits you. Please sit in this chair.' I duly sat uncertainly while she fastened a blindfold about my eyes. Then she led me to the door of the temple where she knocked. I felt the door open, smelling the fragrance of the same kind of incense that Ash used sometimes, but with both a sweeter and more bitter tang to it.

In a ringing voice, the Herald announced, 'I present to the lodge, one who would join our company.' From the way the resonance came back to my body, I was aware of a much larger room beyond: one with few furnishings in it. Then a sudden rush of air as someone came towards me, and I felt the sharp point of a blade upon my breastbone: a male voice asking, 'Stranger at the gate, do you come here of your own free will?'

Clearing my throat, I choked, 'I do,' as a waft of incense caught my breath.

I was guided forward one step.

Another, female, voice asked me, 'Stranger at the gate, are you free to offer your service?'

'I hope I may always ... Yes, I am.' I stuttered. Again, I was gently pushed another step forward.

Yet another male voice asked, 'Stranger at the gate, do you desire to join this lodge?'

'I do.' This time, I both felt, and was, sure. I was guided another step into the temple and the door shut behind me, as the blade was withdrawn from my chest.

'Enter, friend!' The whole lodge spoke together, so that I was able to gage just how many stood here: more than 8, less than 13. With the door closed, the density of the incense smoke became the medium that I moved through. It may explain why I remember the next part less well, but it involved being moved from station to station about the temple, as the words of ritual wafted over me. Pliant under the press of the hands that led me, I experienced the kind of carefreeness that I have not felt since I was a child: as when your parents are looking after you, when you don't have to plan or anticipate anything, when you just live and play in the moment. The woven pacing was making some kind of pattern, like the movements of a dance on the lodge floor. It felt as if I was being observed, not only by the lodge members, but as if I was being presented to those unseen beings who presided here. A part of all this was rendered stranger by the blindfold around my eyes, provoking the same hint of disorientation as in a party game – though here I trusted those guiding me not to harm or trick me.

A voice I knew well asked me, 'Tell us, friend, what you understand by the word "sanctuary?"'

Into my mind came memory of an obscure picture by William Blake: a sketch of a sanctuary in some temple. That was also an empty room. The image had always had a strange effect upon me, gravid as it was with potent, immanent space. I knew it, as I think others had known it through time, as an accessible chamber, full of silence…

I answered, with some searching for words and impressions: 'I conceive of sanctuary as being an empty room with a light in it… The light is in the sanctuary or rather upon it, or even emanating from it… Yet when I am in it, the light is not coming from one place… It is radiantly everywhere… I am one with it…Many others have been here through time, though it has no door. It is the silence that is also singing….'

The blindfold was taken from my eyes by the Herald, and I found I was standing before a wooden altar, with Ash on the other side. He was attired in the same robe but with golden-coloured cope over it. Startlingly, for he could have stepped from some former time in history, he bore a likeness to some engraving I remembered, as a medley of impressions smote upon me: a bewigged divine, an ancient temple priest, an alchemist, a fish-crowned servant of a Sumerian divinity… I could not say.

His dark-rimmed grey eyes smiled at me, 'You have truly described sanctuary. Come now to the altar and place your hands upon it, for you have truly deserved sanctuary.'

I did as he bade me, palms down, pressing my hands upon the wooden surface. I had the weirdest sense that other hands stretched up to meet mine as I pressed down.

Ash's voice shimmered over the incense smoke, 'Do you, Jack Rivers, give gladly of your service – the blessing that you brought into this life is yours alone to bestow? No one may compel you.' And I liked that, who had once had to submit unwillingly to one who was unworthy to admit me.

'I give my service gladly,' I responded firmly.

Facing me across the altar, Ash laid his two hands lightly over mine, his voice ringing with gladness: 'Then, as senior officer of this lodge, I acknowledge your glad gift, and name you my brother in the Great Work.' His hands remained over mine for a long time as we gazed at each other across the altar that witnessed our joint service.

Removing his hands, he said, 'Turn outwards and reflect your blessing – mediating it out unconditionally.'

As I turned and raised my hands palms facing outwards, I was aware of the blessing going forth with strength and support, as solidarity of purpose flowed forth too. It was not undirected, but focused in one sense of service. It felt as though others joined us and sent forth their blessing too, from the depths of wisdom out to the least atom – none were excerpted from the blessing, and I knew myself at one with the light in a different way, at once realizing that nothing now would ever be the same again. The nature of the work I undertook would be infused with this blessing.

While I could not have described it so at the time, it was as though the wisdom and solidarity of the ancients downloaded into my system – a great coagulant mass of understanding which came shooting down through me, so that I became like the delta of many river currents meeting within my being.

Ash was part of it, and Jane, our child to come, and all the clients I had and would see, the Beacon, Melanie, Tryphena, and a host of unknown initiates who had taken on another kind of life, and who were now as stars in a circle of council for our times, mediating what could not be told, and yet was known as the inheritance of all hearts.

The beauty of it broke me open and a deep shuddering began in my body. Like an oak shivering under the lightning flash, I endured its coming through me and was changed. The mystery that had been hidden from me stirred and was fully part of me at last – I understood now why mysteries cannot be told: they come into us in this manner – as initiations joining us to that mightiness that has waited for the right time. At another level, I understood the shuddering within my frame was my body attempting to temper this force and balance it.

From that moment onwards, I was part of the mystery, as a man is joined in love to a woman. I also understood exactly how this work was life and joy to Ash, who had no partner, and how this awesome mercy was unsparing, complete and terrible – not to be obeyed as a tyrant, but as the giving of myself in service.

Lastly, Ash, his fingers dipped in oil, came to sign me on the forehead. The déja vu of Kyriakou making the self-same gesture flashed briefly upon me, and was replaced – but how differently, and with full heart! I knew with certainty that my self-protective prayer of dedication at those unclean hands in the Icenfield Masonic hall, was here made true and perfect within the lodge – for I had already dedicated myself to the light, and now that promise was properly welcomed at the hands of Ash. As the oil touched me, he laughed gently as if in recollection or recognition of this as he anointed me, his gladness evident: 'From a time long past and a place now lost do I derive this office, as magister of this lodge. Now in the name of the Ruler of the Holy and Ancient Mystery, with this touch handed down through the ages, I acknowledge you as a brother who stands with us under the Arch of Stars.'

As the oil flowed down my brows, the words of the psalm came unbidden, 'It is like the precious ointment upon the head, that ran down upon the beard, even Aaron's beard: that went down to the skirts of his garments.' I no longer found those lines amusing, but truly descriptive. Priesthood was here in the anointing oil and my service was my altar – how good and pleasant indeed when we live together in harmony! I was in one flow.

There may have been singing, I cannot say – the mightiness came through me and was one with me, and my gift was met in wonderful completion. My legs would not hold me up any longer, and I fell to my knees.

Time started to run again, and someone was raising a glass of water to my lips. I drank thirstily and was helped to rise in my own time.

'Welcome, brother!' Each member of the lodge acknowledged me thus, with hand and kiss – the kiss of peace that signs us as members of each other. Around my neck was placed the lamen of the arch of stars, with the offering hands beneath it. Which is how I entered into the ranks of those who cannot speak of what they do – not from any sense of superior knowledge or privileged secrecy – but because my life has fallen into different lines: I am upon the path that I always believed to be my own, but now I am accompanied and upheld in strength. For that gift, I am grateful every day of my life.

Although nobody was supposed to know, word had got out that I had joined the ranks of Ash's lodge, and so there was a little reception committee waiting when I returned with Ash later that night. Wendy and Gillespie had laid out a cold collation of meat and cheese, with some freshly baked rolls nestled in a crisp linen napkin. To complete our welcome, they had left a pot of consommé on the chafing dish to keep warm, and a bottle of champagne in the ice-bucket.

Jane flashed one look at me and marched up to Ash with, 'What *have* you done with my husband?' Then, examining me very curiously, rather as a mother cat examines her kittens, 'You don't look very different.' She poked me in the chest, 'Still human, that's good!'

'I think you will find he has all his faculties,' Ash said, peeling off the cap from the bottle of champagne before popping it.

Anastacia peered over the bannisters curiously and we called her down to enjoy the celebrations. It was not until the early hours that we all went to bed, where I went deeply down into dreamless, nourishing sleep.

The report when it came the following Monday was quite shocking. Among the staff comments were recommendations that Wendy and Gillespie be pensioned off and younger staff engaged; apparently I myself was labouring under the pernicious influence of Ash, with what they perceived as some kind of hero-worshipping complex, which might be 'affecting my judgement;' Jane's lack of practice hours (which had necessarily been curtailed by her pregnancy) were criticized, and they hinted at irregularities with her registration to practice outside Australia; but they saved their worst ammunition for Ash who was seen as promoting unprofessional and New Age views not in alignment with MHRC policies. He would be called to answer at a tribunal as to his fitness to practice or direct the Beacon, date to be announced. Only Will came away with a clean report, with a recommendation that he might run the Beacon in future, should all the recommendations and changes be made in accordance.

Even the Beacon itself was found wanting: recommendations included separating staff and guest eating areas, and the acquiring of a fully-trained arts therapist for our art room. There was a whole paragraph about religious images in the Sanctuary making it an unsuitable area for inmates to be exposed to, since it ran the risk of fueling fantasies or religious obsessions, which was clearly Flicky's view. Suggested solutions were to white-wash or cover over the wall paintings if the space were to be used for any kind of treatment or assembly area. Yet they had still managed to come up with a recommendation that a suitable prayer-room for Muslims should be provided – possibly in the waiting room. The shrine to Melanie was to be moved to a private area, as it was a clear fire-hazard, quite apart from giving the unhealthy impression that patients were entering of some kind of cult. The lack of ensuite facilities in all of our guest rooms was criticized strongly – but this was something that would be impossible to correct without wrecking the whole interior structure of the Beacon, of course. They could not fault us on health and safety, however, and our care in the security of medication storage was commended. Between these recommendations, and proposals, and the tribunal they wanted to hold upon Ash's fitness, we had very little wriggle room.

To say that there was uproar, would be putting it very mildly: indignation boiled over on every side. Ash let everyone say their piece, then added, 'We will have to come up with a compliance and recovery action plan for this.'

There was utter silence in the room as we all stared at him, followed by a volley of protest.

'We are not going to lie down under this farrago of nonsense?' Wendy insisted.

Gillespie shook his head, 'Man, you must have really pissed off Dicky of Alamein!'

Jane just came over and squeezed Ash's hand, standing silently beside him.

'For the sake of the Beacon, we are going to have to make some changes,' he said. 'A lot of the recommendations are just that – recommendations that are not obligatory. I am thinking of things like our literature: if we make plain the kind of place we are on paper, we are being open and transparent. A lot of the nastiness is Faulkner's revenge, and I am certain we can prove that it is so. For myself, Jack will help me get together evidence for the case going to tribunal.'

We were all suddenly aware of how devastated Wendy and Gillespie looked. Ash took each of them by the hand, 'Dear friends, I would no more dream of sacking or replacing either of you, you know, than I would of cutting off my own head. The report was framed to hurt us all.'

'Bless you! Well it did hurt, and badly,' Wendy cried into her tissue. She shook her head at the thought of it, 'Whitewashing the Sanctuary, for goodness sake!'

Ash sought me out and we went over the awful report together for about an hour and half, until we couldn't bear to look at it any more. He pushed the paperwork away, and said in a more cheerful voice, 'I know things have been difficult over the last few weeks, and I wish I had been able to offer you this a little earlier, but it's been held up by a great number of difficulties. At least let something good come out of today!'

Ash handed me a large fold of papers sealed with pink ribbons, and a crumbly red stamp affixed to it, 'These are the deeds of Capricorn House, which I hope you will accept as a very belated wedding present. - I have been over the house with the handyman to ensure everything works alright. About the décor – well, Jane will have her own views, I know. But it is all yours to live in.'

I stupidly dropped the papers, in my bemusement. Ash patiently picked up and handed them me again.

'But this is your ... family home... how can you...'

He shook his head: 'It was never my family home. I was born in Andover, remember? It is precious to me, yes, because it was Tryphena's home and, but I never lived there. It's been empty too long. All the difficulties about making this transfer have been solely because of her uncle, Sebastian Ellis Hands and his legacy. The house is a grade II listed property and there are a number of conditions attached to its upkeep and use which I had to iron out with the National Heritage List, as well as keeping sweet the Arts and Craft Guild trustees who felt they had certain rights over it, so I will have to explain those to you. These include all kinds of ferocious proscriptions against any building alteration, so you may not feel it is for you. For the moment, the most important thing is that you and Jane have a place to call your own, where you can raise a family.'

I thought swiftly, weighing up this immensely generous offer: Nutbourne was a good three quarters of an hour drive on a good day – far enough from the Beacon to offer Jane and our child a safe haven from the vagaries of our guests and their conditions, but equally far enough for me to have to travel every day and night.

'Can I discuss it with Jane?'

'Of course. I haven't discussed it with anyone at the Beacon yet, so take your time.'

I brought Jane up a small bunch of hot-house freesias that Wendy had brought back with the shopping, and had made her a pot of her favourite hot chocolate, by way of an introduction to Ash's wonderful offer. 'What is that under your arm?' she asked, pointing curiously to the bundle of deeds.

'It's a late wedding gift from Ash,' I said, dropping them in her lap.

She supped her chocolate and looked at the deeds, 'But isn't this Tryphena's old house?'

I nodded, keeping my expression blank, lest she take against the idea and I had to embarrassingly hand back the deeds to Ash.

'But this is so lovely!' Holding the deeds to her chest, her face working with emotion, she became inarticulate with tears. Between the sobs, I gathered that she had been as worried as myself about bringing her first child into the life of the Beacon, about not having our own place to be. She had given up so much in her life to become part of the household, but now the rules were changing as the birth drew nearer.

When the tears subsided, she asked, 'What's the matter?' she asked, pressing a questioning finger into my mask-like face, 'Don't you want to be there?'

Attempting to unfreeze my features, I nodded, 'It is the most beautiful house I've ever seen, bar this one – overlooking the sea too. I don't know what we've done to be so honoured.'

Putting aside the deeds with a secret smile, Jane swung her legs off the couch and started to firkle around under it for a pair of shoes she could still get into.

'What are you doing?' I asked, anxiously.

Cocking her head on one side as if I was a simpleton, she said, in a tone that brooked no stay, 'Getting ready to go and see it, of course, Jack.'

I ran into Ash's study, 'Is it alright if we go and look? Jane wants to see the house now!'

Ash unhooked the elaborate Arts and Craft key from the key-board, giving it into my hand with a fond look, 'Take your time.' He called after me to catch, throwing a steel tape measure towards me, 'Women usually like to measure things, I believe.'

We drove by the quickest route, avoiding the coast road as much as possible until the very last. Jane sat as bolt upright as 9 months of pregnancy will allow, perched on her comfort cushion, peering keenly out at everything, for it had been a very long time since we were both out in the car together. The February day was cold, and the wind blew from the west with drizzle, but it helped us both to be away from the Beacon.

Jane had never seen Capricorn House before, and a deep quietness fell upon her as we drew up outside and stepped through the tall wrought iron gate embedded in the hedge.

She fingered the Heritage plaque proclaiming Sebastian Ellis Hands' dates and his original building of the house, as I opened the door with the beautiful stylized Capricorn key. We entered the front room where I had first met Tryphena at the beginning of that year, and Jane stood on the spot, slowly turning. She exclaimed, 'This house.... It's like a museum – all these beautiful things!' She went through each room, touching and exclaiming at the rich and precious objects, and thrilling at the inset niches that Sebastian Hands had so thoughtfully included in his design of the house.

Truly, the proportions, the décor, and furnishings all went to make a lovely house. In the back linen-fold paneled room was a portrait of Vivian Rich,

Tryphena's lover, set where no-one but she would have seen it. 'It's like living with the Pre-Raphaelites!' Jane expressed my own feeling perfectly. Now that we were physically in this house – and I had clearly no idea quite how richly and expensively it was appointed - I kept my counsel. I didn't want to pour doubt upon the advisability of a small child let loose among all these extravagant things, at this juncture, as Jane moved slowly around the house with growing amazement and glee.

But when we reached the upstairs main bedroom that looked out upon the sea, we literally stood back in amazement, mouths open, as we entered what appeared to be green and golden forest. The wooden bed had pillars like slender tree trunks rising from its corners, supporting a canopy of leafy hand-made tapestry. The mattress was high, with a golden velvet bedspread.

Jane and I looked at each other in awe, and delight, then, as one person, we swooped upon it and threw ourselves down upon it, kicking off our shoes.

It was Jane who began the giggling. We lay on that great museum-piece bed, letting our delight percolate up to the tapestried forest canopy.

'So, will this do?'

'Do!?' Jane hit me with a tapestried cushion. 'Do?! – It's the house of a dream. I'll never live it down in the Northern Territory, you know? I'm a right Pom, now!'

She sat upright suddenly, 'Aaarghh! – Quick! Grab some towels from the airing cupboard!' She attempted to move her body off of the bed but got stuck, so I pulled her forward.

'Oh no! Not the carpet!' she wailed, clutching the windowsill as her waters soaked into the Persian rug.

'Carpets can be cleaned!' I said, as I pulled a bunch of towels off the shelf on the landing.

'But I can't have the baby in *this* room!'

Amused at her distress, I enquired, 'Why ever not? It's your room now! Where else would you suggest? In the linen-fold dining room? Or perhaps in the temple room at the back, among the indigo draperies?'

She dithered for as long as it took me to tear the golden velvet coverlet off and throw down massed ranks of towels upon the sheets beneath, before she subsided upon the bed again.

'Do you have your bag of things for the hospital?' I asked, foolishly.

She winced and shook her head, caught in a contraction. Then, after a few more breaths, she countered with 'Did *you* bring your bag of tricks for doctoring with?'

Of course, I hadn't! 'I'll phone for an ambulance,' I said, going to find the phone.

Jane caught me back urgently, hissing between her teeth, 'Count - on your watch. These contractions are coming quite fast..... Damn! I don't want to do this without any drugs.'

But do it without them she did, just as handily as she would have delivered a woman in the bush, only with inexperienced me on the receiving end instead. Fortunately, we had boiled the kettle on arrival, before we got sucked into the glorious richness of the house. Tryphena's work basket yielded a pair of sharp scissors and some silken sutures for the cord, and our daughter tumbled into the world upon the most beautiful bed in Britain, just a bare half-hour later.

While I tidied Jane up, she lay quietly with the child upon her breast, smelling her, taking her all in, 'She looks like you, Jack.'

'God help her!'

'*And* a bit like my Great-Auntie Mabel.'

'Is that good?'

'My Great Auntie Mabel made the best lamingtons in Australia.'

'Well, that's alright then!' At that point in the proceedings, I was oblivious to Australian sponge cakes, with or without dessicated coconut on them.

I gave my daughter the professional once over, assessing a full complement of limbs and digits, and that she could hear, see, and drink alright, before handing her back to her mother to be fed.

Jane lay back, with our daughter attached and sucking strongly. 'There are stars!' she said, dreamily after a while.

'What?' I asked, alarmed, thinking she might be hallucinating.

She nodded upwards, 'Up there, look!'

I wedged myself on the edge of the bed and looked up into the canopy to see that, above the pillows, there were indeed stars: the constellation of Capricorn and its accompanying celestial bodies had been embroidered there.

'Well, clever you! Only you could give birth in the northern hemisphere *and* under the Tropic of Capricorn at the same time!'

She smiled dreamily, 'Looks like we might have to live here after all, Jack?'

And I kissed her and the baby.

The birth of our daughter brought a brief calm in the aftermath of the report. Wendy and Gillespie descended on Capricorn House with Ash to bring us all of the baby things that we had stored in an outbuilding, as well as a suitcase each of immediate necessities from our room. The baby was cooed over by the women, while in the kitchen, Gillespie solemnly unscrewed a fresh bottle of

Islay Malt for us to wet the baby's head: all tossed down in bejeweled Arts and Craft goblets from the glass cabinet.

'How many babies have you delivered in your time?' Ash whispered to me as we stood looking out of the window of the beautiful front room at the sea.

Keeping my face straight, I said, 'Just the one.'

His eyes widened, 'The one upstairs?'

I nodded. Ash's roar of laughter brought Gillespie at the gallop to fill up our glasses again.

Wendy finally came down the stairs, to join us with, 'I've never seen a more inconvenient house for having a baby in…It…' And there she stopped, transfixed in the doorway at the spectacle of her employer, husband and colleague downing rainbow goblets of whiskey.

Everything in that first week of parenthood went into slow-motion for Jane and myself, while the world rolled onwards. We made do at Capricorn House for a few days which, as Wendy said, was not the place where we could manage without help. So, leaving Gillespie to cater up at the Beacon, she came over to superintend us. I spoke to Ash on the phone, hearing that Anastacia had made great progress: her time with us was coming to an end, and I dreaded it, because it would mean – to all intents and purposes – the Beacon would have no function.

On the day of Jodie's memorial, which happened a few nights later, I drove over with Jane and the baby to swell the throng. Several of Jodie's friends had come, and a few of Anastacia's fellow musicians from the consort, as well as Marius Tesar, the cellist from the famous Bohemian Quartet who had been a patron of the consort since its foundation. A picture of Jodie was set at the foot shrine with a tall candle, and the friends were able to remember her in their own way, with poetry, song and music in the Sanctuary.

Anastacia kept a very low profile during the evening: allowing Ash to introduce each of the contributions, and oversee the event, 'Because it is your house and your shrine, and I couldn't do as well as you.' But at the end, she shared with us the fruit of her studies.

Looking a lot less fragile than she had done the day she arrived, Anastacia addressed all of us who had welcomed her to the Beacon, 'I knew as soon as I entered peace of this beautiful Sanctuary that I had come to a true place of healing. You have all helped me at a very difficult time and given me welcome, meeting me at the threshold of my pain, and I thank you for coming tonight to remember Jodie with us. When I heard what the Beacon is going through, and what it will mean if the decision goes against you, I knew I had to share this.'

She touched the strings of the psaltery to check the tuning.

Looking out at us all, taking us all in, she said, 'I know better than anyone what it is to be locked in the dark and be unable to find the light, so this text, about the angel Raphael coming to visit poor, blind Tobit when he was sunk in gloom, seemed the right gift for this time.'

Anastacia sat down. Holding the psaltery across her lap, she conjured a flurry of gentle descending chords. Then her voice mysteriously elided with the psaltery: the singing voice that, till now, we had never heard. Wherever it had wondered to, her voice was back with us now - truly that of an angel, as she sang Raphael's entry in a pure, clear stream of sound with no vibrato:

'Ingressus Raphael Archangelus   Archangel Raphael went in
ad Tobiam, salutavit eum dicens: To Tobias, greeting him, saying:
"Gaudium tibi semper."   "Joy be to thee always!"

Then, in the voice of one who knows despair, the psaltery making a querulous tremulo:

'Sit cui Tobias,   And Tobias said,
"Ait quale gaudium mihi   "What manner of joy shall be to me,
Erit qui in tenebris sedeo   Who sits in darkness
Et lumen caeli non video?"   And sees not the light of heaven?"

To which the angel answered in the bright, shimmering tones of eternity:

Cui Angelus dixit;   And the angel said to him,
"Forti animo esto,   "Be of good courage:
In proximo est ut a deo cureris."'   Near to you is the God who shall heal you."'

The psaltery played into us all the strength that only comes in the darkest moments: sure, certain, faithful, and ever true. And we who sat there, crouched like Tobias in his gloom at the prospect of losing the Beacon and our beloved Ash, began to feel the flicker of hope: that we were truly not alone, nor without help.

I got up early the next morning, to say goodbye to Anastasia, whom Marius was going to drive back to his house in the country. She needed a little more time to return to herself, but in the care of friends, and at a discreet distance from the paparazzi from whom we had been thankfully spared during her stay.

Ash and I watched as the car sped off. I said to him, 'I don't know who did most healing, you know? The Beacon or us?'

'Oh, that's easy,' he said. 'Anastacia herself found the tincture that 'turneth all to gold,' and she fed it to us all last night!'

He blithely turned to go in, as if the threat of tribunal was not still over his head, but I stood taking in his enigmatic words. It felt to me like one of those cases where the guest gives forth more healing than she receives, but his alchemical reference to the Philosopher's Stone was not lost on me either.

Going upstairs to bring her a drink, I found Jane out of bed, and not in the loo. The baby was not in her cot. Looking anxiously out of the window, I saw that she was wandering about in the Wilderness behind the house, pulling up the spent stalks of lemon balm and staring up at Hartworth Beacon. It took a lot to keep Jane out of the garden at the best of times. The baby was a papoose, wrapped up against the cold against her front, and Jane was talking to her. Some of her words drifted up to me, as I stood at the window, 'And that big hill is the real Beacon where people used to light fires when danger threatened, to warn every one. Someone would light that fire, and the people down the way would see it and light theirs, from hilltop to hilltop, so that the whole South Coast would know the danger within minutes.'

'What are you doing out of bed?' I exclaimed, coming out to join her.

She turned, 'You're not going to play the heavy doctor with me, are you? I couldn't stay in bed when Seren was keen to see where she has come to live, could I?'

I stopped in my tracks, 'Seren?' I had never heard the name before.

Calmly Jane said, 'I thought we could call her Seren. It's Welsh for "star." Then she can be Star Rivers, like the Starr River near where I used work in Northern Territory.'

I put an arm around her and the baby, pulling them close, 'What? No middle name?'

She pondered, 'Well, I was wondering whether she could cope with Tryphena, but it's such a big name for so small a person. It's easier to go through life with a name people can say *and* spell.'

'Maybe she could have the option of using it for best, and be just Seren for everyday?'

'So, do you like it?'

I regarded them both closely, 'It suits her.' I tried it aloud, 'Seren Tryphena Rivers. It will please Ash, that's for sure.'

'And not you?' She turned an anxious triangle of face up to me, she was so wrapped up in woollens.

I reassured her with a hug, 'It pleases me too, of course.' And I suddenly understood why Jane needed to be outside today, and why it was good for us to name our daughter under the light of the afternoon sun, under the shadow of Hartsworth Beacon. A sense of deep happiness, born out of relief after pain, enveloped me. There was suddenly not a striving bone in my body.

The birds were making that peculiar chibbling sound that that they make when they are building their nests, when the Spring is not quite come, but is edging into sight. Everywhere the buds were reddening on the bough, and the snowdrops were about to give way to daffodils in a sudden rush. Violet leaves were unfurling under our feet and the tree branches up the Beacon in the distance were turning redder every day.

Jane's eyes fell upon the old summer house which was looking beaten up from the recent gales, 'It needs a bit of help.'

'Gillespie said that the wood was nearly rotten, and would need replacing.'

'While I was drowsing the day after she was born, I dreamt that there was a little place for people to sit in up there.' Jane pointed up to the back of the Wilderness. I looked to where she was pointing.

'It's awfully steep up there. I know, I had to go up and rescue an owl chick a couple of years ago.'

'But with some steps and a bit of under-shoring, there could be a real beaut little place up there, so that our guests could sit quietly up under the trees, like a joey in its pouch. A chance to be really in the heart of nature rather than this…'

Her gesture made the little summerhouse look very tame, like an abandoned beach hut.

'What's your idea about it?' sensing there was something more she wasn't saying.

'Well, I don't think it's *my* idea really. It was a kind of fusion of Melanie and Tryphena who showed it me. I was lying in bed, just drifting in and out, but it seemed like both of them. I think *they* want a sanctuary of silence to be built up there, where people who are too traumatized can just be made whole again.'

'A sanctuary of silence?' I said nothing at first, as it seemed too extraordinary a coincidence. Jane had somehow touched near to my experience of initiation at the lodge.

I kissed her head and thrust my finger into Seren's fist, 'That sounds like a wonderful idea.'

Ash came out to join us, 'How are mother and baby doing?

'Fine, thank you,' Jane said. 'The baby is a very good girl, but her mother is needing a lie down, so maybe the father would like to take over?' She passed Seren to me and told him the names we had chosen for her. We were both rewarded with a hug, 'That's is splendid! Tryphena is so glad to know that!' And it is a testament to our belonging to the Beacon, that neither of us thought that a strange statement.

We watched Jane go in down the path.

'Did you know that I would come here to the Beacon?' I asked him, attempting to rock my daughter to sleep.

Ash nodded imperceptibly.

'You not only knew I was coming, but you made me come, didn't you?' I demanded.

He shook his head, stopping to regard the high scudding clouds in the cold blue sky, 'Let's say, I could feel the *coming* of you from afar. I didn't know your name or where you were, only that you would come....'

'What? In the same way house sellers know that the right tenant will come?'

'Something like that,' he smiled.

A companionable silence fell between us.

After a while, I said, with realization, 'I came when I was ready.'

He nodded, 'Exactly.'

'Just like clients do!'

He agreed with me, with a twinkle, 'Well, the readiness is all!'

'Will the Beacon continue, do you think?

'We have taken every care that it does, but the heart of the hearth has to be rekindled in every generation.' We both considered Seren, her blue eyes peering up at us. 'We cannot say what comes after us, but we and others before us have brewed the alchemical tincture...'

'What?...medicinally taken, in small doses, at regular intervals?'

'It is the true gold that fails not.' He turned back to the Beacon, as a dark cloud passed over the sun. 'But the assayers will come to test it, nevertheless.'

Anger blotted everything out suddenly and found myself about to curse Faulkner and his crew to perdition, but caught myself back, for here I was with my daughter in my arms. Anger was replaced immediately by a fierce sense of protection.

Ash was no fool's gold to be unmasked at the first assay, but our true Philosopher's Stone, our 'immortal wheat, which never should be reaped, nor was ever sown.' As in Thomas Traherne's poem, 'I thought it had stood from everlasting to everlasting.' His was the true gold, and no piratical inquisitor was going to steal him away from us, I was determined.

And then I remembered what the Archangel Raphael said to Tobias, and I repeated it to him, as sincerely as my heart knew how, 'Be of good courage: near to you is the God who shall heal you!'

'From your mouth to God's ear,' he said.

www.ingramcontent.com/pod-product-compliance
Lightning Source LLC
Chambersburg PA
CBHW071143160426
43196CB00011B/1993